DISTANT STRANGERS

Debate about the responsibilities of affluent people to act to lessen global poverty has dominated ethics and political philosophy for forty years. But the controversy has reached an impasse, with the main approaches either demanding too much of ordinary mortals or else letting them off the hook. In *Distant Strangers* Judith Lichtenberg shows how a preoccupation with monistic moral theories and concepts such as duty and obligation has led philosophers astray. She argues that there are serious limits to what can be demanded of ordinary human beings, but that this does not mean that we must abandon the moral imperative of lessening poverty. Drawing on findings from behavioral economics, psychology, and other disciplines, she shows how we can harness the efforts of better-off people to lessen poverty without excessively taxing their moral virtue. Lichtenberg argues convincingly that this approach is not only practically, but morally, appropriate.

JUDITH LICHTENBERG is Professor of Philosophy at Georgetown University. She is editor of *Democracy and the Mass Media* (1990), and co-author of *Leveling the Playing Field: Justice, Politics, and College Admissions* (with Robert K. Fullinwider, 2004).

D1452392

DISTANT STRANGERS

Ethics, Psychology, and Global Poverty

JUDITH LICHTENBERG

 CAMBRIDGE
UNIVERSITY PRESS

CAMBRIDGE
UNIVERSITY PRESS

University Printing House, Cambridge CB2 8BS, United Kingdom

Published in the United States of America by Cambridge University Press, New York

Cambridge University Press is part of the University of Cambridge.

It furthers the University's mission by disseminating knowledge in the pursuit of
education, learning, and research at the highest international levels of excellence.

www.cambridge.org
Information on this title: www.cambridge.org/9780521763318

© Judith Lichtenberg 2014

First published 2014

Printed in the United Kingdom by Clays, St Ives plc

A catalogue record for this publication is available from the British Library

ISBN 978-0-521-76331-8 Hardback
ISBN 978-0-521-12462-1 Paperback

For David

Contents

Preface

This book has been a long time coming. In graduate school, many years ago, I was inspired by the crystalline version of libertarianism articulated in Robert Nozick's 1974 book *Anarchy, State, and Utopia* – inspired, that is, to show why this view was dead wrong. My dissertation argued that libertarianism rests on an undefended and indefensible distinction between "negative" duties not to harm and "positive" duties to aid, and in turn between action and omission. I wouldn't put the point quite this way today, but the animating idea persists as one of the main themes of this book. In the course of writing my dissertation I was lucky to meet Henry Shue, whose book *Basic Rights: Subsistence, Affluence, and U.S. Foreign Policy* was soon to appear. Henry's work helped push my thinking further along.

I continued to think and write about these questions over the years while working on other projects. But the plan to write a book took shape only much later. Like many other moral philosophers over the last decades, I was interested in the question "What are the moral responsibilities of comfortable people to alleviate poverty?" But I became convinced that to decide what people ought to do, we need to know what it is reasonable to expect them to do, which requires an understanding of human motivation and behavior. Defending this idea and exploring its implications have been the central themes of this book.

Another theme is that we are indebted, for who we are and what we achieve, to more people than we know – literally and figuratively. But it is gratifying to be able to acknowledge some of these debts explicitly. I spent twenty-five years at the Institute for Philosophy and Public Policy at the University of Maryland, where there really was a "we" constituted not only by great colleagues but also good friends. Other colleagues at Maryland, and at Georgetown, where I have taught in the philosophy department since 2007, have also provided support and constructive feedback. And my students in both graduate and undergraduate courses over several decades of teaching have impelled me to sharpen my thinking about these issues.

Two idyllic visits away from my academic home gave me the intellectual space and leisure to write the book. Early on in its development, I spent a wonderful year, 2005–6, at Stanford University's Humanities Center, where my fellow fellows, mostly from other disciplines in the humanities, cast a somewhat skeptical eye at my way of formulating the questions and answers but in so doing pushed me to sharpen them. Other friends in the Stanford community also improved my thinking on these subjects. In 2011, as a fellow at the Institute for Advanced Studies at the Hebrew University, I wrote much of what was to become the final version of the book in the company of a group of scholars and friends with complementary interests. With less leisure but a still wonderfully stimulating environment, I completed the book in 2012–13, while teaching at the Center for Transnational Legal Studies, a consortium of law schools from around the world based in London. Presentations that year at CTLS, University College London, Nuffield College, Oxford, and the University of Edinburgh helped bring the project to fruition.

I presented earlier versions of these ideas at numerous places in the United States and elsewhere and published some papers whose descendants appear in the book. Members of those audiences and readers of those earlier works, as well as others in conversation along the way, helped me write a better book than I would otherwise have done. Among those I especially want to thank (aware that I am forgetting others) are Charles Beitz, Stephen Campbell, Alexandru Cojocaru, David Crocker, David Enoch, Arthur Evenchik, Kyle Fruh, Verna Gehring, Ralph Glass, Robert Goodin, Karla Hoff, Stacy Kosko, Daniel Luban, David Miller, Edward Minar, Nate Olson, Gwen Pearl, Matthew Pianalto, Joel Roberts, Jeffrey Schaler, Jorn Sonderholm, Karen Stohr, and several anonymous reviewers of articles previously published. I have also benefited from the experience of friends and family members who have participated in humanitarian efforts on the ground. Among them are Patrick Byrne, Nate York, Arthur Evenchik, Rachel Luban, Alec Lichtenberg, and Michelle Sullivan Lichtenberg.

Thanks to Hilary Gaskin, my editor at Cambridge University Press, especially for having confidence in the project; Anna Lowe, assistant editor at Cambridge University Press, for help of various kinds; Lydia Wanstall, who provided expert copy-editing; and Rachel Luban, who did the index. I also want to acknowledge several research assistants over the years who waded through some of the voluminous literature on aid and provided other help as well: Kaily Lam, Jessica Robbins, Paige Kirby, and LiJia Gong.

Claudia Mills, David Wasserman, Rachel Luban, and David Luban read the entire manuscript. I am enormously appreciative of their good sense, intelligence, and verbal gifts, not to mention many specific comments that have improved the manuscript. Also valuable were the comments of an anonymous reader for Cambridge University Press.

Finally, I am deeply grateful to my friends and to my family for love and support over the years. When this book began gestating I had no way of knowing that my children, Daniel and Rachel, would contribute to it intellectually as well as providing emotional sustenance. But I owe most to my husband, David Luban. As no one who knows him will be the least surprised to hear, David has provided unending encouragement and enthusiasm, not to mention being a continual fount of ideas, information, arguments, stories, and (not least) laughter and wit. I could not have written this book without him.

Earlier versions of parts of the book have appeared elsewhere, although in all cases there have been revisions, often substantial, since the original publications.

Some of Chapter 3 appeared as "Are There Any Basic Rights?," in *Global Basic Rights*, a festschrift for Henry Shue, edited by Charles Beitz and Robert Goodin (Oxford, 2010).

Most of Chapter 4 was published in *Ethics* 120 (2010) as "Negative Duties, Positive Duties, and the 'New Harms.'"

Much of Chapter 5 appeared as "Oughts and Cans: Badness, Wrongness, and the Limits of Ethical Theory," in *Philosophical Topics* 38 (2010).

An ancestor of part of Chapter 6, "Consuming Because Others Consume," was originally published in *Social Theory and Practice* 22 (1996).

Part of Chapter 8 was published in *Philosophy & Public Policy Quarterly* 29 (2009) as "What Is Charity?"

Part of Chapter 9 appeared in *Philosophy & Public Policy Quarterly* 28 (2008) as "About Altruism."

CHAPTER I

Introduction

In 2008, 1.29 billion people – 22.4 percent of the world's population – lived below the World Bank's international poverty line of $1.25 a day. In sub-Saharan Africa, 47.5 percent of people live below the line.[1] This absolute poverty line aims to denote the income "needed to purchase a very basic basket of food items, chosen to meet minimal nutritional requirements, and a similarly minimal set of essential nonfood items."[2] A "second tier" international poverty line of $2 a day puts 2.47 billion people in poverty.[3] About one third of all deaths worldwide – 18 million a year – result from poverty-related causes;[4] about 7 million children a year die of hunger and preventable diseases.[5] The malnutrition rate for sub-Saharan Africa is 42 percent, for South Asia 47 percent.[6] By contrast, about a billion people – including myself and just about anyone reading this book – live well by any reasonable standard. In North America the malnutrition rate is 4 percent.[7]

This is a bad situation. It just doesn't seem right. It shouldn't be. What more can be said and what more should be said?

---

[1] World Bank 2012a; 2012b.   [2] Stern, Dethier, and Rogers 2005, 5.

[3] World Bank 2012c. What is it like to live below these poverty lines? See Banerjee and Duflo 2007, summarized at GiveWell 2012. For criticism of the World Bank's poverty measures see Pogge 2010, chs. 3 and 4. For discussion of the complexities of measuring poverty see Alkire 2010 and OPHI 2013. Here I ignore the complexities. The World Bank estimates are staggering even if they are underestimates.

[4] Pogge 2002, 2.   [5] UNICEF 2012.   [6] World Bank 2011.

[7] World Bank 2011. Poverty lines in developed countries are often defined relationally, incorporating the idea that "people are poor if they cannot afford the patterns of activity of the society in which they live" (Stern, Dethier, and Rogers 2005, 6). I discuss relational aspects of poverty in Chapters 6 and 7.

From one point of view I have already said too much, or too little. "The death of a single Russian soldier is a tragedy. A million deaths is a statistic," Stalin is supposed to have said. Recent studies confirm that statistics do not move people to act; stories of "identifiable victims" do.[8] Psychologists continue to investigate the reasons, but the conclusion surprises no one, least of all relief and development organizations, which have always known that the way to a donor's pocketbook is via her eyes and heart.

I begin with statistics because my primary aim in this book is not to move people to act to lessen poverty, although moving them is also a goal. My immediate aim is to understand the nature of the responsibilities comfortable people have to alleviate poverty, and to see how we might implement those responsibilities on a large enough scale to make a real difference. I assume that anyone who has started this book will respond not only to heart-rending pictures and stories (as almost everyone does) but to analysis and argument (a rarer trait), which is what the reader will find here. In this context the cold, bare facts seem appropriate.

Questions about human beings' moral responsibilities to alleviate poverty go back a long way in human history, pervading ethical and religious teachings. To take just a few ancient examples:

> If there is a poor man among you . . . you shall not harden your heart, nor close your hand to your poor brother; but you shall freely open your hand to him, and generously lend him sufficient for his need in whatever he lacks.[9]

---

[8] See, e.g., Small, Loewenstein, and Slovic 2007, 143–53. In an experiment subjects were given the chance to give $5 to the organization Save the Children. In one treatment, subjects saw only an identifiable victim, a girl named Rokia; in a second, they saw statistics about victims of hunger and malnutrition; in the third, they saw both. Not surprisingly, donations were far greater among subjects in the first treatment than among those in the second. But they were also greater among those in the first treatment than among those in the third; in other words, seeing statistics *in addition* to an identifiable victim reduced people's likelihood to contribute. See also Slovic 2007, 2. For possible explanations see Jenni and Loewenstein 1997, 14 and Slovic 2007.

[9] Deuteronomy 15:7–8 (New American Standard Version).

Sell what you have and give the money to the poor.[10]

Let the man with two tunics share with him who has none; and he who has food is to do likewise.[11]

Take stock then: not only can you manage on a few things only, but God himself asks very few from you. Ask yourself how much he has given you and then pick out what you need; all the rest of your things lie there as superfluities, but for other people they are necessities. The superfluity of the rich is necessary to the poor. If you hold onto superfluous items, then, you are keeping what belongs to someone else.[12]

There is a time when we sin mortally if we omit to give alms; on the part of the recipient when we see that his need is evident and urgent, and that he is not likely to be succored otherwise – on the part of the giver, when he has superfluous goods, which he does not need for the time being, as far as he can judge with probability.[13]

If a poor person comes and asks for what is sufficient to fill his needs and one does not have the means to provide it for him, one gives according to his means. How much is this? One-fifth of one's assets is the best possible way, but one-tenth is the usual way.[14]

. . . to parents do good, and to relatives, orphans, the needy, the near neighbor, the neighbor farther away, the companion at your side, the traveler, and those whom your right hands possess.[15]

Today these problems press on us especially hard, for several reasons. One is that the ubiquitous mass media make the rich everywhere visible to the poor and the poor to the rich. No one can pretend not to know how the others live. It may also seem that poverty is no longer inevitable – that now we could be done with it, whereas earlier in human history it was inevitable. There are the sheer numbers of very poor people in the world. Although the number living below the $1.25 poverty line declined from 1.9 billion to 1.29 billion between 1990 and 2008 – and from 43 percent to 22.4 percent of the world's population – the figures remain staggering. More very poor people

---

[10] Luke 12:33 (Contemporary English Version).
[11] John the Baptist, in Luke 3:11 (New American Standard Version).
[12] Augustine 2004, 454 (psalm 147, para. 12).
[13] Aquinas 1916, vol. II, q. 32, art. 5, ad. 3.   [14] Maimonides 2003, ch. 7, 5.
[15] Qur'an 4:36.

are alive in the world today than constituted the total world population less than 200 years ago.[16] And the decline in the poverty rate has taken place almost entirely in East Asia, mainly in China. Excluding China, the poverty count in all other developing countries is around 1.1 billion, just as it was in 1981.[17] Moreover, in many developing – and developed – countries the gap between rich and poor has widened.[18]

The contemporary philosophical debate

What ought a comfortable person do to remedy these conditions? For several decades now, this question has penetrated the ivory tower and become the focus of intense philosophical scrutiny. It's not an exaggeration to say that the contemporary debate began with an article the Australian philosopher Peter Singer published in 1972. In "Famine, Affluence, and Morality," Singer asserted what seemed (but only briefly) an innocuous premise: "if it is in our power to prevent something bad from happening, without thereby sacrificing anything of comparable moral importance, we ought, morally, to do it."[19] Echoing Augustine, he concluded that the comfortable ought to give up all luxuries, and reduce themselves to the point where if they reduced their standard of living further they would be as badly off as those they are trying to help. Similarly, the American philosopher Peter Unger argues that "on pain of living a life that's seriously immoral, a typical well-off person, like you and me, must give away most of her financially valuable assets, and much of her income, directing the funds to lessen efficiently the serious suffering of others."[20]

Few people accept this conclusion, and even those who acknowledge its validity intellectually rarely live up to it. (Critics gleefully

---

[16] United States Census Bureau 2012b.   [17] World Bank 2012c.
[18] World Bank 2012d, 3–4. Why we should be concerned about inequality – as opposed to poverty – is a question I take up in Chapters 6 and 7. The World Bank focuses on the detrimental effects inequality may have on economic growth, "thereby hindering further poverty reduction," as well as on the perception and reality of fairness and equality of opportunity.
[19] Singer 1972, 231.   [20] Unger 1996, 134.

note that even Peter Singer falls short.[21]) Believing Singer and Unger is just too painful: either we must give up our comfortable lives, or we must live with the guilt that failing to do so – doing wrong – brings. (A less painful third set of alternatives, probably commonest of all, is forgetting, willful blindness, or self-deception.) It's not surprising that a cottage industry of very able critics has emerged since the publication of Singer's seminal article, employing their intellectual firepower and the exacting tools of analytic philosophy to show that Singer and his ilk go too far: the better-off cannot be morally required to give up most of their worldly possessions and creature comforts to aid the poor.[22] The critics vary in their own conclusions, with some arguing for a more demanding standard than others – although all give answers that fall far short of Singer's and Unger's views. Relying on ideas like integrity and autonomy and the inherent moral permissibility of leading a life of one's own, they defend the commonsense view that we are not morally obligated to spend most of our time and resources in the service of benefiting others in need.

My conclusions are not so different from the moderating critics of Singer and Unger. I too believe that we cannot be morally required to transfer nearly so much as they think. But I come at these questions from different starting points than the moderating critics, and the inferences I draw take us in different directions. The critics treat the moderate view as a conclusion to be argued for in the face of the unquestionable moral pull of Singer and Unger's demanding view. Even if they are not themselves utilitarians or consequentialists, they are powerfully drawn to what might be called the consequentialist problematic, which has had a dominant influence in Anglo-American philosophy for many decades. That is, they take seriously the idea that one *might* be morally obligated to do what is best overall – that

---

[21] According to a 1999 profile in *The New Yorker* (Specter 1999), Singer gives away 20 percent of his income – far more than most people do and more even than the familiar tithe some religions counsel, but still much less than the demanding standard set out in "Famine, Affluence, and Morality."

[22] See, e.g., Cullity 2004; Miller 2010, ch. 1; Mulgan 2001; Murphy 1993; Scheffler 1994.

one is not permitted to give preference to one's own interests (or to
the interests of those near and dear) but rather must treat all agents'
interests equally. According to Brian Barry, G.E. Moore was the first
to maintain that "the assertion 'I am morally bound to perform this
action' is identical with the assertion 'this action will produce the
greatest possible amount of good in the Universe.'" Barry describes
this view as "the time-bomb that has been ticking away ever since" –
and that "has at last blown up utilitarianism."[23] Many of the moderating critics seem to take the demanding view as the default, the
presumptively correct position against which one must offer compelling arguments.

A great deal in philosophy – as elsewhere – depends on defaults
and presumptions. Because the critics begin where they begin, they
spend their efforts establishing what to most people – including the
ordinary person in the street who has never heard of consequentialism – already seems clear. At the same time, when we look closely at
their philosophically sophisticated arguments we seem to find our
commonsense beliefs embedded therein: that you have your own life
to live and cannot be required to put aside all your goals and purposes
to help others. Perhaps it's a fallacy to think this is a defect in their
reasoning; it may be inevitable. You can't get something into the
conclusion of an argument that isn't already in the premises. Unless
we somehow begin with the assumption that one is morally permitted
to lead what Garrett Cullity calls a "non-altruistically-focused life,"[24]
it may be impossible to defeat the maximizing view.

On the other hand, you don't have to begin with maximizing
consequentialism to doubt the moral legitimacy of the current global
distribution of wealth. Many people who have never heard of consequentialism, who have missed Philosophy 101 altogether, worry
about whether it is right to live well while so many others live on the
brink of subsistence. No moral or philosophical theory is needed to
generate concern about the coexistence, in the real world, of wealth
and excess on the one hand with extreme poverty on the other.

---

[23] Barry 1979, 639 n. 37.   [24] Cullity 2004, 133.

An alternative approach

I begin with different defaults and presumptions than do both proponents and critics of the demanding view. I embrace two working assumptions that appear to be at odds; my aim in this book is to reconcile them. One is that a world in which some live very well while others barely survive is morally repellent and that those who are able should work to alter it. The other is that morality is made for ordinary human beings, and cannot continually and on a regular basis test their capacities, their inclinations, and their characters too severely. So a moral view that as a general rule demands a great deal from individuals is misguided, not only practically but (more controversially) in its very nature.

In calling these propositions presumptions I do not mean I leave them undefended. The first is discussed most explicitly in Chapter 2, where I explore the various grounds of moral responsibility for alleviating others' suffering; I offer five kinds of moral reasons for thinking one person or group ought to benefit another and explain their relevance to the problem of global poverty. The second presumption takes up most of Chapter 5, where I ask whether demandingness – cost to the agent in satisfying a moral requirement – is relevant to determining moral responsibility. Against the view that "Morality Demands What It Demands," paying no heed to how people are built, I argue that morality cannot require too much of ordinary human beings.[25] Arguments in support of these presumptions are found elsewhere in the book as well. In Chapter 3, for example, I try to show how we came to frame the problem in these terms – what is the moral obligation of the individual to alleviate the suffering of others? – why it leads us down a dead end, and how we might find a better way.

In describing the two propositions as defaults or presumptions I mean that it would take a lot for me to give them up. I take them as relatively fixed points in my moral outlook, and what I aim to do is to show how, despite their apparent incompatibility, we can continue to

[25] The phrase "Morality Demands What It Demands" comes from Scheffler 1986.

believe both, having our cake and eating it too. How is that possible?
A central idea, defended in Chapter 6, is that demandingness is not a
fixed quantity. It varies greatly depending on many factors. If we can
control even some of these factors we can make acting to alleviate
others' suffering easier – less costly – for the agent. My general
strategy depends on the fact that, as many psychological experiments
over the last fifty years have shown, the particular circumstances in
which people find themselves exert enormous influence over human
behavior. (Whether "situations" are *more* important than deep-seated
and fixed psychological traits in determining behavior or simply
important – a controversial question among social scientists – doesn't
matter much for my purposes; it's enough that they are very important.) So if we can manipulate the environments in which people act
(without, of course, doing anything illegitimate), we can greatly
increase the probability of their acting in ways that benefit others.

A more specific application of this general strategy underlies my
argument. For an interesting variety of reasons, it is much easier to
act or refrain from acting (e.g., to act in a way that seems to sacrifice
your interests) if other people around you – in your reference group,
your community, or society – are doing so as well. The reasons have
to do with the effects of infrastructure and networks, habituation and
the psychological salience of certain kinds of goods, and status
considerations. It follows, I argue, that if the acts to alleviate poverty
are carried out by many people together they will be much less
demanding of agents, and not only for the obvious reason that each
person will bear only a small share of the burden.

The "elasticity of demandingness" is a powerful reason for conceiving the responsibilities of individuals as elements of collective
responsibilities. The thorny individual/collective nexus is important
for a variety of other reasons as well. Is our standard question about
the responsibilities of individuals to alleviate poverty? Or is it about
the responsibilities of groups – rich or developed countries or the
global North – to poor or developing countries, the global South?[26]
For the most part these questions have not been adequately

---

[26] For more about terminology see the section on "How to talk" below.

disentangled; or perhaps it's more accurate to say that those who address one tend to ignore the other without explaining why, and without elucidating the relationship between them. States and nations and countries are composed of individuals. What states do must be carried out ultimately by individuals. And individuals belong to collectives such as nations; individuals tend to think of themselves as Americans or Chinese or Kenyans, affiliations that constitute an important part of their identities. If they live in democratic states their relationship to the government that acts on behalf of the collective is even closer. Moreover, individuals participate, albeit usually in small ways, in activities that contribute to the global institutions in which people live as rich or poor.

I begin by asking about individual responsibility: what should *I* do? That is how the question first appeared to me and how, it seems, it must appear to all of us. But I have come to believe we can best answer this question, and best solve the problems it poses, by relating it to the collective one: what should *we* do? And who *are* we? Weaving the connections between the individual and the collective is an element in the argument of this book.

How to talk

Defending the centrality of freedom of expression in *On Liberty*, John Stuart Mill asserts that when it comes to the realms of "morals, religion, politics, social relations, and the business of life, three-fourths of the arguments for every disputed opinion consist in dispelling the appearances which favor some opinion different from it."[27] Because the subject of this book lies right smack at the messy intersection of these realms, it is important to acknowledge from the outset "the appearances which favor" opinions different from mine and to suggest how I propose to engage with them. Yes, one might say, of course it's a bad thing that poverty exists and so, yes, we should act to alleviate it – except for all the reasons that we shouldn't,

[27] Mill 1978, 35.

can't, or don't have to. So it is worth staving off several sources of misunderstanding at the outset.

First, let me say something about the language and the terms I employ in what follows. How shall we describe these individuals or groups who bear responsibilities and those to whom they bear them? How shall we characterize the nature of their responsibilities? These abstract and seemingly pedantic questions mask the moral and political delicacy surrounding such choices. It is difficult to find terms that are not offensive or ideologically loaded. Of course, nothing is more common these days than accusations of hypersensitivity and political correctness. But there is probably no one on the planet who is indifferent to how he or she is described or named.

There are difficulties with both nouns and verbs: how to name people (individuals or groups), and how to describe what they do or what is done to or for them. Every choice seems to carry ideological baggage or at the very least contestable presuppositions. We are walking on eggshells, or through landmines.

How should we describe those people whose responsibilities (if any) form the subject of this inquiry? Sometimes I use the term "the comfortable." In describing this project over the years, I have learned that if you tell people you are interested in the responsibilities of the "rich" to alleviate poverty, almost everyone in the United States (and probably other developed countries too), no matter what their income level, will conclude you are not talking about them. How well off does a person have to be in order to bear some responsibility for benefiting others? I discuss that question, and questions about the relativity of affluence and poverty, in Chapters 6 and 7. Nevertheless, for the sake of simplicity I sometimes use the terms "rich" and "poor," or even occasionally the capitalized Rich and Poor, as stand-ins or ideal types.

The word "poor" is equally problematic. It can evoke pity or victimhood or suggest a more global assessment than simply lack of material resources. (A person who is poor is a *poor person*. Are ambiguities inevitable? "Needy" is even worse.) Still, I have not found a better word for many of my purposes, although I sometimes talk about the better-off, the worse-off, and the least well-off.

When talking about nations or countries, we have accumulated an abundance of terms. For one group: rich, developed, industrialized, North, West. For the other: poor, underdeveloped, developing, South, Third World. Again, for simplicity I often use "rich" and "poor," sometimes "developed" and "developing." Obviously, these terms mask great differences between countries possessing different degrees of wealth and poverty and other relevant features.

Now to action words, as school teachers might call them. How shall we describe what it is (if anything) that the rich ought to do to alleviate poverty? Should they provide aid or assistance? Terms like *aid*, *assistance*, and *help* suggest certain contestable assumptions. When we talk about helping or aiding or assisting people we may imply (intentionally or not) that the would-be aider is a mere bystander: one who has played no role in bringing about or reinforcing the situation for which aid is needed. This assumption is problematic because it can misconstrue the nature and causes of the global distribution of wealth and poverty; insofar as the poor are poor partly as a result of things the rich have done, to ignore this fact is to misunderstand the moral and/or political nature of the problem. So, for example, in one common version of this view, the responsibilities of the rich rest on harms they have inflicted on the poor.[28]

In Chapter 2, I canvass the possible arguments for the conclusion that the rich ought to benefit the poor. (I use the word "benefit" here as the most neutral term available, to avoid any implication one way or another about prior connections between rich and poor that might underwrite responsibilities or entitlements.) I endorse the harm argument, but I doubt that it takes us as far as some believe. Do centuries of Western colonialism explain why the rich are today indebted to the poor? Probably not. Genuine harm arguments must appeal to baselines: in what condition would those harmed be had the harm not occurred? Such baselines are impossible to establish when a lot of time has passed; in addition, there are "moral statutes of

---

[28] A different strand of argument focuses on "exploitation." I discuss both harm and exploitation in Chapter 2.

limitations" on holding descendants of wrongdoers liable.[29] So harm arguments, to be convincing, must be confined to the relatively recent past. There is also a good deal of legitimate disagreement about when even current or recent activities of the rich have harmed the poor.

For these reasons harm arguments only take us so far in establishing responsibilities to act. Arguments from exploitation also have their limits, as I shall contend. But leaving aside the actual limitations of these approaches, I believe it is crucial to ask what the responsibilities of people are to others in dire need *even if* the first have had no part in bringing about the condition of the second or have not exploited them. I call these humanitarian responsibilities.

Here again we find critics who chafe at the very idea. Some suspect that despite any insistence to the contrary, one who puts the question in terms of humanitarianism *is* implicitly denying or at the very least understating the causal role the rich have had in making the poor poor. But no such denial is required.

Others believe this way of asking the question reeks of condescension, suggesting the tainted attitudes the rich, the white, the West, the global North, the developed countries (take your pick) have held for centuries. We rich people should do something for those poor people (those poor, poor people), out of the goodness of our hearts! Noblesse oblige. My station and its duties. The white man's burden. But it is no necessary part of the humanitarian argument that the responsibilities of the rich imply anything about the goodness of their hearts. As for condescension, there are dangers lurking here that must be taken very seriously – Chapter 8 is devoted to discussing the many pitfalls of aid. These dangers underlie some of the reason for thinking, as I do, that we should conceive the responsibilities of the rich as corresponding to *rights* on the part of the poor. Rights undercut any reason for associating duties to act with condescension, hierarchy, or inequality.

Some who believe that poor people have rights to a decent standard of living, and also some who reject the language of rights (or

---

[29] Richard Miller uses this term in Miller 2010, 163.

even morality) altogether, object to the humanitarian argument because it seems to leave the poor to await the action (if not the kindness) of strangers. What is wanted and needed, these critics insist, is an end to such thinking. The emancipation of the poor must mean that "the final hour of colonialism has struck, and millions of inhabitants of Africa, Asia and Latin America rise to meet a new life and demand their unrestricted right to self-determination."[30] Demands, rights, independence, self-determination, rising up – this is the appropriate language, one might think, because it is action on the part of the poor rather than on the part of the rich that is necessary.

What can be said in response to this objection? Nothing in what I say contradicts the idea that those who have been deprived of their rights should take charge of their own destiny. Still, insofar as *I* am not *you* or *he* or *she* and *we* are not *they*, it is appropriate for *me* and for *us* to ask what, if anything, *I* and *we* should do.

What, if anything, is to be done?

This answer brings us to another source of skepticism, discussed in detail in Chapter 8. It arises from the assumption, implicit when we ask about responsibilities to alleviate poverty, that it's *possible* to achieve such benefits. Since starting to think about these questions years ago, I have accumulated an ever-growing stack of books and articles that seem to demonstrate the contrary: that attempts by the West to aid the Rest (to put it in William Easterly's terms) have failed dismally and are doomed to do so. Some of the titles of these works – *The White Man's Burden, Dead Aid, The Road to Hell, Famine Crimes, The Dark Sides of Virtue, Lords of Poverty* – speak for themselves.[31] The logic of these assaults on aid seems to imply that the best thing we can do is to stay away and do

---

[30] Guevara 1964.
[31] Easterly 2006; Moyo 2010; Maren 1997; de Waal 2009; Kennedy 2005; Hancock 1994.

nothing. Take the advice of the physicians' Hippocratic oath: first, do no harm.

Doing no harm is itself no mean feat, as I argue in Chapter 4. Still, in embracing the conclusion that we need take no positive steps to benefit others – since we will fail at the very least and perhaps make things worse – some will take great comfort. Be selfish! Me first! Charity ends at home! At least one writer has suggested that the best way to help the poor may be to buy luxury goods from exotic (read poor) places.[32] Who knew that shopping till you dropped could be the quintessence of altruism?

The conclusion is all too convenient, of course, and we need to be wary of it. Still, there are good reasons to be cautious before concluding that one can succeed in benefiting others – not only in the international arena but domestically, not only in large-scale contexts but one-on-one. Some of the reasons have to do with the importance of self-reliance, concerns about perpetuating dependence, or the already-mentioned dangers of arrogance or condescension or lack of respect for others that sometimes accompany people's efforts to advance others' interests. A related idea, well-supported by psychological and anthropological research, is that giving to others almost inevitably creates debts.[33] Feelings that you are indebted to others or that others are indebted to you can poison relationships.

Other reasons for pessimism center on problems more specific to the international context. There is, in the first place, much disagreement about the extent to which aid has already worked to improve the lives of poor people.[34] One source of misunderstanding comes from confusing two questions. The first is whether external agents can produce enduring economic development in poor countries. The second is whether external agents can do anything to improve the lives of poor people.[35] Many believe the answer to the first question is no, because change has to come from within poor countries themselves and serious impediments to development often exist therein.[36]

---

[32] See Kuper 2002, 111.   [33] See Chapter 8 for further discussion and references.
[34] See, e.g., Risse 2005, 10–12.   [35] See Easterly 2006, 28–9.
[36] See, e.g., Easterly 2006, 29, 77; Collier 2007, xi, 12, and passim.

But that doesn't answer the second question. In fact, few people believe we can do nothing to alleviate poverty. When you examine the (voluminous!) collected work of those pessimists who, on a variety of grounds, doubt the effectiveness of past or present efforts to benefit the poor, you see that all have prescriptions and proposals for how to make things better. No one says we should simply wash our hands of these problems and do nothing.

This point brings us to another source of misunderstanding. It arises from the belief that the kinds of actions and policies up for debate from the moral point of view are limited to aid in the narrow sense. (This is one of the pitfalls in using words like "aid" or "assistance," and why it may be better to talk about the responsibility to benefit.) In fact, other changes – in the domestic laws of rich countries, in international law, in trade policy, in public opinion – may be more important in effecting change in poor countries.[37]

Unless we have very good reason to believe that anything that outsiders can do will be completely ineffective or even harmful, the moral questions I address in this book – What are the responsibilities of the comfortable to alleviate poverty? What are their grounds and sources? How far do they extend? How should they be realized? – remain on the table.

Us and them

Let me mention one other obvious question that any defender of global responsibilities must address. It concerns the apparent conflict between benefiting "distant strangers" and benefiting members of one's own community or society. (I explore this problem briefly in Chapter 2 and in greater depth in Chapter 7.) Shouldn't people take care of their own poor before the poor of faraway places? How we answer this question depends partly on whether we think the rich are partly responsible causally for global poverty, partly on how badly off poor people in one's own society are compared to those in other

---

[37] See, e.g., Collier 2007, chs. 8–11. I discuss these issues further in Chapter 8.

societies (taking into account that poverty has both absolute and relative dimensions, as I argue in Chapters 6 and 7). It also depends on whether one believes there is such a thing as the human community. This idea is not a modern invention but goes back at least as far as the Roman Stoic Marcus Aurelius.[38] Even if we are sympathetic to this cosmopolitan idea, however, the question is how to reconcile global with local responsibilities.

On the one hand, some arguments supporting the global alleviation of poverty – including those directed against the libertarian claim that we have no duties of aid at all – apply at home as well as abroad. In this respect, the arguments for alleviating poverty are not either/or, and do not entail sacrificing the interests of poor compatriots to those of the global poor. That may sound naïve or disingenuous, since (on the other hand) some ways rich countries have of addressing global poverty – for example, abandoning their own agricultural subsidies – could hurt the least well-off people in those countries. One response is that those harmed within the borders of rich countries can be compensated; governments could cover the costs of their integration into other sectors of the economy.

But this is not to deny that there may be difficult tradeoffs. My aim in what follows is to chart a course for resolving them – in the best case showing why conflicts are more apparent than real. Where conflicts inevitably remain, it will be useful to see where the hard choices lie.

Outline

In Chapter 2 I examine and evaluate the various kinds of arguments – based, roughly, on contract, community, harm, exploitation, and humanitarianism – for the conclusion that people in developed countries ought to benefit the poor in developing countries.

In Chapter 3 I look closely at the form of argument that has probably received most attention in the contemporary philosophical debate: that we as individuals have demanding moral *duties* to aid the

---

[38] Aurelius 2006, bk. IV.

poor. The problem is with both the terms *individual* and *duty*. I challenge the fittingness of the language of individual duty and obligation on a variety of grounds. And I argue that it is often more appropriate to think of these moral responsibilities as belonging to collectives than individuals.

In Chapter 4 I examine the distinction between so-called negative and positive duties, around which the debate about our global responsibilities has crystallized. The standard view is that negative duties (i.e., duties not to harm) are in some sense stricter than positive duties (duties to aid) – you can't wriggle out of them. But negative duties are simultaneously thought to be less demanding than positive duties. Positive duties seem voracious, always asking for more from the agent, while negative duties seem to require something easy: "just stop." In the contemporary philosophical debate Thomas Pogge advocates the negative duty approach to global responsibilities, Peter Singer the positive. I challenge the view that negative duties are necessarily less demanding, and cast other doubts on the negative/positive distinction. If I'm right, appealing to negative duties will not solve the problem of demandingness.

Chapter 5 delves deeper into moral theory, showing how traditional ethical theory has led us to the current impasse about our responsibilities to alleviate global poverty. A common assumption is the view I mentioned earlier that Morality Demands What It Demands – with the implication that if that's hard on us mere mortals, too bad. By contrast, I argue that a valid morality must be much more sensitive to demandingness considerations than traditional moral theories (whether in their usual consequentialist or deontological guises) have been.

But this conclusion need not lead to pessimism about the prospects for lessening poverty, for two related reasons. One is that demandingness is not a fixed quantity but is, rather, elastic. In Chapter 6 I show how demandingness can diminish very significantly if we pay attention to what we know about human behavior, most importantly the many reasons people have for doing as others do and wanting what others want. It follows that changing norms can reduce demandingness and make behavior we wish to encourage easier for the agent. We act more easily, and more effectively, when we act together. This brings us to the second reason more modest moral expectations of human beings need not breed pessimism: the burden of responsibility for action should shift to groups rather than individuals.

In Chapter 7 I consider implications from the thesis of Chapter 6 – that what others have and do is central for individual well-being – for comparing the situations of the poor in developed countries and in developing countries. Such comparisons matter for deciding whether or in what circumstances the poor in developed societies, despite being apparently much better off than the poor in developing societies, might nevertheless have an equally strong or stronger claim to assistance. The choice is not always either/or, but conflicts are possible and priorities important.

Chapter 8 considers the many perils of giving, addressing skeptics who think giving aid is wrong, ineffective, or counterproductive.

In Chapter 9 I take up the objection that motives are central to morality and that my approach ignores them. I ask whether altruistic motives are essential, whether they are possible, and how and to what extent they can or should be incorporated into our expectations of human behavior and into the approach I defend in this book.

Chapter 10 summarizes the main conclusions of the book and offers some suggestions, drawing on work among practitioners and in the social sciences, about how its ideas can be put into practice.

CHAPTER 2

Entanglements and the claims of mere humanity

In this chapter I explain and assess the different kinds of moral reasons one might have for thinking that people ought to act to mitigate the conditions of global poverty.

Nonrelational reasons: need and ability

Broadly speaking, we can divide these reasons into two main kinds. The first is simply the existence of suffering on the part of one person alongside the ability to alleviate it on the part of another. When Peter Singer argues that a passerby ought to save a child drowning in a shallow pond when he can do so with no risk and virtually no cost to himself, he implies the principle we can put this way: where there exists *need* on the part of one person and *ability* (to satisfy that need) on the part of another, there is some moral reason — call it *moral force* — to alleviate the need.[1] The slogan "Can Implies Ought" (turning the philosopher's more familiar one on its head) captures this idea. In general, the degree of moral force depends on the stringency of the need on the one side, and the degree of ability on the other.

Of course, the bare description of a person in need — let's call him Poor — and a person who can easily satisfy that need, Rich, does not by itself tell us whether Rich ought to help Poor. To settle that question, other pieces of information may be important — for example, how Poor became poor and how Rich became rich.[2] If the poor

---

[1] Singer 1972. Singer, of course, puts the argument for helping differently.
[2] Other matters are also relevant. In Chapter 8 I consider the common accusation that "helping" people just as often harms them.

person is the grasshopper who played instead of working, and the rich person is the industrious and thrifty ant, some might conclude that Rich is under no obligation or even moral force to help Poor. So the principle that the intersection of need and ability creates moral force on the part of the able person to alleviate need is best understood not as an invariable truth but as a presumption that might be rebutted in light of further evidence.

The question of the degree of moral force – how strength of need and ability bear on a person's responsibilities to help – I leave open for now. Philosophers – but not only philosophers – tend to speak the language of moral *duty* or *obligation*.[3] Whether we answer yes or no, the question we tend to ask is whether a person has a moral duty or obligation to act. I believe this language obscures as much as it reveals; I defend this view in Chapters 3 and 5, arguing that we should expand our moral vocabulary and rethink the way we express the moral importance of reforming the global distribution of wealth and the responsibilities of individuals and collectives (such as countries). Where it is not awkward I speak instead of *reasons* or *responsibilities* to act, which avoids the categorical connotations of duty. But the language of duty and obligation cannot, at least for the time being, be completely expunged from our discussion. So I want to emphasize that the formulation in terms of duties or obligations is provisional and should not be taken as the last word on the subject.

Instead of the ant and the grasshopper, imagine two individuals not responsible for the situations in which they find themselves. Poor and Rich live on separate islands with no interaction.[4] Poor's island is barren; on Rich's lush paradise, manna grows on trees, there for the plucking. The two become aware of each other's existence, and for the first time it is possible for Rich to transfer some of her wealth to Poor. Should she? By hypothesis, neither is responsible for her own situation, whether miserable or fortunate. Equally important, neither

---

[3] Although some philosophers distinguish between duties and obligations, I use them synonymously and interchangeably.

[4] This "Robinson Crusoe" example comes originally from Milton Friedman (Friedman 1962, 12–13). Robert Nozick utilizes it in *Anarchy, State, and Utopia* (Nozick 1974, 185).

is responsible for the *other's* situation: Poor did not help enrich Rich, and Rich did not exploit or impoverish Poor.

Readers may rightly be impatient with the use of contrived examples like Rich and Poor. Artificial examples, which pervade contemporary philosophy, are problematic in a number of ways. But the example of two inhabitants of isolated islands with no interaction between them illustrates this question: what are a person's moral responsibilities, if any, to alleviate the suffering of others with whom she has no discernible relationship except common humanity? (We might even call into question the special relevance of humanity. Members of other species, as well as aliens or even sophisticated machines, could have a claim on what it is difficult to avoid calling humane treatment.) What claim does humanity alone make? "Claim" here is ambiguous, refer- ring both to the claim of the person in need of assistance and to the claim on the person who is able to help.

Call the idea that Rich ought to help Poor just because she can and Poor needs her help "the humanitarian argument." In the real world such unalloyed cases may be rare. Human beings are entangled with others, near and far, in many ways. The suggestion that rich people should do something to alleviate global poverty simply in virtue of their ability and others' need rather than (for example) because they have played some role in bringing about or perpetuating that pov- erty, or because they have benefited from it, will irritate some. And that brings us to the second broad kind of reason why Rich might have reason to alleviate Poor's suffering. Understanding this reason will illuminate the humanitarian argument – to which we shall return – as well.

Relational reasons

The Rich often stand in relationships with the Poor that explain why the former ought to act to mitigate the conditions of the latter. They may be bound by mutual agreements. Rich and Poor may be citizens of, or at least inhabit, a single political community – or some other kind of community – that binds them. Within a political community or across national borders, Rich and Poor may stand in morally significant political or economic relationships; Rich may have harmed Poor or may have taken advantage of or exploited Poor. Each of these might be a reason for thinking Rich ought to benefit Poor, over and above the mere fact that Poor is poor and Rich is *able* to do something about it.

Over the last several decades, an extensive philosophical literature has explored these grounds of responsibility, with philosophers debating their various scopes and implications. Although the grounds just described differ from each other, they share an important feature and for that reason can be subsumed under one general heading. Given two agents A and B, each of these grounds rests responsibility on *something A has done with respect to B* (harmed B, entered into a contract with B, etc.) or on *some role or relationship in which A stands toward B* (such as being a compatriot or an employer). The common element has been variously described as *contractual*, *transactional*, *interactional*, or *relational*. (For simplicity I will mostly use the term *relational*.) By contrast, the other source of what I have called moral force is not transactional or relational: it grounds a reason to act only on the intersection of need and ability, or, to put it differently, on purely humanitarian grounds. It pictures the agent as a bystander or witness to suffering but not one whose responsibility derives from his previous behavior, role, or special relationship to the person in need.

This distinction is exhaustive: a reason to act is either relational or it is not. But the two are not mutually exclusive: a person may have both relational and nonrelational reasons to alleviate another's suffering. And, as I argue later in the chapter, there is one case that eludes easy classification.

Although the distinction between relational and nonrelational duties has played an important role in discussions of the responsibility to alleviate global poverty (and suffering more generally), its significance has been obscured as philosophers have heaped most of their attention instead on the distinction between negative and positive duties. A negative duty is said to be a duty to *forbear* or *refrain* from doing something; a positive duty is a duty to *do* something, to *act*. For reasons that will become clearer in this book, the distinction between negative and positive duties is problematic in a variety of ways.[5] One reason is that it rests on the more fundamental distinction between relational and nonrelational duties, as I shall argue here.

Minimalist views: libertarianism

It will be useful to sketch a taxonomy of moral views that bear on relational and nonrelational duties. Let me begin by setting out three outlooks at one end of the moral-philosophical spectrum. At the extreme end is *amoralism*, by which I mean the view that a person has no moral responsibilities, relational or nonrelational, negative or positive, of any kind. The second is what I shall call *tribalism*. This is the view that *all* responsibilities are relational: one has no moral responsibilities of any kind except to members of one's group, but to members one may have both negative and a rich assortment of positive duties. Typically, the relevant groups have been understood in terms of ethnicity, religion, or nationality.

I shall have little or nothing to say about these two views. The first has been held mainly by sociopaths and devil's advocating students (at least we hope that's all they are) in introductory philosophy classes. The second is, alas, probably not uncommon in the world but has few serious defenders.

The next most minimal view is what we may call *moral libertarianism*. This is the position that all nonrelational duties are negative: people have positive duties only to those with whom they stand in certain kinds of relationships. So people have no moral duties to aid others, if we understand "aid" to imply the lack of a relationship on which duties to benefit rest. In short, people have no humanitarian duties. As we shall see, moral libertarianism also holds a minimalist view of relational duties. Because moral libertarianism, unlike amoralism and tribalism, plays an important role in contemporary philosophical discussions about the responsibilities of the rich to alleviate poverty, it is worth discussing at some length.

---

[5] See especially Chapter 4.

Moral libertarianism resembles, but is not apparently identical to, *political libertarianism*, an outlook that is familiar in our political-philosophical landscape. Strictly speaking, political libertarianism claims only that the state may not *force* A (one of its citizens) to aid B (another citizen).[6] In theory, this position is consistent with the view that A has a (nonenforceable) moral duty to aid B. But the distinction between moral and political libertarianism does not survive close scrutiny. Let's begin with the political version, taking as our model the position described by Nozick in *Anarchy, State, and Utopia*. In Nozick's view, "individuals have rights, and there are things no person or group may do to them (without violating their rights)."[7] There are no uncontracted or nonrelational individual rights to positive goods or positive action, only to noninterference. Corresponding to these uncontracted negative rights are negative duties not to kill, commit physical aggression, rob, and the like, and rights of the state to enforce such individual rights and duties.

Individuals can, according to political libertarianism, acquire enforceable duties to act and not merely to forbear. They can do so in two ways. One way is by entering into agreements or contracts: if you agree to do something then you acquire an enforceable duty to do it. *Pacta sunt servanda*: agreements must be kept. The other is by harming another.[8] One who harms another acquires an enforceable positive duty to rectify or compensate the injured party for the damage done. But each of these positive duties is relational, resting on some prior conduct of the agent.

Political libertarianism holds a minimalist view of the kinds of relationships giving rise to enforceable positive duties. They are limited to the two just mentioned: harming (however defined) and contracting.[9] Political libertarians deny that membership in a political

---

[6] See, e.g., Nozick 1974, ix.   [7] Nozick 1974, ix.

[8] Nozick speaks of harming as making someone worse off "in specified ways" (1974, 32).

[9] The existence of enormously complex fields such as contract law and social contract theory attests to the fact that agreements do not wear their implications on their sleeves. But the more libertarians depart from explicit agreements, the more they risk straying from their libertarian commitments.

community in itself entails enforceable positive moral obligations to fellow members – as is clear in their rejection of the legitimacy of the welfare state, which would transfer goods from rich members to poor. A fortiori, nonmembers also have no claim to having their basic needs met. Libertarians also deny that certain kinds of economic relationships create enforceable moral duties to treat others in certain ways – that is, they deny the moral significance (or perhaps even the possibility) of exploitation when exploitation does not entail harming in the sense of making a person worse off. I discuss exploitation later in this chapter.

It might be argued that political libertarians can nevertheless acknowledge that individuals are sometimes *morally* obligated to aid others. On the face of it, the two positions seem compatible: what people's individual moral obligations *are* is one thing; what the state may force people to do is something else.

But are the two views truly compatible? The answer depends partly on what it means to be morally obligated or to have a moral duty to do something. I examine this question in detail in the next chapter, but preliminary discussion is necessary here. Some connect the concepts of duty or obligation directly with the legitimacy of coercion: if A has a moral obligation to do x, then it is permissible for the state to coerce A to do x. On this interpretation, libertarians must deny that we are morally obligated to help others. On another common interpretation, however, to say that you are morally obligated to do something is simply to say it would be wrong for you not to do it. Of course, right and wrong don't always come in black and white. But the realm of moral obligation occupies the end of the spectrum: when we assert that a person has a moral obligation to do (or not to do) something, we are staking out the area of clear moral wrongness. In this sense, to assert that aiding is a moral duty or obligation is simply a way of insisting on the moral unacceptability of not helping or the moral necessity of helping, with no implications about the legitimacy of coercion. On this interpretation, it seems that libertarians could acknowledge a moral duty to aid others.

But the question then is why one who conceded that helping is morally required would in principle oppose government enforcement. And it is clear that libertarians' opposition is principled, not merely practical or contingent. Libertarians object, for example, to Good Samaritan laws that would require drivers to stop at the scene of an accident, not simply because such laws involve messy questions about bystanders' liability for subsequent harm or because these laws are difficult to enforce. Their opposition to forced aid extends to (indeed, centers on) welfare policies, which can be accomplished via taxation and raise no such difficulties. There must be some *principled* difference, then, between moral duties not to harm, which libertarians believe are enforceable, and moral duties to aid, which are not. And only two possible explanations for the difference are available, I believe. One is that, however small the cost to the donor and however large the harm to the recipient, not helping is never as bad as harming. The other is that not helping does not rise to the level of wrongness or moral unacceptability that justifies state coercion.

There is at least one sense in which the first explanation is plausible. Having harmed someone always provides an important reason to alleviate her suffering, beyond the mere fact that she is suffering and that you *can* alleviate it. Almost tautologically, then, the person who omits to aid another has failed less badly than the person who has not rectified a harm he has created, because the latter has *both* failed to rectify the damage he has done and failed to aid. But it does not follow that the ability to aid a person in need is insufficient to justify coercion. Libertarians provide no argument for this further categorical assertion, which is necessary to justify principled opposition to the state's coercing people to aid others. At bottom, the libertarian view seems to imply a kind of existential claim: you may be held responsible for making the world worse than it would have been had you never been born, but you may not be held responsible for not making it better.[10]

It follows that libertarians do in fact rely on the claim of a crucial moral difference between harming and not aiding. More to the point, they assume the difference is sufficient to ground a prohibition on

---

[10] I owe the "never been born" formulation to Thomas C. Grey.

forcing people to aid others. I conclude, then, that political libertarianism entails moral libertarianism. In what follows I speak of them interchangeably and sometimes use the simpler term "libertarianism."

We find two broad kinds of challenges to libertarianism. One – introduced in the last section – denies the libertarian's claim that all nonrelational moral responsibilities are negative. In other words, it asserts that we sometimes have nonrelational responsibilities to help other people – just by virtue, we might say, of their need and our ability to meet it. I call this the *humanitarian* challenge. The other strategy challenges the libertarian's minimalist conception of relational positive duties. It includes a variety of objections that I group under two main headings: the *communitarian* challenge and the *expansionist* challenge. The approaches are not mutually exclusive, and in fact can work in tandem to ground responsibilities of some people to others. But I shall consider them separately.

First, however, a remark to the reader who may wonder why I make so much of libertarianism – in its pure form a rather minor political orientation, especially outside the United States – and why I structure my discussion around it, framing all arguments for benefiting the global poor as challenges or responses to libertarianism. There are two reasons. First, in thinking about what the libertarian denies and rejects (as I have done ever since writing my dissertation many years ago in reaction to Nozick's *Anarchy, State, and Utopia*), I have been led to all the reasons I can think of for the view that one person or group might have a responsibility to aid another – whether we accept them or not. Second, even though only a small number of people are self-consciously or explicitly libertarian, libertarian thinking underlies the defense of capitalism and pervades public and private rationales for not benefiting those in need. So to frame our discussion in terms of libertarianism and its challengers is, I believe, to cover all or most of the bases.

The humanitarian (liberal) challenge

A central disagreement between libertarians and their critics rests ultimately on a brute difference in moral intuition or sensibility concerning the responsibility to aid others in need. To dissuade a person of his libertarian or humanitarian proclivities seems to require a kind of Gestalt switch. Devices like the Golden Rule, Kant's categorical imperative, or Rawls's veil of ignorance can produce such changes in outlook, but mere argument is inert because the disagreement is so basic.[11] Either you see it or feel it or believe it, or you don't.

And many *do* see it, feel it, believe it. Their outlook is rooted in the stark recognition of the role of luck and arbitrariness in influencing the social order and the fates of human beings. Differences in natural abilities and social advantages at the starting line exert enormous influence on how the good things of life are distributed, both within and across national boundaries. To have been born in a rich country is already an advantage of spectacular proportions. Likewise, having affluent or educated parents. Genetics plays a part. Yet, as John Rawls famously puts it, "no one deserves his greater natural capacity nor merits a more favorable starting place in society."[12]

Such reflections help explain the humanitarian view that those who have been blessed by fortune have moral responsibilities to aid the less lucky. When we see the miserable conditions many people face, we know that "there but for the grace of God go I." On this view, refraining from harming others – not making them worse off – is not enough. The luck of the draw that lands some in rich countries and some in poor, some in fortunate families and others in disadvantaged ones, should not be allowed to stand. The beneficiaries of life's lottery are under some moral pressure to give to others who, through no fault of their own, have fared badly.

Those who share this outlook may disagree among themselves about the relevance of fault. Some will want to withhold aid from the grasshoppers of the world who have themselves to blame for their plight; others are more forgiving of human weakness, at least in some

[11] See Rorty 1993, for the view that changes in moral outlook arise from seeing pictures or hearing stories, not from considering arguments. This nonrationalist conception of moral change has to be somewhat depressing news for philosophers, whose stock-in-trade is reasoned argument.

[12] Rawls 1971, 87.

cases. But we can ignore these differences for the moment. What the liberal outlook requires at least is compassion or sympathy for suffering a person has not brought on himself, and consequent responsibility – to some degree or other – on the part of the fortunate agent to offer assistance. Libertarians, by contrast, demand that agents benefit others only if those agents have had some part in creating the suffering that needs repair.

A central question for liberals, of course, is how strong the moral force is. Is there a moral *duty* to aid the unfortunate? Or is the nature of the responsibility weaker than or different from duty? I leave these questions aside for now, but return to them in Chapters 3 and 5.

The communitarian challenge: membership in groups

Many of libertarianism's critics agree with liberals that the mere fact of dire need creates moral force, and that the haves ought to benefit the have-nots simply for this reason. But some will also emphasize other sources of responsibility. What binds communitarians and expansionists together under one general heading – in contrast to libertarians – is their more robust picture of the kinds of relationships that can give rise to responsibilities of some to others. But the similarity between communitarians and expansionists ends there.

Many philosophers and probably the typical "person in the street" believe that people have special duties to compatriots and perhaps to members of other groups to which they belong. Religious and ethnic groups are common candidates, but I shall not discuss the criteria for deciding which groups qualify, and will focus on nationality, which is both most relevant for our purposes and probably least controversial.[13] Such a view is likely to go along with a "concentric circles" picture of morality asserting special duties to people in the inner circles – family and intimates first and foremost – with responsibility declining as the circles move out from the center. On this outlook, comfortable people might have some responsibilities to aid the global

---

[13] I take for granted that relationships to family and other intimates create special responsibilities. "Nationality" is an ambiguous term that can refer to groups

poor, but their responsibilities to their own poor compatriots take priority.[14]

As to exactly how and why membership in a political community generates special responsibilities to compatriots, philosophers disagree, or at least express themselves differently. Thus, for example, while acknowledging minimal humanitarian duties (nonrelational duties, as I have called them) to noncompatriots, Thomas Nagel argues that the more pressing duties – duties of justice – are inherently relational: "Justice is something we owe through our shared institutions only to those with whom we stand in a strong political relation," i.e., joint membership in a state.[15] Such duties obtain only among compatriots because members are "both putative joint authors of the coercively imposed system, and subject to its norms" – both subjects, and "those in whose name ... [the state's] authority is exercised."[16] Richard Miller defends special duties to compatriots on the grounds that "the diverse and vitally important roles of a modern state in creating and shaping opportunities for those who live in its sovereign territory generate a rich array of political duties toward disadvantaged compatriots." These duties include "civic friendship ... fair provision of benefits, mitigation of socially created disadvantage, and trusteeship over the territory in which wide-ranging, exclusive sovereign power is asserted."[17]

These and other views of the grounds of duties to compatriots raise further questions. For example, philosophers disagree about whether or to what extent, deep down, the reasons for preferring compatriots are instrumental or intrinsic. Utilitarians may argue that

---

bound by ethnic, religious, social, or political ties. In what follows I am generally talking about relationships among people (generally citizens) within a state – such as the relationship that those in the United States, who may come from very different ethnic groups, have to each other. See Chapter 7 for further discussion of the issues in this section.

[14] Caution may require a *ceteris paribus* clause here. Compatriots' well-being takes priority, other things being equal, but particular circumstances may add weight to the claims of strangers.

[15] Nagel 2005, 121. But "there is some minimal concern we owe to fellow human beings threatened with starvation or severe malnutrition and early death from easily preventable diseases" (ibid., 118). See Chapter 7 for further discussion.

[16] Nagel 2005, 128.   [17] Miller 2010, 43.

a world divided into nation-states more efficiently maximizes welfare; if so, then special duties among compatriots are justified. To many, however, the utilitarian account misses the nature of these special responsibilities. The point is easy to see if we consider the family. Human well-being may be enhanced overall if people take care of their own children, parents, and partners, but that does not seem to fully explain why we have these duties.

For present purposes we can leave this dispute aside.[18] I shall simply assume that there are good reasons for thinking people have some such special responsibilities to compatriots. Thus, for example, citizens of the United States had special reasons to assist residents of New Orleans after Hurricane Katrina – reasons that Hungarians, Indians, and Egyptians did not have.

Membership or communitarian reasons are typically taken to limit responsibilities to the global poor, not to ground them. Communitarians explain that people have duties to aid their own citizens, which libertarians deny, but this is generally thought to justify restricting benefits to distant strangers in favor of the local poor. Suppose, however, it is argued that we ought to help the global poor *because* we belong to a single community. What defines this view – cosmopolitanism – is the idea that our primary community is the human community and our first duties are to other human beings. The Roman Stoic Marcus Aurelius grounded this view on the faculty of reason.[19] We are, by virtue of reason or something else, first and foremost citizens of the world.

It is worth making several points about this view. First, even if we are members of the human community, we are also members of other communities – most important, probably, for our purposes here, national communities. A central question, then, is what the priority

---

[18] I return to it in Chapter 7.

[19] "If mind is common to us all, then we have reason also in common – that which makes us rational beings. If so, then common too is the reason which dictates what we should or should not do. If so, then law too is common to us all. If so, then we are citizens. If so, we share in a constitution. If so, the universe is a kind of community. In what else could one say that the whole human race shares a common constitution?" (Aurelius 2006, bk. IV, sec. 4).

relationships are between these memberships. The true cosmopolitan believes that membership in the human community is primary, but she need not deny that we have other morally important member-ships.[20] Thus, even if we have responsibilities to other human beings because of our shared humanity, we might have further responsibil-ities to compatriots with whom we share membership in a smaller community. Still, membership in the human community can serve as a ground of responsibility to other members.

Second, we may wonder what the relationship is between the cosmopolitan argument for benefiting the poor and the humanitarian argument outlined earlier. In some ways they seem similar. Both are highly inclusive, and both make reference to humanity. But the humanitarian argument relies on the suffering of one party and the ability of another to alleviate it; the common humanity of the two parties is seemingly incidental to the reasoning. After all, the argu-ment can also undergird the conclusion that one ought to alleviate the suffering of nonhuman animals, or any being capable of suffering, for that matter. The cosmopolitan argument, by contrast, appeals to some kind of commonality between one in need of assistance and one who could help him – essentially, a community of equals to which both belong.

Finally, some may argue that the idea of a human community makes no sense because communities always imply the existence of outsiders as well as insiders. Is it sufficient for a meaningful cosmo-politanism to exclude nonhuman animals?[21] Or would the existence of the human community only make sense once we encounter aliens, who would unite us by contrast? My own sense is that aliens who were sufficiently similar to us would qualify for inclusion in this cosmopolitan community, although we would, of course, then no longer describe it as "human."

---

[20] Gillian Brock argues that principles of cosmopolitan justice must be determined first; only then can we know what duties we have to compatriots, family members, and the like (Brock 2009, 15).

[21] Excluding them would not entail that we can treat nonhuman animals however we please, of course.

The first expansionist challenge: harm

We saw earlier that libertarians take an agent's having harmed another party as the only ground, apart from agreement or contract, for the conclusion that the agent has a responsibility to benefit that party. One basis for what I call the expansionist view is a widened understanding of the seemingly uncontroversial principle that agents must compensate those they have harmed. Thomas Pogge, a leading advocate of the expansionist view of harm, puts the point this way:

> I agree [with libertarians] that the distinction between causing poverty and merely failing to reduce it is morally significant ... My argument conceives, then, both human rights and justice as involving solely negative duties: specific minimal constraints ... on what harms persons may inflict upon others.[22]

But the libertarian and the expansionist differ in their assumptions about the harm the rich inflict on the poor. The expansionist points to the intricate causal nexus characterizing the contemporary world. Modern transportation and telecommunications enhance action at a distance. Borders are porous. Environmental harms, climate change in particular, are perhaps the clearest example: they have been caused mainly by members of rich, industrialized countries, who have also been their main beneficiaries. Their worst effects will be on the poor in developing countries.

Pogge describes other ways the actions and policies of those in developed countries can harm people in poor nations. If a group controls "a preponderance of the means of coercion within a country," it will be "internationally recognized as the legitimate government of this country's territory and people," irrespective of how it "came to power, of how it exercises power, and of the extent to which

---

[22] Pogge 2002, 13. For a persuasive argument that Pogge does not, in fact, rely solely on negative duties see Daskal 2012. For another approach that argues from libertarian premises, attempting to show that "a negative right against coercion actually entails positive rights to things like basic food, water, shelter, and so forth," see Hassoun 2012, 18.

it may be supported or opposed by the population it rules."[23] International recognition confers on such groups the "international resource privilege," making them free to dispose of the country's resources, and the "international borrowing privilege," allowing them to borrow in the country's name – often with disastrous consequences. "Tyranny, corruption, coups d'états, civil wars" – factors many will point to as the local causes of poverty – are encouraged by the global economic order.[24] Leif Wenar argues that Western consumers routinely "buy stolen goods when they buy gasoline and magazines, clothing and cosmetics, cell phones and laptops, perfume and jewelry."[25] These harms result from flaws in the international system of global commerce, which allow corrupt dictators in resource-rich countries to profit hugely at the expense of their impoverished citizens.

Harm can also result from seemingly innocuous and even well-intentioned actions. Environmental harms generally result from the aggregation of individual actions that, taken one by one, are morally neutral.[26] Policies intended to relieve worker shortages in the United States can drain talent from sending countries.[27] The actions of corporations and even apparently humanitarian efforts can, notoriously, go awry.[28] That such conduct lacks malicious intent does not relieve actors of liability.

In theory, there is nothing to prevent libertarians from acknowledging the existence and importance of some of these harms. After all, they hold no brief for the moral significance of national

---

[23] Pogge 2002, 112.   [24] Pogge 2002, 115.   [25] Wenar 2008, 2.
[26] See Chapter 4 for further discussion.
[27] Dugger 2006. An obscure provision in a Senate immigration bill aimed at remedying a nursing shortage in the United States "would throw open the gates to nurses and, some fear, drain them from the world's developing countries."
[28] An example: in some places mosquito nets introduced by international nongovernmental organizations (NGOs) to prevent malaria were used by the intended beneficiaries as fishing nets instead. Their use depleted the tiny creatures the fish eat; as a result the fish died and the local population lost its source of food and income. This story was told to me by the head of a small NGO that carries out projects to alleviate poverty in developing countries.

boundaries or special duties to compatriots. One question, then, is how much libertarians and expansionists disagree. The answer will vary, no doubt, from libertarian to libertarian and expansionist to expansionist. Another question is whether or to what extent their differences rest on empirical disagreements about the facts (did action x or policy y in fact cause harm?), or on differing conceptions of what constitutes harm.

Disagreements about the facts no doubt play a part, as they often do when people differ about apparently moral questions. Two people may disagree about the legitimacy of the death penalty because one believes in retribution and the other does not – a disagreement about moral principle – but also because one thinks the death penalty deters crime and the other does not. But alternative conceptions of harm also matter. Pogge, probably the leading contemporary exponent among philosophers of the expansionist view, explicitly relies on two notions of harm. One is the traditional idea that "someone is harmed when she is rendered worse off than she was at some earlier time, or than she would have been had some earlier arrangements continued undisturbed."[29] Pogge takes this criterion to be satisfied for many harms he believes the rich have inflicted on the poor, including those resulting from the "very violent history through which the present radical inequality accumulated."[30] But he also relies on a different notion of harm, which sees it in terms of "an independently specified conception of social justice." On this view, "we are *harming* the global poor if and insofar as we collaborate in imposing an *unjust* global institutional order upon them."[31]

Libertarians would certainly reject this moralized conception of harm, instead limiting harm to a species of making someone worse off. On their view, harm is prior to justice, indeed the ground for determinations of justice, not vice versa. To reverse this priority, they would argue, is to beg the question. Not all instances of making someone worse off, however, count for them as harming in the

---

[29] Pogge 2009, 311.   [30] Pogge 2009, 308.
[31] Pogge 2009, 311 (emphasis in original). For criticisms of this conception of harm see Howse and Teitel 2010, ch. 21.

relevant sense. The obvious exception is competition. One person's opening a coffee shop may make a competitor worse off, but we do not for that reason alone deem the first's action impermissible. Nevertheless, libertarians insist that making someone worse off than she would have been in the absence of one's action is a *necessary* condition for harm, even if it is not sufficient.

So Pogge's second conception of harm diverges significantly from the libertarian conception, taking us into a realm that we might think is better described in other terms. At least part of what he intends is probably captured in the second expansionist challenge – exploitation – which I shall discuss shortly. But first it's important to note that even what we might call the classical view – harm-as-making-someone-worse-off-plus[32] – is problematic as a basis for compensation to the poor by the rich.

The reason is that the traditional view of harm implies a baseline or benchmark that is not always available. Our paradigm of harm is one person committing aggression against another. If A punches B in the face, we can say with confidence that A has harmed B, because we know what B's face would have been like had A not struck him: if A had not struck B, B would not have required stitches in his forehead. Similarly, we can know that driver D has harmed pedestrian P because if D's car had not crashed into P, P would not have suffered a broken leg and internal injuries. But when harm occurs over an extended period and involves long causal chains and many intervening people and occurrences, it will generally be impossible to establish the baseline or counterfactual: to know *how things would have been* if the allegedly harmful event had not occurred. We do not know what the Congo would be like today if Belgium had not colonized it in the nineteenth century. We do not know where contemporary descendants of American slaves would be or how they would be faring in the absence of the slave trade and the taking of slaves to

---

[32] The "plus" is meant to take account of whatever other feature must be present (so as to exclude, e.g., legitimate competition). For simplicity I omit the "plus" in what follows.

America hundreds of years ago.[33] Moreover, as Derek Parfit has pointed out, if harmful events like the Belgian conquest of Congo or the slave trade had not occurred, different individuals, with different descendants, would have been conceived; since those now living would not have been born, they cannot have been harmed by the events in question.[34]

One response to the nonidentity puzzle is that, even though contemporary people would not have existed in the absence of the old harms, their interests are affected – and they can perhaps be said to be harmed – because of their emotional connection to those originally harmed. As a member of a particular ethnic or national group, I can be negatively affected (albeit usually to a lesser degree) by the harms inflicted on earlier members, even if they were not my actual ancestors.[35]

This response takes us a certain distance, but still short of an argument for full compensation or reparation. Moreover, it seems plausible that a moral "statute of limitations" makes it problematic to hold descendants responsible for the sins of their remoter ancestors.[36] The conclusion that descendants ought to be at least partly responsible must rest, I think, on benefits the descendants have gotten as a result.

None of this is to deny that contemporary poverty results in part from harm inflicted by the rich. But the baseline problem and the absence of relevant counterfactuals make it difficult to establish

---

[33] Jon Elster (2004, 36–7) recounts this story, told by historian G. de Bertier de Sauvigny (1999, 79): after the French Revolution the restored Bourbon regime offered its supporters reparations for lost property and even lost career opportunities. Sometime after May 1814, "a former officer of the royal navy who had not seen service since 1789, at which time he was a mere cadet," petitioned to receive "the grade of rear admiral, arguing that this would have been his position had his career taken its normal course." The secretary of the King's Council told the Secretary of the Navy, who had brought the petition: "Answer him . . . that he has only forgotten one essential fact: that he would have been killed in the battle of Trafalgar."

[34] Parfit 1984, ch. 16. This is the famous nonidentity problem.

[35] I am grateful to Tamar Meisels for this point.   [36] See Miller 2010, 163.

claims to reparation or compensation when the actions in question are long past.

The second expansionist challenge: exploitation

Those who are not libertarians (or amoralists or tribalists) will probably agree that it is possible for an agent to treat another person badly, perhaps even impermissibly, short of harming her – i.e., making her worse off than she would have been had the agent not done what he did. I gather these nonharm forms of mistreatment under the general heading of *exploitation*. Perhaps there are other species as well, but this term appears to adequately capture the kinds of behaviors we are interested in. In its most general sense, exploiting someone means taking advantage of her.[37] Richard Miller zeroes in on the distinction between harm and exploitation in the context of global poverty: exploitative conduct consists "of making improper use of the desperate neediness of people in developing countries, not imposing it on them."[38] Examples are not, of course, limited to the international realm. They include relationships between people in developed countries – for example, between employers and employees who do not earn a living wage such as farm workers and hotel chambermaids.

Defenders of such arrangements, whether domestic or international, are likely to argue that these workers act voluntarily.[39] No one forces them to take the jobs; they can turn them down if they choose. In trying to resolve this disagreement, it's easy to get bogged down in disputes about the meaning of "freedom," "coercion," "force," "choice," and "voluntariness." Although nothing substantive should hang on terminology, everyone wants these words on their side. To some it seems clear that poor workers, whether in developed or developing countries, "have no choice": if they want to eat, and to

---

[37] Wertheimer 1996, 10.   [38] Miller 2010, 59.
[39] See, e.g., Columbia University economist Jagdish Bhagwati, describing women in China who leave the countryside to work in factories twelve hours a day, six days a week (quoted in Miller 2010, 65).

support their families in any way whatsoever, they must work at the wages offered. But libertarians like Nozick assert that

> whether a person's actions are voluntary depends on what it is that limits his alternatives. If facts of nature do so, the actions are voluntary ... Other people's actions place limits on one's available opportunities. Whether this makes one's resulting action non-voluntary depends upon whether these others had the right to act as they did.[40]

This passage is shot through with contentious assumptions. First, whether employers have the *right* to act as they do, offering poor wages, is precisely the question at issue, and Nozick does nothing to resolve it. He simply assumes from the outset that people have only negative duties not to make others worse off unless they have explicitly agreed otherwise. Second, even if employers did have the (moral) right to act as they do, it doesn't follow that it is right for them to do so or that, all things considered, they ought to. Rights do not exhaust all moral categories.[41] Finally, we may ask what Nozick means by "facts of nature" as the source of the limited alternatives that might lead a poor person to accept substandard working conditions and that, in his view, render such actions voluntary.

Nozick is probably imagining the old Robinson Crusoe example, where the poor guy who happens to have been born on a barren island is now negotiating with the lucky one in the lush paradise. To assimilate the situation of poor workers in developed or developing countries to this fable is a distortion. It doesn't *just so happen* as a result of "facts of nature" that poor workers find themselves without bargaining power. That situation results partly from contemporary political and economic institutions that structure negotiations and decisionmaking in ways that benefit the already advantaged.[42] It may result also from old wrongs – the effects of colonialism. Although, as I argued in the last section, construing these effects as harms may be problematic because there is no appropriate baseline against which to compare them, and because descendants of those harmed might not

---

[40] Nozick 1974, 262.   [41] For further discussion see Chapter 5.
[42] For discussion see almost any of the works of Pogge; Miller 2010, ch. 3; Wenar 2008; Benvenisti and Downs 2007.

have existed absent those harms, it does not follow that the situation of poor workers is simply a "fact of nature." On the contrary, it grows at least partly out of historical and contemporary entanglements between rich and poor.

But suppose instead that the inferior bargaining situation of poor workers did *not* result in any way from past actions or current institutional arrangements. Suppose instead it did grow out of "facts of nature" – perhaps a deficit of individual talent on the part of workers, perhaps a naturally barren environment from which they come, perhaps a combination of the two. We might still ask whether, when employers offer jobs to workers, the latter deserve or are entitled to better treatment than "take it or leave it." Miller's position, with which I agree, is clear. He argues that

> a person takes advantage of someone if he derives a benefit from her difficulty in advancing her interests in interactions in which both participate, in a process that shows inadequate regard for the equal moral importance of her interests and her capacity for choice. In the case of globalization, the central difficulties are bargaining weaknesses due to desperate neediness.[43]

Of course, a lot of people in the world are desperately needy. Are poor workers entitled to something that other people, perhaps even poorer, are not? Does our neglect of these latter people show "inadequate regard for the equal moral importance" of their interests? Miller thinks not. One of his overarching concerns is to pull back from Singer's radically demanding view, which would require large sacrifices on the part of the rich to aid the poor purely on what I have been calling humanitarian grounds. What Miller calls sympathy, which he believes is owed to all people regardless of one's relationship to them, doesn't demand very much; one is not required to do things that "would impose a significant risk of worsening one's

---

[43] Miller 2010, 60. Miller insists that these bargaining weaknesses do not result from mere "facts of nature" – he spells out in detail the institutional arrangements that contribute to these weaknesses – although his claim in this passage does not depend on that view.

life."[44] But something more is required, he believes, once one is engaged with others in labor or power relationships.

We see at work here the subtle but fundamental distinction between relational and nonrelational responsibilities. On the one hand, it might seem paradoxical that respect for other people's interests is not violated provided we ignore them entirely, if we have nothing to do with them. And, of course, some might claim that we do in fact violate respect for them in these circumstances. On the other hand, taking this view pushes us to the radically demanding conclusion that so many find implausible.

So what is the moral basis for thinking that exploitation violates respect while complete neglect does not (or at least does not *necessarily*)? One difference follows almost inevitably from the fact that two people are in a relationship. Once you enter into relations with another person you cannot fail to be aware of him and thus in some sense to acknowledge his existence; his humanity and his interests come within your purview. At least as important is what is implicit in the idea of exploitation: taking advantage of another. To take advantage of other people is to *benefit* from or even celebrate their bad circumstances – even if one does not make them worse off than they would have been in the absence of interaction – and that seems to amount to using them as a means in a way that is objectionable. By contrast, simply to fail to aid poor people on the other side of the world is not to use them, however else it might be described.

Recognizing, no doubt, that we cannot avoid using people partly as means, Kant asserts that we may not use another *solely* as a means. When I altogether avoid interacting with you I do not use you as a means; once I interact with you, Kant's stricture would demand that I also take into account your humanity in appropriate ways. In something like this way we might explain what makes the relationship described by critics as exploitative morally troubling.

[44] Miller 2010, 13.

Some further considerations

When we talk about nonrelational responsibilities we call the benefits in question "aid" or "assistance."[45] When, on the other hand, people have had a role in creating others' need, or benefit from it or from the inferior bargaining situation of those in need, we use different terms. If we think there has been harm we talk about compensation or reparation. In cases of exploitation we are likely to talk about fairness. With communitarian arguments the language is less clear: communitarians may talk about aid or assistance (e.g., for poor compatriots) even though the responsibilities in question are relational.

There is a lot of disagreement about the extent to which relational considerations support responsibilities to alleviate poverty. I have discussed briefly four different relational considerations: agreements, membership, harm, and exploitation. Agreements and harm are in principle uncontroversial. If you have agreed to benefit people then you ought to do it, unless there are very strong reasons to the contrary.[46] If you have harmed people you owe them compensation. We can see why harm-based arguments seem to possess certain advantages (and why, for example, Pogge wants to insist that he relies solely on negative duties – i.e., harm-based arguments); few

---

[45] There are also the terms "charity" and the philosopher's "beneficence," which I discuss in later chapters.

[46] So, for example, the United States and other developed countries have committed themselves through agreements to reducing poverty in the poorest countries. At the Third United Nations Conference on Least Developed Countries (LDCs) in Brussels in 2001, restating commitments made originally decades earlier, the United States asserted: "We affirm ... that official development assistance (ODA) has a critical role to play in support of LDC development. We take upon ourselves not to spare any effort to reverse the declining trends of ODA and to meet expeditiously the targets of 0.15% or 0.20% of GNP [gross national product] as ODA to LDCs as agreed ..." (United Nations, 2001, 8). This agreement is still unmet. In fact, total ODA of the United States in 2006 was 0.17 percent of GNP (ibid., 10). But only about a fifth goes to LDCs; much is directed to countries because of their role in the war on terror (Singer 2010, 105). So although the commitment requires that about a fifth of 1 percent of ODA go to LDCs, only about a twenty-fifth – a fifth of a fifth – has been directed to that purpose.

people reject the premise that harm justifies compensation. But harm is a more problematic basis than it appears. We saw one reason earlier: the baseline problem limits credible harm-creating responsibilities to the recent past. We will examine another reason in Chapter 4: it is difficult for individuals to avoid participation in the machinery of harm, but equally difficult to know what conclusions to draw about their accountability.

Moreover, the facts on which harm arguments rest are often contestable and contested. Facts can be contested in any of three ways. One might deny that x, the harmful consequence, has occurred: the inhabitants of the city did not, in fact, die of starvation. One might deny that agent A did y, the action that caused x: the inhabitants did die of starvation as a result of y, but it was B who did y, not A. Finally, one might deny that y had the causal properties attributed to it: A did y (blockaded the city) but y did not cause x (which resulted instead from an epidemic unrelated to the blockade). In political discourse each of these strategies is common.

Still, harm-based arguments play an important role in establishing responsibilities to alleviate poverty. One ought to compensate others for harm one has caused them by making them as well off as they would have been in the absence of the harm.

One reason harm arguments are contested is that people sometimes fail to distinguish harm from exploitation: they claim the former when what is at issue is the latter. Exploitation mostly involves cases where the weaker party is better off than she would have been in the absence of the interaction. Its wrongness in such cases is more controversial than harm. Libertarians will simply deny that it is wrong to exploit people – to take advantage of others' inferior bargaining situation – even though they agree that it is wrong to harm them. (Or at least they will deny that exploitation violates people's rights or that agents do not have the right to act in such exploitative ways.) In this respect exploitation arguments resemble those resting on nonrelational responsibilities; they do not depend on facts in the way that harm-based arguments do, but rather on a philosophical principle or intuition, in this case about the unfairness (or some other variety of moral "ickiness") of benefiting from others' weakness.

Yet the line between harm and exploitation is not always sharp. Think again of the workers for transnational companies in developing countries whose wages and working conditions are poor but who (we will assume) are nonetheless better off than they would be without such jobs. This appears to be a clear case of exploitation rather than harm. We can assume that if these workers could organize into unions, they would be able to improve their working conditions. What prevents them from organizing? All too often, it is the actions of their governments with the collusion (implicit or explicit) of the companies. So, in fact, someone (the governments, the companies, and/or their agents) is actually harming the workers: if they refrained from these union-busting activities the workers would be better off.[47] This example provides one reason for thinking the distinctions between harming and exploiting, harming and not aiding, and negative and positive duties are much less sharp than is usually thought. We will see other reasons in Chapter 4 and elsewhere.

Whereas arguments from harm and exploitation are often employed to defend responsibilities to alleviate global poverty, communitarians emphasize special duties to members of one's own community or nation. In theory these communitarian duties – whose precise nature and source, as we saw earlier, is explained differently by different thinkers – could coexist with responsibilities to those outside one's community. But in practice the tendency is for the first to supplant the second, at least in part. Still, communitarian arguments provide a grounding for responsibilities to alleviate poverty and other suffering to one's compatriots – something that libertarians reject. Those concerned about lessening global poverty might be consoled by *any* arguments that comfortable people have responsibilities to alleviate poverty, even if only among the poor in rich countries.[48]

Nonrelational responsibilities possess a certain simplicity. They rest only on the unseemliness of dire need coexisting with abundance

---

[47] I am grateful to Michael Walzer for this point.
[48] See Chapter 7 for further discussion.

and the moral force that such situations create. The cosmopolitan argument may be similar in this respect. No facts about the cause of people's need are assumed. Libertarians deny that these situations create moral force on the prosperous agent (just as they deny the problematic nature of taking advantage of another person). But even if one acknowledges in principle a responsibility to aid, the question is how much is required beyond the easiest rescues.

In this respect, however, relational responsibilities are not so different from nonrelational ones. There is no simple answer nor a precise way to "measure" how much one "owes" as a result of harm or exploitation or membership. I develop this point further in subsequent chapters. But here are two further observations that support it.

First, few people are pure libertarians. Most of us acknowledge that the coexistence of dire need and easy ability creates some moral force on the part of the agent to act, and similarly that it is not nice (to use a technical term) to take advantage of or benefit from other people's weak bargaining positions, especially if they are in particularly dire straits. Even some libertarians would probably agree. What makes them and others pull back is the stronger claim some make that a person is *morally obligated* to help another in need when she can do so without significant sacrifice, or that a person has a *moral duty* not to take advantage of another's weak bargaining position. In the next chapter I examine this language and its significance more carefully, showing how it leads us astray in determining the responsibilities of individuals and groups.

Second, assuming that each of these sources of responsibility for alleviating poverty – harm, exploitation, and membership in a community, among the relational ones, and the coexistence of need and ability, the nonrelational one – possesses at least *some* moral force and also that the preconditions of each are satisfied in our world, then it would seem that adding them all together will result in a very heavy burden of responsibility on the part of the better-off.[49] Philosophers

---

[49] By preconditions I mean empirical preconditions: that there are good grounds for thinking that people in developed countries are causing some harm to the global

have tended to concentrate on one source of responsibility and neglect the others – without denying that other sources have a role to play. Singer does not assume that the rich have harmed or exploited the poor, and defends extremely demanding duties simply on utilitarian principles. Pogge explicitly relies on negative duties not to harm, without denying that there might also be positive duties to aid. Miller rejects Singer's onerous standard, replacing what he calls Singer's "principle of sacrifice" with a fairly anemic "principle of sympathy."[50] But just as readers might be getting ready to breathe a sigh of relief that their comfortable lives will remain morally intact, Miller provides devastating arguments for the conclusion that as a result of harm and exploitation, people in rich countries have "a vast, largely unmet responsibility," imposing "significant costs" on them, to alleviate global poverty.[51]

I believe each of these sources of responsibility – humanity, harm, exploitation, community, agreements – possesses moral force. They are not all of the same kind or degree; as I have argued, where agreements or harm exist, we have more precise guidelines about the benefits that are called for. In the next chapters I look more closely at the humanitarian argument, on which this book centers. This is not to downplay the force of the other arguments. I focus on the humanitarian argument not only because it avoids the contingency surrounding arguments depending on harm and agreements but also because it seems to me to have a great deal of moral power of its own. How *much* power? What does the argument commit us to in the way of action? The answer to that question is not straightforward, for reasons spelled out in the next few chapters.

It would surely be anticlimactic if that were the end of the story. Fortunately, it's only the middle.

poor, and that they are benefiting from the poor's weak position, and that they live in societies with others with whom they have special relationships.
[50] Miller 2010, ch. 1.   [51] Miller 2010, 1.

CHAPTER 3

Duties and rights, charity and justice

Suppose you are convinced by one or more of the arguments outlined in the last chapter not only that global poverty is a great evil but that it exerts some moral force on you. I believe each of these arguments – agreements, harm, exploitation, community, humanity – has merit. If so, we then confront the question of how much in the way of responsibility they imply, separately or together. Leaving aside their aggregate force, let's focus now on the humanitarian argument. Recall its simplifying advantage of not relying on possibly controversial empirical assumptions – assuming neither that agents who may be responsible for alleviating poverty have contributed to causing it nor even that they benefit from it or take advantage of its victims. This assumption is also in some ways a drawback, insofar as evidence of harm creates greater moral force than the simple conjunction of need and ability assumed by the humanitarian argument. Still, the latter possesses a certain power of its own.

The clearest way to express the idea of moral force is to say that a person's claim of dire need gives others some reason to act to alleviate it. But how much reason does it give them? This question has preoccupied contemporary moral philosophers ever since Peter Singer published his groundbreaking article "Famine, Affluence, and Morality" in 1972. As we saw in Chapter 1, Singer there argues that a person ought to aid the poor up to the point where giving more would make the agent as badly off as those she is helping.[1] Singer seems to mean (and others have taken him to mean) that it is *wrong*

---

[1] Singer 1972. In later works Singer has moderated his conclusions, whether for philosophical or practical reasons. See, e.g., Singer 2010, ch. 10.

not to give this much and that one is *morally obligated* to do so. Most people, including most philosophers, disagree with this radical conclusion. They think Singer demands too much of ordinary people, who cannot be obligated to give so much, especially to those with whom they have no special relationship – and much effort has gone into explaining why he is mistaken. Since Singer offers a utilitarian argument, it may seem easy to reject his conclusion by rejecting utilitarianism, which many do. Still, the thrust of his view – that it is wrong for some to live in luxury or great comfort while others barely survive – possesses power even when shorn of utilitarian connections. And so even those not tempted to go as far as Singer may worry that they do not go far enough, and that comfortable people are morally obligated to do a great deal to alleviate poverty.

Moral philosophers in the modern era have tended to discuss these issues in terms of moral duties, obligations, and rights.[2] They have interpreted "You ought to do *x*" to mean "You are morally obligated to do *x*." In many ways this is not surprising; the legalistic language of rights and obligations is compelling, seeming to leave little room for ambiguity or interpretation, and its appeal is widespread. Beyond academic philosophy, Americans talk promiscuously in the language of rights – although, tellingly, much less often in the language of duties. And at least since the adoption by the United Nations of the Universal Declaration of Human Rights (UDHR) in 1948, talk of human rights has also become common in the international arena. Among the thirty articles in the UDHR, Article 25 is of special interest for our subject:

> Everyone has the right to a standard of living adequate for the health and well-being of himself and of his family, including food, clothing, housing and medical care and necessary social services, and the right to security in the event of unemployment, sickness, disability, widowhood, old age or other lack of livelihood in circumstances beyond his control.[3]

---

[2] As I explained in the last chapter, I use "duty" and "obligation" interchangeably.
[3] *Universal Declaration of Human Rights* 1948.

What does it mean to say that the basic need for a decent standard of living is a moral *right*? Do those who already enjoy a standard well above this line have moral *duties* to bring about this standard for those beneath it? How should the relationships between rights and duties be characterized? In this chapter I examine the language of rights and duties and its implications.

The standard view of duties to aid

I think it's fair to say there is a standard philosophical approach to the problem of humanitarian assistance. It is that negative duties – which, as we saw in the last chapter, have been largely assimilated to duties not to harm – are strict or "perfect," in Kant's terminology, while positive duties, which include duties to aid, are imperfect. (Unless otherwise noted the duties in question are moral duties.) On the traditional Kantian view, humanitarian responsibilities are described as "imperfect duties" of beneficence, allowing a great deal of latitude on the part of agents as to time, place, manner, and extent.[4]

The difference between perfect and imperfect duties is most commonly put in terms of this idea of latitude or discretion: agents have a great deal of leeway in how to discharge imperfect duties of beneficence, including not only the manner or style of discharging them (whether to give to Oxfam or Save the Children, to volunteer in

[4] The man for whom "things are going well, sees that others (whom he could help) have to struggle with great hardships, and he asks, 'What concern of mine is it? . . . I will not take anything from him . . . but to his welfare or to his assistance in time of need I have no desire to contribute.'" Kant concedes that it is possible to *conceive* of the maxim of nonaiding "as a universal law without contradiction." (This is not possible in the case of perfect duties like promise-keeping; the impossibility of conceiving of a maxim as a universal law without contradiction is the defining feature of a perfect duty.) But he argues that it is nevertheless impossible to *will* that the maxim of nonaiding become universal law. "For a will which resolved this would conflict with itself," since the willing person might need the help of others but "would have robbed himself, by such a law of nature springing from his own will, of all hope of the aid he desires" (Kant 1997, Ak. 4, 423). From the impossibility of willing the maxim of nonaiding as a universal law it follows, for Kant, that aiding is an imperfect duty.

a soup kitchen, or to tutor disadvantaged children) but also just how much time, effort, and financial resources to expend.

But another feature of some duties is also thought to render them imperfect. Some duties correlate with rights of others, and some do not. Barring a few exceptions, everyone has a moral duty not to kill or commit violence against others, and all those who are owed such duties (i.e., everyone, barring the few exceptions) have correlative rights not to be killed or have violence committed against them. Barring some exceptions, everyone has a moral duty not to lie or take others' property, and all those owed such duties have rights not to be lied to or to have their property taken.

Rights, on the standard view, necessarily entail or correlate with duties on the part of others: for it to be meaningful – more than simply the expression of an aspiration – to assert that someone has a right to x (whether x is a good, an act, or a forbearance), duties of at least one other person must be specified. It is easy, then, to see the difficulty with positive rights to aid or a universal right to a decent standard of living: for them to be real and meaningful, we must be able to say *who* has the duty to fulfill them or not to violate them and exactly what and how much such agents must do. No such difficulties seem to attend negative rights. The answer to the question "Who has the duty not to kill A and B and C?" is "Everyone!" There is no difficulty, it seems, because the duty is merely negative, a duty to refrain from acting rather than a duty to act; and it is a refraining that we take to be not overly demanding. Requiring people not to kill others, commit aggression against them, lie to them, rob them doesn't seem to be asking very much. But requiring them to help others, in particular strangers with whom they have no special tie, immediately raises several questions. Who has the duty? How much does a person have to do? Is there a limit to what can be demanded?[5]

---

[5] Onora O'Neill casts doubt on the universality of rights such as those embodied in Article 25 on precisely these grounds – that unlike negative rights, they do not clearly imply what duties follow. The corresponding duties, she argues, must belong "to specified others rather than to all others" (O'Neill 2005, 428).

On the standard view, the correlativity of rights and duties goes only in one direction: rights entail duties on the part of others, but duties do not necessarily entail others' rights. Whatever humanitarian duties or duties of beneficence there are, on this view, lack correlative rights-holders.

So we have two sets of distinctions among duties: whether or not they admit of latitude as to the manner and extent of their fulfillment, and whether or not they correlate with individual rights. These properties are distinct. In theory, a person could have a strict or perfect duty to donate some part of her income to alleviating others' suffering even though no particular person had a right to her donation. But in practice the two conditions – the strictness of the duty, concretely specified, and the existence of a correlative right-holder – have usually been conflated.

Moral obligation

If we think abstractly and generally about individual duties of aid or beneficence, almost inevitably they must be imperfect both in the sense of being vague – leaving a lot of latitude in terms of the manner and extent of fulfillment – and in the sense of not carrying correlative rights. Suppose, however, we think instead about particular examples.

Think first about cases of easy rescue. Does A have a moral obligation to tell Z that "a river is swollen so high that Z cannot safely attempt to ford it"?[6] Does a passerby have a duty to rescue a drowning child, when she can do so with no cost to herself?[7] In the latter case – Singer's much-discussed drowning child example – the pond is shallow and the passerby risks nothing more than muddy clothes. What could be easier than doing what is necessary to save the people in these examples? There are no conflicting demands, and costs to the agent are nil or minuscule. Still, in discussing such

---

[6] The example comes from the English historian Thomas Babington Macaulay, chair of the commission to draft the Indian Penal Code, which was ultimately adopted in 1860 (2013, 704–6).

[7] Singer 1972.

examples with students, I have gotten different answers depending on exactly how the question is posed.

Ought you (or should you) save the drowning child? Of course you should, students say.

Are you a jerk (creep, morally challenged, other unprintable words) if you don't save him? Definitely.

Is it morally wrong not to save him? Yes.

Do you have a moral duty or obligation to save him? Students are often more reluctant to answer yes to this question than to the others. In fact, the terms *duty* and *obligation* sometimes seem to catch them up short.[8]

Why might someone be reluctant to assert that a person has a *moral obligation* to save the drowning child? One reason is that they connect the concept of moral obligation with the legitimacy of coercion. The belief is not entirely without warrant. For example, in his classic essay "Are There Any Natural Rights?," H.L.A. Hart argues that the most important characteristic of the concepts of justice, fairness, right, and obligation is that there is a "special congruity in the use of force or the threat of force" to secure the good in question – that "it is in just these circumstances that coercion of another human being is legitimate."[9] It is easy to see why, on this view, libertarians might feel compelled to deny that people are morally obligated to aid others.[10]

Elizabeth Anscombe goes further, claiming that terms like "moral obligation" and "moral requirement" presuppose a "law conception of ethics" and that "it is not possible to have such a conception unless you believe in God as a law-giver."[11] Probably few contemporary philosophers find the latter requirement plausible; suffice it to say that

---

[8] In thinking about these distinctions I have benefited from Maggie Little's work on "deontic pluralism."

[9] Hart 1955, 17. Hart here follows John Stuart Mill's understanding of a right in *Utilitarianism*: "To have a right . . . is, I conceive, to have something which society ought to defend me in the possession of" (Mill 1979, 52).

[10] See Chapter 2, where I argue that political libertarianism, the view that the state may not force one person to aid another, entails moral libertarianism, the view that individuals are not morally obligated to aid others.

[11] Anscombe 1958, 6.

anyone who wishes to speak of moral or human rights outside a theistic framework must reject it. One reason Anscombe holds this view may be a commitment to the connection between moral obligation and coercion: not only does moral obligation require a lawgiver, she suggests: it requires a law-enforcer.

But it is nevertheless clear that, conceptually, we can separate the claim that one has a moral obligation to do something from the claim that the state is justified in coercing one to do it or that God will punish one for not doing it. In that case, to say that "A has a moral obligation to save the drowning child" would be just another way of saying "It is wrong for A not to save her."[12] I believe this way of speaking is at least as prevalent in ordinary discourse as the meaning that links obligation and coercion.

Of course, we may still ask *why* it is wrong not to save the drowning child or not to warn the traveler of the rising waters. At this point some will appeal to one or another moral theory – as Anscombe suggests we must do to make the claim coherent. Others will take the assertion as more obvious than any theory that could be employed to explain its wrongness.[13] In any case, once the linkage with coercion is severed, most people will probably agree that one is morally obligated to save the drowning child and to warn the traveler.

Should we also say that the traveler and the drowning child have a moral *right* to be rescued? There seems no reason to deny it, since the duty in this case is a duty *of this particular traveler* to rescue *this particular person* in dire need. The reason for asserting the duty seems to correlate precisely with the legitimate claim of the endangered person to assistance.

But it is easy to see why many are reluctant to acknowledge a *right* to aid, even if it seems plausible in this case. The correlation of a right to aid with a specific individual's duty rarely holds. Suppose, for

---

[12] Hart would probably reject this approach. He notes disapprovingly that many philosophers use "obligation" as "an obscuring general label to cover every action that morally we ought to do or forbear from doing" (Hart 1955, 178). And he might say the same about using it for every action that it would be *wrong* not to do.

[13] For further discussion of the link with moral theory see Chapter 5.

example, you agree that anyone with an income above x is morally obligated to give away y percent of her income to alleviate poverty. Does it follow that any particular person has a *right* to a portion of your income? Clearly not. Who could it be? A chambermaid in Tucson? A farmer in Sudan? A fisherman in Burma?

My point is that what philosophers have called duties of beneficence – nonrelational duties to aid others, or what I have described as humanitarian responsibilities – possess two distinct features that come into view when we consider particular cases. Sometimes (e.g., in easy rescues) such duties might both specify concrete actions and correlate with rights-holders at the other end.[14] But duties to aid could specify concrete requirements (for example, give away y percent of your income) even in cases where no particular individual could justifiably claim a right to your assistance.

Rights, thin and thick

If rights must ultimately be cashed out in terms of duties on the part of someone to satisfy the rights, why speak of rights at all? Why not speak only of duties, since that's where the action is? Rights express something over and above what can be said in terms of duties alone. It is the idea that people sometimes have legitimate claims that ought to be met, that they are sometimes *entitled* to goods, actions, or forbearances on the part of others. The word "entitlement" has legalistic overtones, but the entitlement in question here is moral.[15]

---

[14] For a useful interpretation of the Kantian approach see Stohr 2011. Stohr argues that "decisions about whom to help, when to help, and how much to help are a matter of judgment and hence, admit latitude. But beneficence also carries with it a narrow duty to avoid indifference to others as end-setters. It is wrong not to help when helping is the only way to avoid indifference" (2011, 67). Not to perform an easy rescue (such as warning the traveler of the rising waters or saving the drowning child in Singer's example) is to exhibit gross indifference, and thus these rescues are morally required.

[15] People often speak interchangeably of entitlement and desert. We sometimes say people *deserve* to be treated in certain ways (e.g., in ways that respect their dignity), sometimes that they are *entitled* to certain treatment. There are often good reasons for keeping these concepts distinct, as Joel Feinberg explains in "Justice and

Americans in particular throw around rights-talk promiscuously. And not all moral rights are equally important. Still, most will agree that there are legitimate moral claims individuals may make, some concerning matters of fundamental significance. Least controversial are rights not to be killed or subjected to violence.

What does the assertion of moral rights or entitlements mean or imply? At least two dimensions must be fleshed out. One concerns the corresponding duty-holders, which could be individuals or collective entities such as governments. A second question is whether the duties are single-layered or multi-layered – in a sense I shall explain shortly. Each of these distinctions could be described in terms of "thinness" and "thickness."

Philosophers often talk in ways that suggest moral rights are thin in both senses: the duties are held by individuals, and they are single-layered. The rights carry correlative duties – otherwise they would be merely aspirational – but these duties are obligations to refrain from violating the right (if the right is "negative") or duties to satisfy or fulfill it (if the right is "positive"). Negative rights are thought easy to satisfy because they entail duties only to refrain from acting; the duties correlating with would-be positive rights seem to be indeterminate, potentially very demanding, or both. And that explains why many people think these humanitarian duties or duties of beneficence must be severely limited at best.

As we saw in the last chapter, libertarians deny such rights and duties altogether. Nozick, for example, argues that

> the major objection to speaking of everyone's having a right *to* various things such as equality of opportunity, life, and so on, and enforcing this right, is that these "rights" require a substructure of things and actions; and *other* people may have rights and entitlements over these ... There are particular rights over particular things held by particular persons ... No rights exist in conflict with this substructure of particular rights ... The particular rights over things fill the space of rights, leaving no room for general rights to be in a certain material condition.[16]

Personal Desert" (1970). Still, it's not clear in cases such as these that the distinction is sharp.

[16] Nozick 1974, 238 (emphasis in original).

Nozick begs the central question. It could just as plausibly be argued that rights to "be in a certain material condition" (e.g., to have enough to eat) limit the particular rights of others (e.g., their property rights).

Leaving aside arguments about just what rights and duties there are, the thin view of rights fails to capture the way certain basic rights are understood in popular and political discourse. Think again of Article 25 (and many other articles) of the Universal Declaration of Human Rights, and of many articles in the International Covenant on Civil and Political Rights (ICCPR); the International Covenant on Economic, Social and Cultural Rights (ICESCR); the European Convention on Human Rights (ECHR); and American Convention on Human Rights (ACHR).[17]

If the language in these documents is not merely aspirational – expressing hopes and desires for what might be in some better world than ours – then there must be a conception of rights at work other than the thin conception. And there is. This thicker view articulates a more complex, political conception implicit in talk of human rights.

A leading proponent is Henry Shue, whose 1980 book *Basic Rights* sets out this political conception in detail. According to Shue, "a moral right provides (1) the rational basis for a justified demand (2) that the actual enjoyment of a substance be (3) socially guaranteed against standard threats."[18] Central to this conception is the idea – which could slip past the unsuspecting reader almost unnoticed but which fundamentally alters the nature of basic moral rights – that such rights must provide *social guarantees* against standard threats. Rights do not simply entail moral duties on the part of other individuals or even governments; the performance of these duties must be assured so rights-holders can count on having the substance of their rights fulfilled. These social guarantees are most typically political guarantees.

---

[17] *International Covenant on Civil and Political Rights* 1966; *International Covenant on Economic, Social and Cultural Rights* 1966; *European Convention on Human Rights* 1950; *American Convention on Human Rights* 1969.
[18] Shue 1996 (1980), 13.

The claim of social guarantees points to a persistent ambiguity in the notion of a right. Abstractly, a person can have a *right* to another's action or forbearance without a *guarantee* of action or forbearance. This is the standpoint of the thin conception. On this view, moral rights are simply imperatives about what people may legitimately claim and about what others must as a result do or not do. Although conceptually it is important to distinguish the moral imperatival aspect of rights from any idea of enforcement, guarantees of enforcement are, as we saw earlier, often thought implicit in discussions of rights, from John Stuart Mill to H.L.A. Hart to Robert Nozick. Shue probably does not intend to make social guarantees essential to *all* moral rights. But basic rights, which concern "the morality of the depths . . . the line beneath which no one is to be allowed to sink," must, he believes, include such guarantees.[19] Shue includes both what he calls "security rights" against physical aggression and violence and "subsistence rights" to a decent minimum among the basic rights.

Once we grant that rights require social guarantees, Shue argues, the sharp distinction between the apparently undemanding negative rights and the apparently demanding positive rights fades. Security rights – what most people call "negative rights" – necessarily require complex and expensive institutions like police, courts, and legal systems. And, on the other hand, subsistence rights to a decent standard of living, usually considered "positive rights," need not mean being provided with food, clothing, and shelter but instead with "some opportunity for supporting oneself."[20]

Who bears the duties corresponding to moral rights – in particular to these crucial basic or human rights? The abstract philosophical

---

[19] Shue 1996 (1980), 18.
[20] Shue 1996 (1980), 40. Shue expands on this point in the afterword to the second edition: the right to have x may entail "a duty to stay out of people's way while they take x for themselves, or a duty to teach them to read so they can figure out how to make or grow x, or a duty to let them form a political party so that they can effectively demand that the government stop exporting x" (ibid., 164). Some of these duties may be positive and some negative; in general, however, they require less intervention of the micromanaging variety that concerns many welfare-rights skeptics.

conception suggests that individuals are their main addressees, and this explains much of the skepticism about rights to basic necessities such as food, shelter, and healthcare. A thicker, political conception, on the other hand, denies that individuals bear the primary duties corresponding to these rights. James Nickel writes that "human rights are political norms dealing mainly with how people should be treated by their governments and institutions. *They are not ordinary moral norms applying mainly to interpersonal conduct* (such as prohibitions of lying and violence)."[21] Similarly, Thomas Pogge argues that "human-rights violations, to count as such, must be in some sense official . . . human rights thus protect persons only against violations from certain sources."[22] This view is built into the structure of all human rights instruments – such as the ICCPR, the ICESCR, the ECHR, and the ACHR.

Shue probably agrees with Nickel and Pogge that governments are the primary bearers of duties corresponding to human rights, but he goes further, multiplying the kinds of duties that correlate with rights. To every basic right, he believes three kinds of duties correspond: "I. Duties to *avoid* depriving. II. Duties to *protect* from deprivation. III. Duties to *aid* the deprived."[23] This is a very thick conception! Some of these duties fall on those outside a person's government – not only on collective entities (including other governments and NGOs) but also on individuals. If governments were the only addressees, there could be no recourse when governments violated their citizens' human rights. Since governments are often the prime violators, this outcome would largely defeat the purpose of rights. When people's basic rights are violated, others besides their government – whether individuals, other governments, international agencies, or other collective bodies – sometimes have responsibilities to act.

---

[21] Nickel 2010, sec. 1 (emphasis in original). See also Nickel 2007, 10.

[22] Pogge 2001 (1995), 192. A somewhat different version appears as ch. 3 of Pogge's 2002 *World Poverty and Human Rights*.

[23] Shue 1996 (1980), 52.

On any conception of rights, it is necessary to specify what duties fall on which individuals, governments, and other collective entities. If the corresponding duties fall on individuals, would-be rights to a decent standard of living or to some minimum level of subsistence immediately raise the problem of demandingness (or over-demandingness). How much is an individual required to do? In answering this question there is an almost inevitable tendency among philosophers to make the duties either quite lax or very demanding. It is tempting to say "too lax" and "too demanding," but for the moment I will leave the claims in more neutral terms.

A few, like Singer and Peter Unger, demand that people sacrifice a great deal – more than almost anyone believes is morally required and more than almost anyone in fact sacrifices. Like Singer, Unger believes that "on pain of living a life that's seriously immoral, a typical well-off person, like you and me, must give away most of her financially valuable assets, and much of her income, directing the funds to lessen efficiently the serious suffering of others."[24] Critics of this standard, largely relying on common sense, defend duties that are much less demanding and that do not entail others' rights to our assistance. Liam Murphy, for example, argues that we are required to do our fair share (e.g., to eliminate poverty), which is that amount that would be needed if everyone did her fair share. It may well be that if everyone did her fair share then no one would have to sacrifice a great deal. But, of course, not everyone does; on Murphy's view, however, one is not required to take this into account and make up for the slack in a way that might be truly demanding.[25]

Similarly, as we saw in the last chapter, Richard Miller pulls back from the very demanding standard, offering a principle of sympathy to replace what he calls Singer's principle of sacrifice. Sympathy is owed to all people regardless of one's relationship to them, but it does

---

[24] Unger 1996, 134. Singer is less judgmental and doesn't use words like "immoral," although his requirements are similar.

[25] Murphy 1993.

not demand very much; one is not required to do things that "would impose a significant risk of worsening one's life."[26]

What *are* governments' duties?

The thick, political view of rights does not escape demandingness problems. It must also explain just what and how much governments, outside entities, and individuals must do to satisfy human rights. But there are prior questions that need to be answered about this conception.

One is how well the distinction between the duties of institutions and the duties of individuals holds up. There are at least two reasons to believe it is exaggerated. The first is conceptual: the duties of institutions ultimately fall on individuals, because institutions are ultimately constituted by individuals, and it is they who render institutions actors. Government neglect or abuse of human rights means the neglect or abuse by *human agents* within the government. Of course, the acts of institutions often depend on the aggregate or joint acts of individuals, not on individuals acting alone. And they are acts of individuals in their capacity as agents of government, not as private persons. So to say human rights make demands on institutions and not individuals is to say that they make demands on individuals in their roles within institutions, not individuals in their private capacity.

More important than this conceptual point is a moral one. If human rights held solely against governments, then those outside government or in their nongovernmental capacities might be disempowered from acting and beyond the reach of criticism for failing to prevent, protest, fight, or compensate for government violations of human rights. For human rights to be able to do what we want them to do, they must impose burdens not only on governments but on

---

[26] Miller 2010, 13. But Miller takes back with one hand what he gives with the other: while endorsing a weak principle of humanitarian assistance, he argues for powerful global duties of justice of the rich to the poor based on harm and exploitation.

individuals and institutions outside governments, who will often be the violators of their citizens' rights.[27]

Even to the extent that duties corresponding to human rights fall primarily on people's own governments, this claim is open to a variety of interpretations, narrow and broad. The breadth of interpretations is reflected in deep ambiguities in the phrase "how people should be treated by their governments." For example, does it imply only government action, or does it encompass omissions as well? What constitutes "treatment"?

The US Supreme Court asserted a narrow interpretation in *Deshaney v. Winnebago County Social Services Department*. It held that a state's failure to protect a boy who became profoundly retarded after he had been violently abused by his father over a long period, even after the state received repeated reports of abuse, did not violate the boy's rights.[28] Such conduct would violate Article 3(2) of the Convention on the Rights of the Child (CRC),[29] as well as Article 3 (asserting a right to the security of the person) and Article 5 (prohibiting torture and "cruel, inhuman or degrading treatment or punishment") of the Universal Declaration of Human Rights. The question is whether the government is implicated when the acts have been committed by private persons. The Supreme Court said no.

By contrast, consider Pogge's account of the ways governments can disrespect human rights:[30]

---

[27] Despite what he describes as his institutional understanding of human rights, Pogge makes the very strong individualistic claim that "since citizens are collectively responsible for their society's organization and its resulting human-rights record, human rights ultimately make demands upon (especially the more privileged) citizens" (2001 (1995), 200). See also Charles Beitz's *The Idea of Human Rights* for a pragmatic account of human rights that justifies international responses to rights violations by governments (Beitz 2009).

[28] *Deshaney* 1989.

[29] "States Parties undertake to ensure the child such protection and care as is necessary for his or her well-being, taking into account the rights and duties of his or her parents, legal guardians, or other individuals legally responsible for him or her, and, to this end, shall take all appropriate legislative and administrative measures" (*Convention on the Rights of the Child* 1989). The United States and Somalia are the only countries that have not ratified the CRC.

[30] Pogge 2001 (1995), 193–7.

1. Governments can create or maintain "(unjust) laws that permit or require human-rights violations."
2. They may do so "under the color of law," i.e., "by perversely construing existing legislation as licensing human-rights-violating policies."
3. A government may refrain from human-rights violations but "reserve for itself the legal power to order or authorize" them.
4. It may pass human-rights legislation but not enforce it.[31]
5. It may organize or encourage private groups to violate human rights.
6. Even if it does not organize or encourage them, a government may "stand idly by" when private groups violate human rights.
7. Citizens may fear "violent interference or punitive measures" so much that they refrain from conduct protected by human-rights standards or legislation. In such cases, lack of government interference in protected conduct does not signify respect for human rights.

Pogge divides government misconduct regarding human rights into two categories: official government violations, and manifestations of "official disrespect."[32] The line between these is not always clear; Pogge includes the first two in the above list as violations, whereas the others presumably constitute less serious but nonetheless unacceptable offenses. Others might draw the line in a different place. By including manifestations of official disrespect as impermissible, Pogge elides the distinction some would make between violating a person's rights and allowing them to be violated.

Cases like *Deshaney* fit under the sixth category: the government "standing idly by" while a private person violates a person's human right not to be subjected to cruel and inhuman treatment.[33] "Standing

---

[31] Although Pogge mentions passing human-rights legislation but not enforcing it as one way to violate people's human rights, it seems clear that such legislation being "on the books" is not necessary, according to Pogge, to violate human rights. Human rights are pre-existing, whether or not they are legally in force.

[32] Pogge 2001 (1995), 192.

[33] If human rights are in the first instance rights against a person's government, how can we talk about "a right not to be subjected to cruel and inhuman treatment" full

idly by" suggests that the government is aware of the mistreatment. In *Deshaney* this was so: the Winnebago County Department of Social Services had taken steps to protect the child, so it was clearly aware of the abuse; the problem was that the agency did not remove the child from his father's custody. But perhaps a stronger condition is appropriate: the government shows official disrespect in those cases when it *ought* to be aware of (private) mistreatment, whether it is, in fact, or not.

This complex spectrum of types of problematic government conduct and attitudes toward mistreatment of individuals leaves several questions unanswered. If we distinguish between direct violations of human rights by governments and manifestations of official disrespect ("standing idly by" and the like), do governments have strict duties to avoid both? When we consider civil, political, and security rights, duties to refrain from direct violations are much easier to satisfy than duties to refrain from all possible manifestations of official disrespect; and committing direct violations may seem to demonstrate greater *mens rea* and be particularly reprehensible. Are the duties to be distinguished in terms of strength, and, if so, how? Shall we say all these duties are strict, but some are stricter than others?

Pogge's list and the accompanying descriptions suggest violations of civil, political, or security rights. With rights to a decent standard of living or economic rights, the distinction between direct violations and manifestations of official disrespect becomes harder to draw. Suppose one endorses a basic right to subsistence as in Article 25 of the Universal Declaration of Human Rights, and suppose this is a right in the first instance against one's government. When people lack basic necessities, it will often be difficult to tell whether their government has engaged in direct violations or is manifesting official disrespect – or what the difference amounts to.

---

stop? Is it part of the very meaning of the right that the correlative duty is a duty of government? I take it the answer is no, otherwise a violation by a private party would not be a violation of a human right. But it appears that even those who believe human rights are rights against governments talk as if private violations are violations.

On Shue's view, although the duties to satisfy human rights fall in the first instance on governments, individuals are not off the hook. They have duties when governments fail, as governments so often do. But in addition they have ongoing indirect duties "to create, maintain, and enhance institutions that directly fulfill rights."[34] That these duties are indirect does not, Shue admits, mean "they are any less onerous in the magnitude of time, money, energy, and so forth that they require to be invested. In principle, indirect duties could be more demanding than direct duties."[35] The thought that, although people might not be required to contribute a large portion of their incomes to relieve suffering, they are morally obligated to invest a great deal of time attempting to influence the political process or reform social institutions, will not comfort those concerned about the demandingness of human rights. Indeed, Shue's view might be thought to suggest a glut of duties, even a regress of duties. But we should resist the temptation to return to the thin conception, attributing duties to individuals, or assuming the duties of individuals or governments are single-layered. These approaches are too anemic to serve the purposes of rights.

Rights, urgency, and justice

One might despair at the enormity of the demands talk of rights makes, whether on the thin or the thick conception, and conclude we should avoid it altogether. And yet something important would be lost if we did. Rights (at least these rights, what Shue calls basic rights, for the "morality of the depths") express not only urgency but entitlement – what a person may appropriately demand. You don't have to ask nicely to have your rights fulfilled.

This sense of urgency coupled with entitlement explains the connection between the language of rights and the language of justice. Rights carry correlative duties; or, putting it the other way round, some duties are perfect and correlate with rights. In these

[34] Shue 1988, 696. And Pogge agrees, as we saw earlier (2001 (1995), 200).
[35] Shue 1988, 697.

circumstances – where rights are concerned – we speak of matters of justice. Whether or not we accept Rawls's view that "justice is the first virtue of institutions,"[36] it is impossible to deny the rhetorical and moral primacy of justice.

In an essay celebrating the fiftieth anniversary of the founding of Oxfam – an organization that, like others with similar missions, is typically called a charity – Philippa Foot describes a time in the 1960s when "the call began to be heard [among members of Oxfam] to replace the concept of charity with that of justice." What, she asks, does this shift amount to?

> Fundamentally, it means that the help that is given to those who need it is seen as something *to which they have a right* rather than solely as something which, from compassion, we want them to have. As a motive, compassion still comes into it, or at least a strong sense of solidarity with others; but now the idea is that what is given is in some sense or other what we owe them. For if anybody has a right to something, he or she has what ... Herbert Hart ... has called "a piece of moral property"; that is, a valid claim which others are morally wrong to disregard.[37]

Similar problems attach to the philosopher's idea of "beneficence" as to Foot's understanding of charity. Beneficence, which "connotes acts of mercy, kindness, and charity,"[38] has no ordinary meaning outside philosophical circles. It suggests virtuous character traits. Insofar as these terms do suggest acts, beneficence and charity seem to imply imperfect duties lacking rights attached at the other end, or even supererogatory acts – those above and beyond duty. The ideas of charity and beneficence suggest that a person who fails to act charitably or beneficently does not do wrong. Words like "aid," "assistance," and "help" have similar connotations. As Foot suggests, the language of charity lacks the assertion of human dignity associated with the concepts of right and entitlement, and seems tinged with condescension.

---

[36] Rawls 1971, 3.
[37] Foot 1993, 7 (emphasis in original). Foot was involved with Oxfam almost since its beginnings in the 1950s. Motives are a different matter, which I return to in Chapter 9.
[38] Beauchamp 2008.

Is the idea of charity necessarily condescending? After all, it is conceptually possible, I have argued, for a duty to aid to be perfect in the sense of determinate (e.g., give 10 percent of your income) even if no particular individual has a right to your donation. In that case the agent really has a duty to perform the action, and it would seem that overtones of generosity and "the goodness of your heart" are misplaced. But if "charity" and "beneficence" by definition imply that the recipient is not *entitled* to the agent's assistance, that the agent does not *owe* something to the recipient, then it is easy to think the recipient ought at the very least to be grateful for what is given.[39]

Some, of course, will happily agree that the deeds are unowed. Amoralists believe nothing is owed. Libertarians think only duties not to harm are owed unless one has contracted otherwise or has previously harmed someone and owes compensation. Even some nonlibertarians argue that "justice is something we owe through our shared institutions only to those with whom we stand in a strong political relation," i.e., a state.[40] On this view duties to noncompatriots lie outside the realm of justice. Others may think owing is just the wrong terminology for describing what is at issue here.[41]

On the other side, as we saw in the last chapter, many who insist that people have rights to a certain standard of living believe that these people – whether in developing countries or in our own – have in fact been harmed by others and that such harm is sufficient to justify their rights and the language of justice. Perhaps they would also endorse the humanitarian view that all human beings have the right to a decent minimum, irrespective of whether their plight results from harms of others who now bear corresponding duties. But these expansionists, as I call them, often insist that harm suffices to explain why we in the developed world owe the poor in developing countries something. Their view of harm is broader than that of

---

[39] See Chapter 8 for further discussion of defects in the concepts of charity, beneficence, and aid – among them the suggestion that the recipient is indebted to the donor.

[40] Nagel 2005, 121.

[41] Whether for the kinds of reasons Anscombe gives – that it suggests a law-giver or law-enforcer – or for other reasons. See Chapter 5 for further discussion.

libertarians, and they will call for rectification, reparations, or compensation.[42] Like libertarians, expansionists often associate nonrelational sources of duty with beneficence or charity – and it is difficult not to characterize their attitude by prefacing these terms with the qualifier "mere." A true commitment to human rights, including the right to a decent minimum, must avoid downgrading the humanitarian argument in this way.

Rights without duties?

Wouldn't it be nice if there could be rights without correlative duties? Every decent person agrees that dire poverty is a very bad thing and that poor people do not deserve to be deprived of the basic necessities of life. We would probably all like to say the poor have rights to these necessities, but for the inconvenient fact that such claims by their nature come with strings attached. Duties without rights makes sense, but rights without duties does not. Rights by their nature impose demands and constraints on other people. The problem is partly demandingness – how much is it reasonable to ask people to do? – and partly a matter of identifying exactly those agents who must act. These things cannot be left to chance.

A promising way to mitigate these problems is to collectivize and thereby institutionalize duties. Suppose the locus of responsibility for relieving dire poverty was not *I*, the individual, but *We*, the society or community. As an American, I focus on the United States; residents of other developed countries can think of their own societies and governments. Explaining the metaphysical and moral relationships between I and We is a difficult task and I will not attempt to shed much light on it here; instead, I assume that we have some kind of rough understanding of and belief in the idea that individuals are members of groups such as societies and partake in collective

---

[42] Expansionists may also speak of exploitation, but they may use the term differently than I do (see Miller 2010, 59). To exploit people in my sense is to treat them badly by taking advantage of them in some way but *not* by making them worse off than they would have been had one not so treated them; expansionists do not necessarily adhere to this condition.

enterprises, intentions, and moral responsibilities.[43] Although in a democracy we identify the people with their government, the communal view I have in mind is not equivalent to the idea examined earlier in this chapter that the addressees of human rights are governments or that governments have the primary duty to protect their citizens' interests. For one thing, our subject here is the responsibility to benefit people *outside* one's own society.

Why should we conceive of duties as belonging to collectives rather than individuals? There are several related reasons. First, it is easier to identify the agents (countries, for example, are easy to spot); specifying those responsible for acting is one of the main problems with so-called positive duties. Second, many of the problems in question are most appropriately viewed as arising from the collective behavior of groups or the aggregation of many individuals' behavior. Third, institutions can address these problems much more efficiently than can individuals. Last but not least, such a shift would reduce the demands on individuals, and this is one of the great stumbling blocks to eradicating poverty. Let me briefly elaborate on some of these points, particularly the last and its relation to the others. They are developed in subsequent chapters.

First, when a community acts together it can have a much greater impact than isolated individuals can: "the aggregate of individually small investments by large numbers of persons could reach a significant sum, especially if cooperation and coordination occurred among those acting in fulfillment of duty."[44] Less obvious is the motivational value of this fact. When people act together rather than as isolated individuals, each putting a drop in the ocean, they can see significant results.[45] They may even be inspired.

---

[43] For investigations of these issues see, e.g., May and Hoffman 1991.

[44] Shue 1988, 695. "Isolated and uncoordinated efforts by individuals are materially wasteful and can be psychologically oppressive to no good purpose" (ibid., 697).

[45] In the decisionmaking literature "the common tendency to put little weight on very small outcomes – both gains and losses" – is called the "peanuts effect" (Loewenstein, John, and Volpp 2013, 364). The peanuts effect explains why people buy lottery tickets at a dollar apiece despite the minuscule chances of winning. In the context of humanitarian assistance the peanuts effect may seem particularly irrational. The

Second, if a community acts together each person needs to do much less in absolute terms than he would if acting in isolation. Peter Singer estimates that if all comfortable people were doing their fair share to alleviate poverty, the amount each would need to give "would be in the hundreds, rather than thousands, of dollars per year."[46] Acting alone, they might have to make large sacrifices, and, equally important, they would have to think, worry, and decide what sacrifices to make.

Third, the fact of collective action suggests (although it does not entail) that the acts are compelled rather than voluntary, ensuring nearly full compliance. Perhaps under the influence of libertarian thinking, many people believe that it is wrong to force people to do things, such as help others, even if they are under a moral obligation to do them. But the reverse is sometimes more accurate. As Thomas Nagel argues:

> Sometimes it is proper to force people to do something even though it is not true that they should do it without being forced. It is acceptable to compel people to contribute to the support of the indigent by automatic taxation, but unreasonable to insist that in the absence of such a system they ought to contribute voluntarily. The latter is an excessively demanding moral position because it requires voluntary decisions that are quite difficult to make ... This is partly due to lack of assurance that others would do likewise and fear of relative disadvantage; but it is also a sensible rejection of excessive demands on the will, which can be more irksome than automatic demands on the purse.[47]

Nagel here alludes to at least two distinct reasons why coercion can be less burdensome than voluntary action. The first has to do with "excessive demands on the will." It's easier to contribute to others' welfare automatically – as, for example, through taxation – than to have to continually think about it and decide to contribute.

The other reason – fourth – has to do with relative disadvantage. As I argue in detail in Chapters 6 and 7, for a variety of reasons – having to do with such things as infrastructure, habituation,

value of saving one person's life, even out of a total of millions or more who need assistance, can hardly be denied.

[46] Singer 2010, 142.   [47] Nagel 1975, 145–6.

psychological salience, and status – well-being is largely relative, so even apart from the motivation that comes from seeing substantial change occur through widespread action, giving up goods can involve much less cost to the agent if others give them up too.[48] In a community with good public transportation where few people have cars, you will not be disadvantaged without a car. Conversely, as Adam Smith famously noted, if respectable people in your society wear linen shirts or leather shoes, you need them as well to be respectable. Compelling everyone to act eliminates the free rider problem, and individuals then have one further reason not to resent contributing to others' welfare.

Finally, it seems appropriate that the locus of responsibility for alleviating poverty should be the group rather than the individual, since the existence of massive global poverty cannot be disentangled from deep-seated structural features of institutions in the contemporary world. Better-off people participate in these institutions as small elements in a large, complex web. But in many respects they cannot make significant differences acting alone.

Summarizing, and a look ahead

Among philosophers the most common language for addressing the problem of global poverty morally is the language of rights and duties. According to the standard analysis, rights entail duties, but duties do not necessarily entail rights. A thin conception of rights prevailed in philosophical circles for many years. It can be thin in either or both of two senses. First, it might posit that individual rights correlate with individual duties – thus, an individual right to x (whether x is a good, an act, or a forbearance) entails a duty or duties of one or more individuals to satisfy the right (whether by transferring a good, performing an act, or refraining from acting). Second, and perhaps more important, on the standard analysis the

---

[48] The point assumes that the way to raise the well-being of the poor is to lower the well-being of the rich. This assumption is not always well-founded, but for my purposes here it will do.

duties (even if they are duties of collectives such as governments) corresponding to rights are conceived as single-layered. Putting it in Shue's terms, they are duties to avoid depriving, but not duties to protect from deprivation or to aid the deprived.[49]

Even in the absence of a right (to a decent standard of living, for example), philosophers have asked how much a person "owes" in the way of assistance to others – distant strangers – in dire need.[50] Philosophers who frame these questions in terms of individual duties tend to conclude that they are either very demanding or rather lax. Demanding duties might be problematic on moral grounds – they might require more than is reasonable to ask of ordinary human beings. They might also be problematic simply on pragmatic grounds – it might be unrealistic to expect people to act in accordance with them. (In Chapter 5 I argue that the moral and the pragmatic are not easily distinguishable.)

The thick, political conception of rights and duties includes not simply moral obligations but social guarantees of their fulfillment. Once we acknowledge social guarantees it is inevitable that the duties corresponding to rights will be multi-layered; even if the first-line duties belong to governments, there must be back-up duties belonging to other collectives and to individuals if the rights are to be meaningful.

The thick conception might seem to avoid demandingness problems, since the bearers of duties corresponding to basic or human rights are primarily governments rather than individuals. But satisfying human rights, such as the right to a decent standard of living, can be demanding for governments too. In addition, since governments may have problems fulfilling their citizens' human rights and are sometimes the prime violators of them, the question is what other agents, whether individual or collective, must do in such cases. Demandingness worries again rear their head.

---

[49] Shue 1996 (1980), 52.
[50] In accordance with the structure outlined in Chapter 2, I focus here on nonrelational obligations – those not grounded in previously having harmed or exploited others and not grounded in shared nationality or other relevant group-hood.

We cannot make demandingness problems disappear entirely. Eradicating global poverty (to mention only the basic human need that is my focus in this book) is not easy. But we can make some headway. In the next several chapters I argue that abandoning the focus on individual moral duty – with emphasis on both the *individual* and the *duty* – is an important step to mitigating the problem of demandingness.

One piece of the argument rests on a close examination and critique of the entrenched distinction between negative and positive duties. In the standard formulation, negative duties are duties to *refrain* from doing things – duties not to harm – while positive duties are duties to *do* things, such as to give aid. In the next chapter I argue that problems of demandingness plague so-called negative duties as well as positive duties. Thus, we cannot dismiss or minimize positive duties on the grounds that they differ radically from negative duties, with the latter being strict or perfect and the former imperfect. Moreover, the distinction between negative and positive duties (or responsibilities, as we should call them in order not to beg the question of whether they *are* duties) is exaggerated in at least two other important ways that have already emerged; I discuss them at the end of the next chapter.

CHAPTER 4

"Negative" and "positive" duties

A reasonable morality cannot continually require us to make very large sacrifices to our own well-being. Both common sense (of which we have reason to be deeply suspicious, of course) and widely accepted philosophical approaches tell us that such requirements impermissibly infringe our autonomy and our ability to live our lives as *our* lives. This critique has commonly formed part of an attack on utilitarianism and consequentialism, but it exerts influence beyond moral theory. The view underlies the popular idea that duties to render aid to others are very limited. Much of its persuasive power lies in the supposed contrast with our "negative" duties not to harm people. Although we have at most imperfect duties to aid people, the argument goes, we have strict or perfect duties not to harm them. And one thing that gives *this* position its persuasive power is the suggestion that not harming people is for the most part straightforward and easy. Don't kill people, don't rape them, don't attack them, don't rob them: if you follow these simple and indisputable rules you are doing what you ought to do and cannot be faulted; at least you have fulfilled your obligations.

But over the last few decades something has changed. We see – or, in many cases, others inform us in no uncertain terms – that our most humdrum activities may harm people in myriad ways we have never thought about before. And because these activities are seamlessly woven into our normal routines, ceasing to engage in what we may call these "New Harms" is not at all easy – not simply a matter of refraining from things we never would have dreamed of doing in the first place, like killing and raping and robbing. Not harming people turns out to be difficult, and to require our undivided attention.

The moral contrast between doing what is required not to harm people and doing what is required to help them may once have seemed sharp, but no longer does. Although on some views minding your own business is all a person is morally obligated to do, even this apparently modest injunction now turns out to be almost impossible. Over the last few decades, but especially in the last few years – with economic, environmental, and electronic globalization rapidly increasing; the threat of severe climate change, whose effects will be felt most by the world's poorest people; knowledge that the provenance of products we use every day is compromised in a variety of ways; and, finally, the growing impossibility of remaining ignorant of these phenomena – we have seen how our ordinary habits and conduct contribute to harming other people near and far, now and in the future. The model of harm underlying the classic formulation of the harm principle – discrete, individual actions with observable and measurable consequences for particular individuals – no longer suffices to explain the ways our behavior impinges on the interests of other people.

Turn off the lights. Use compact fluorescent bulbs (even if they contain mercury and produce an ugly glare). Drive a small, fuel-efficient car. Drive less. Take public transportation. Don't fly unless you really need to (no more trips to international conferences, no more exotic vacations). Turn down the thermostat in winter. Turn off the air conditioning in summer. Make sure your appliances are energy-efficient. Take cooler showers. Eat local (except sometimes; find out when[1]). Don't eat factory-farmed meat – leaving aside harm to animals, producing it is not energy-efficient or environmentally sound. Don't buy Chilean sea bass, or salmon, or ... (fill in the blank, depending on which sea food is at the moment overfished or otherwise unsustainable[2]). Don't drink bottled water – the energy costs of producing and transporting it are wasteful (leaving aside that only 14 percent of bottles are recycled). Don't throw away plastic

---

[1] See Kwok 2008.
[2] See, e.g., Bittman 2009. Despite the title – "Loving Fish, This Time With the Fish in Mind" – the article focuses less on harms to fish than to the environment.

bags (not paper bags either!). Recycle. Compost. Don't use chemical fertilizers on your lawn; better still, get rid of your lawn.[3] In this new world in which we find ourselves, "each bite we eat, each item we discard, each e-mail message we send, and each purchase we make entails a conversion of fossil-fuel carbon to carbon dioxide," with possible deleterious consequences for others and for the globe.[4]

Apart from the environmental consequences of our actions, which disproportionately affect poor people, other harms also loom. Don't buy clothing made in sweatshops. Was your oriental rug knotted by eight-year-olds? Do you own stock in a company that exploits its workers? Is the coltan in your cell phone fueling wars in the Congo? (And what is coltan, anyway?) How much effort would it take to get all this information? Leif Wenar explains how Western consumers may buy goods stolen from developing countries when they purchase all sorts of everyday items, including gas, clothes, cosmetics, electronics, and jewelry.[5] These harms result from flaws in the international system of global commerce, which allows corrupt dictators in resource-rich countries to profit hugely at the expense of their impoverished citizens.

Every bite we eat! Every purchase we make! To *not* do these things, to *know* what not to do, to know what to do instead, can encroach on our resources and our autonomy at least as oppressively as any duties of aid or beneficence. As we saw in the last chapter, Thomas Pogge frames "human rights narrowly as imposing only negative duties," in order to rest his argument for human rights on "widely acceptable" premises.[6] His neglect of positive rights as elements of human rights may seem surprising; one might think a progressive, humanistic philosophy of human rights would embrace protecting the vulnerable even when it is not our fault they are vulnerable. I argued in Chapter 2, by contrast, that the humanitarian argument has moral force of its own. But the question here is why negative duties seem so much more "acceptable" than positive duties,

---

[3] See, e.g., Colbert 2008. [4] Petersen 2008, A25. [5] Wenar 2008, 2.
[6] Pogge 2005, 720.

and whether they will remain so once central features of the New Harms are properly understood.

My aim in this chapter is to make some progress toward answering these questions. What accounts for the difference in our attitudes toward would-be negative and positive duties?[7] How does globalization change the way we *do* affect distant people (for the worse) or *can* affect them (for the better)? How should these changes affect our attitudes and our moral responsibilities?

I begin by examining psychological responses and attitudes related to our capacity for acting, or omitting to act, in the world. The point is to help explain why we feel responsible when the effects of our actions, or our omissions, are near and visible to us – and why we do not feel responsible when they are distant.

In the following sections I explore apparent disanalogies or asymmetries between would-be negative and positive duties. Since I want to show that the moral contrast between negative and positive duties is much less sharp than we have thought, such asymmetries could undermine my conclusion. In fact, I argue, at least one of these asymmetries confirms the commonsense view that negative duties take priority over positive duties. But another asymmetry suggests the opposite conclusion. I argue that a third possible disanalogy is illusory.

I go on to consider the question of demandingness, which has already reared its head and which many people think is a defining difference between negative and positive duties. This discussion takes us into the next chapter, but before concluding this chapter I consider some further reasons for thinking the distinction between negative and positive duties is exaggerated.

Causality and psychology

Central to the classical picture of harm on which the primacy of negative duties depends is "the idea that individuals are primarily

---

[7] I use the term "would-be" in order not to beg the question of whether there is in fact a duty in either the negative or positive case. In what follows the qualifier is often omitted but should be understood.

responsible for the harm which their actions are sufficient to produce without the intervention of others or of extraordinary natural events . . ."[8] Two elements are important. One is that an individual's action is sufficient, without the acts or interventions of other people, to cause harm.[9] The other is that the harmful effects a person's action produces are generally near and immediate. My fist comes into contact with your nose; my car runs you over.

This causal picture less accurately reflects the mode of individual agency increasingly prevalent in the world today than it does classic torts, for example. In the cases we are concerned with here – what I call the New Harms – no individual's action is *the* cause of harm; an individual's action makes at most a causal *contribution* to an overall effect that may be large and significant. Samuel Scheffler describes concomitant changes that apply to cases of this kind in what he calls the phenomenology of agency. Individuals may not be aware of the contribution their act makes, they have little or no control over the larger processes, it is difficult to get information about these processes, and equally difficult to avoid participating in them.[10] Psychologically or phenomenologically, "the primacy of near effects over remote effects means that we tend to experience our causal influence as inversely related to spatial and temporal distance."[11] Recent experiments confirm that "up close and personal" harm is more "emotionally salient" than more remote and impersonal forms of harm, and that the difference influences moral judgments.[12] Since an individual's actions contributing to the New Harms do not produce palpable, immediate, visible effects, we are likely to feel no regret, no guilt, no shame, and no drive to act differently.

These psychological states – or perhaps we should say the absence of them – resemble our mindsets when we do not help distant strangers whom we could help. As Scheffler puts it, "we experience

---

[8] Hart and Honoré 1985, lxxx.
[9] Of course, every event is the effect of a concatenation of many prior events and conditions, including human actions. Which one we pick out as the cause depends on context, our interests, and what is unusual or departs from the routine. See Hart and Honoré 1985, 64 ff. for further discussion.
[10] Scheffler 1995, 233. [11] Scheffler 1995, 228. [12] See Greene *et al.* 2001.

our omissions as omissions only in special contexts."[13] If I fail to jump into the pond to save the drowning child before me, or if I do not intervene when I witness a mugging on the street, I am likely to "experience" the omission. But I will not ordinarily experience my failure to aid hungry children half a world away as an omission, much less as a failure. Ordinarily, I will *have* no experience.

Lacking the relevant psychological states, people do not "feel" they are doing anything wrong when they contribute to the production of New Harms, just as they do not feel guilty when they fail to aid the distant poor; changing behavior is correspondingly more difficult.

The moral priority of avoiding harm over helping?

It is widely believed that duties not to harm are more stringent than duties to aid. One basis for this belief is that one who harms another makes that person worse off than she would have been had the agent not done what he did, while one who fails to aid does not make someone worse off in this way. In light of this difference, some assert a kind of existential claim: you are liable for making the world worse than it would have been had you not acted, but you are not liable for failing to making the world better. (In Chapter 2 I described this as the "never been born" view.) Something like this point seems to underlie the view that, as Scheffler puts it, "individuals have a special responsibility for what they themselves do, as opposed to what they merely fail to prevent."[14] This outlook comes in various strengths: in the strongest version, you have no responsibility for not making the world better; in weaker versions, you are responsible, but not to the same degree as if you had made someone worse off. A view of this kind is central to Robert Nozick's claim that the state may prohibit people from harming others, but may not require them to aid

---

[13] Scheffler 1995, 227.
[14] Scheffler 1995, 223. The locus classicus for this view is Bernard Williams's essay, "A Critique of Utilitarianism" (1973, 93–100). See below for further discussion.

others.[15] A central example of Nozick's is the medical researcher who synthesizes an important drug out of easily available materials. According to Nozick, the researcher is not morally obligated to make the drug available to those who need it because, since he has not made any resources more scarce, his actions have not made anyone worse off.

As we have seen, there is much room for disagreement about this fundamental existential claim, especially in its strongest forms: that people are not morally required to aid others, or that the state may never force them to do so. But the disagreement seems to be of the brute variety: certainly, one cannot prove that we have, or do not have, positive duties. Yet one version of the asymmetry claim seems difficult to deny. Having harmed a person always provides a reason to rectify her plight over and above any other reasons one has. Think of the proverbial drowning child in the pond. Most people agree that the bystander ought to wade in to save the child. Yet most would also say that the reason to intervene intensifies if the bystander is no mere bystander but has pushed the child into the water. Even if the pushing were accidental, we are strongly inclined to believe the agent has a greater responsibility to act than does the innocent bystander. And it is not unusual for a person to feel guilty for having harmed another even if her behavior is blameless.

In one sense at least, then, it seems incontrovertible that harming is worse than not aiding – or, in other words, that negative duties are more stringent than positive. However strong the reasons to alleviate a person's suffering, one has an additional reason to do so if one had some role in bringing that suffering about. In this sense, duties not to harm are more stringent than duties to aid – they provide a further reason to act over and above any reason one might have in the absence of having contributed to the harm.

But nothing in this argument tells us how *much* stronger negative duties are than positive duties. True, having reasons x and y for acting provides more moral force than having reason x alone. But if x

---

[15] Nozick 1974, passim, especially 181–2. In Chapter 2 I argued that libertarians are committed to saying not only that the state may not force one to aid others but also that one is not morally obligated to.

is itself a very strong reason, then y may not add much additional force to it. It begs the question to assume that reasons for helping (x) are weak relative to reasons for not harming (y).

Moreover, we can imagine cases where a positive duty to help another person outweighs or takes priority over a negative duty. Suppose I am driving my friend's new car and must crash it in order to stop in time to save a person choking to death on the side of the road. Clearly I ought to crash the car, even if it turns out that I am unable to compensate my friend for the damages. The duty to save the person from choking takes priority over the duty not to harm the property (or property rights) of my friend. Nor does the example depend on comparing two unequal things (physical harm versus mere property rights); we would draw the same conclusion if saving the choking person required slight physical harm to another person.

Efficacy

For most of human history it was probably difficult either to harm or to help people at a distance. No doubt a story can be (and probably has been) told about the evolutionary and psychological repercussions of this fact; the story would explain how we evolved so as to feel no discomfort when we contributed in a small way to faraway harms or failed to aid distant strangers. Causal efficacy at a distance began to increase with the advent of global trade and colonialism, which enhanced human interaction and brought products from faraway places. With these came a growing awareness of the effects of seemingly innocent actions on distant people. For example, starting in the early 1790s more than 300,000 English people (out of a total population of only 8 million) participated in a sugar boycott in an effort to abolish the slave trade.[16] So neither the New Harms nor awareness of them is entirely new.

Still, they exist today on an unprecedented scale. And it might be thought that, considering the matter in terms of an individual's power to make a difference in the world, there is an asymmetry between

---

[16] Hochschild 2005, 192–6.

negative and positive duties: one that – ironically, in terms of the general bias in favor of negative duties – tells in favor of fulfilling positive duties to aid over negative duties not to harm. Along these lines it might be argued that the effects of an individual alone refraining from the New Harms are negligible or nil, while on the other hand a person can through aid single-handedly make a signifi-cant difference to someone's well-being. If this argument is right, then, other things being equal, an individual might have more reason to give aid – to fulfill a would-be positive duty – than to fulfill a negative duty by avoiding participation in a New Harm.

The reasoning underlying the argument is as follows. For a given unit of effort or money, a person can be more certain that her aid (say $100 sent to Oxfam) will help someone than she can be sure that the equivalent amount (for example, spending $100 less in air condition-ing costs) will avoid harm. So, other things being equal, she has more reason to give aid than to reduce her use of fossil fuels. If this argument is sound, then perhaps we should not burden ourselves to consider what we buy, eat, or otherwise consume in the way I suggested at the beginning of this chapter. For, it might be said, people do not have duties to refrain from engaging in harmful practices unless doing so would make a difference to the outcome. And acting alone, individuals do not have good reason to think they will make a difference.

To appreciate the force of this objection, we must explore two possible lines of argument. The first, taken up in the remainder of this section, explores the causal claim that in fact individual attempts to aid in such cases are more efficacious than individual attempts to avoid harm. The second, explored in the next section, asks whether making a difference to the outcome is the only relevant consider-ation. It examines the rejoinder that it is wrong to participate in harmful activities, irrespective of whether one's own conduct makes a difference.

Do I – living in a safe American suburb far from the frontlines of global poverty – have more reason to give $100 to Save the Children or Doctors Without Borders than I do to reduce my energy con-sumption by $100 or to refrain from buying $100-worth of products made in sweatshops, on the grounds that the former acts are more likely to make a difference than the latter?[17]

Answering this question requires facts about both the efficacy of aid and the efficacy of refraining from harm, neither of which is easy to come by. Begin with the question of the efficacy of a person's aid dollars. In recent years, critics – including many former insiders in the world of international aid – have challenged the effectiveness of humanitarian assistance, in the form of both disaster relief and long-term efforts to improve well-being among the world's poorest people. Garrett Cullity summarizes some of the main charges: large-scale aid programs "damage the local economy and pauperize the 'target population' ... The effect is to create aid-dependent economies in which the task of developing economic self-sufficiency has been made much harder than it was before."[18] Aid programs can disrupt traditional institutions, undermine incentives to work, erode recipients' self-respect, and encourage corruption by local governments. Organizations can also fail in more obvious ways: their goods may simply not reach those they are designed to help; they may spend excessively on administrative costs. William Easterly rejects Singer's metaphor of the drowning child. One reason is that we cannot directly save the malnourished child on the other side of the world – we must work through intermediaries, and the question is how they can be made accountable. A second reason is that although it is clear how to save the drowning child – and we need only act once – it is not obvious how to alleviate chronic poverty and the malnutrition and disease associated with it.[19] Some argue that

---

[17] The comparisons are not easy to draw, since refraining from harm, as by using less energy, serves some of the agent's interests and to that extent should not be counted as a cost to him. In these cases, the cost to some of our interests (sweltering without air conditioning, giving up the cherished gas-guzzler) is offset by gains to our economic interests. But not all cases possess this feature, and in any event people do consider many of the demands required by not contributing to global harms a sacrifice to their interests. For present purposes, we can subtract whatever benefit people derive by refraining from harm and consider only the net cost to them.

[18] Cullity 2004, 39.   [19] Singer and Easterly 2009.

poverty eradication can only come from within poor countries themselves.

In Chapter 8 I consider in detail this and other problems with attempting to aid people, and there and in Chapter 10 I discuss some of the most effective and promising approaches. In the meantime, I will simply assume that throwing up our hands and concluding we can do nothing to ameliorate poverty, disease, and ignorance is not justified. In fact, most of aid's detractors have proposals for reducing poverty, even while they are harshly critical of existing approaches. They assume that we are neither morally at liberty to ignore poverty nor utterly impotent to alleviate it.

Nothing is foolproof. Evaluating charities based on the proportion of their costs dedicated to administration may sound plausible, but is not necessarily a good measure.[20] Microfinance is often effective but not always; it must be monitored.[21] Efforts of all kinds must be sensitive to the particular circumstances existing in different places. "There is no generic thing that works," says Easterly, and no doubt he is right.[22] But only willful ignorance could allow the conclusion that we can make no difference at all to the well-being of distant strangers, or that there are no means of judging how best to do so. The inconvenient truth is that figuring out what works takes effort — another face of the demandingness of positive duties.

What about refraining from contributing to harm? It may seem that the probability of making a difference is smaller than in the case of individual aid. If I am careful in how I allocate my donations it seems probable that I can actually help a small number of people, but it is hard to imagine that my solitary boycott of plastic bags will make any contribution to slowing climate change or that my refusal to buy sweatshop-made clothes will alleviate the exploitation of workers even a little bit.

---

[20] Bialik 2008, Karlan 2011. For further discussion see Chapter 10.

[21] Microfinance and microcredit programs, pioneered by Mohammed Yunus, winner of the 2006 Nobel Peace Prize, give loans to poor entrepreneurs who would not qualify for ordinary bank loans.

[22] Singer and Easterly 2009.

But is this right? We have reason to distrust the intuition that our behavior, because it constitutes only a tiny fraction of the total harm, makes no difference. In the first place, since aggregate effects are a function of individual actions (carried out within a framework of institutions and policies), it would seem that tiny individual changes will have at least tiny effects on the outcome, even if psychologically we tend to minimize them.[23] Moreover, people bring about change in other ways than by direct reductions in harm. Driving a fuel-efficient car or carrying reusable bags to the supermarket are publicly visible acts; through them people can set examples or fuel trends that others may imitate, whether out of conviction or conformity. The power of fashion, the desire for approval and avoidance of shame, pride in living up to one's principles, the effects of "tipping points" – via such psychological and social processes actions with negligible direct effects can nevertheless produce widespread changes in behavior over the longer run. And the belief that one's own conduct makes a difference is a potent and probably adaptive human trait.

This discussion is inherently speculative, for at least two reasons. First, because the facts about what conduct does harm and what does good are hard to come by. And second, because the kinds of behavior in question (possible contributions to harm, possible contributions to good) are so heterogeneous as to defy subsumption under a single general principle. Perhaps the most we can say at this stage is that, per unit of human effort (measured in dollars, or some other way), we cannot entirely rule out the initial intuition that, acting on our own, we can make a bigger difference by giving aid than by refraining from contributing to harm.

---

[23] "It is not enough to ask, 'Will my act harm other people?' Even if the answer is No, my act may still be wrong, *because* of its effects on other people. I should ask, 'Will my act be one of a set of acts that will *together* harm other people?' The answer may be Yes. And the harm to others may be great. If this is so, I may be acting *very* wrongly ..." (Parfit 1984, 86). It's true, however, that we are less likely to feel we are making a difference, because of the "peanuts effect" described in Chapter 3, and thus we may not be motivated to change our behavior. This is a central reason for thinking in terms of group responsibilities, as I argued at the end of the last chapter.

It is difficult to entirely bracket the efficacy question or to know how to measure it, especially when we include indirect effects of our behavior such as setting an example or fueling a trend. Is it absurd even to imagine that one can measure or quantify these effects? If so, that's a problem for utilitarianism and contemporary economics. It is unlikely that we can make anything more than very crude judgments about the consequences of our conduct in this realm. Yet there are other moral reasons to refrain from participating in harmful activities, beyond any direct or indirect material effects a person's actions may have.

Integrity

In reflecting on such reasons it appears that the harmful activities we are concerned with divide into two types. One includes the kinds of environmental harms epitomized by the threat of climate change. Such harms are *essentially aggregative*: there is nothing intrinsically harmful to the environment or to other people, nothing inherently problematic morally, in burning fossil fuels; the harms depend on the joint effects of many people's actions. By contrast, other kinds of harms – buying products whose manufacture exploits workers or that deprive owners of their rightful property – involve actions that are *intrinsically* wrong, irrespective of what others do. Although the commercial practices under scrutiny would not exist without the participation of many people, each individual act of theft or exploitation is wrong.

The distinction between intrinsic and essentially aggregative harms affects the moral reasons to refrain from participating in harmful activities. Consider a person who chooses not to eat meat because he believes killing animals is morally wrong.[24] Most people would probably agree that given his beliefs his choice is appropriate, even if it will not significantly affect the lives and well-being of any

---

[24] For anyone who believe that animals' interests should not count in a serious way in our moral reflections or calculations, this example can be seen as an analogy; for those who think animals' interests should count, it's simply another relevant case.

animals, and irrespective of whether other people eat meat or not. Although I have no control over what other people do, the agent may say, I can at least control what *I* do, and I choose not to contribute to these wrongs. This reasoning might apply both to individual and aggregative harms, but intuitively at least seems to hold more sway in the former case, where it is more plausible that the wrongfulness of my conduct does not depend on what others do.

The decision to refrain from acts complicit in aggregative harms arises from different reasoning. Imagine an agent employing the categorical imperative, who performs only those actions she would be willing to allow everyone to perform. Since allowing everyone to consume energy at the rate consumed by the average American leads to disaster, she concludes it is unfair for her to consume at that rate. The vegetarian's decision not to eat meat, by contrast, does not depend in this way on fairness.

Recall the point of this discussion: to consider possible asymmetries between negative and positive duties. In the last section, I considered the following argument:

1. In the kinds of cases we are considering, an individual acting alone can be more certain that her aid will be effective than that her refraining from harm will be effective.

2. Therefore, per unit of effort (measured in dollars or some other way), an individual has more reason to give aid than to refrain from harming.

3. Therefore, from the point of view of efficacy, duties to refrain from contributing to the New Harms are, other things being equal, weaker than duties to give aid.

4. And, in absolute terms, since refraining from harm is not effective in these cases, the duty to avoid harm is at best weak.

I concluded that the empirical claim in the first premise might be correct; if so, this argument – which only concerns efficacy – cannot be faulted. Now the question is whether causal efficacy in bringing about a desired result is the sole criterion by which to judge whether one ought to refrain from participating in harmful activities.

The answer is no. Another reason is simply that one should do the right thing, irrespective of effectiveness. In the case of aggregative harms, doing the right thing involves an appeal to the unfairness of acting inconsistently with how one thinks others ought to act. With intrinsic harms (like eating meat, according to the moral vegetarian's view) it's not a matter of unfairness but something we are inclined to describe as acting on principle.

We possess rich linguistic resources to describe what is objectionable even where a person's behavior makes no difference to the outcome. We talk about the expressive or symbolic meaning of conduct, about personal integrity, or about "participating" or being "complicit" in harmful activities. Yet these ways of talking – all of which bypass questions of efficacy – raise further questions about the distinction between negative and positive duties.

The assertion that one should do the right thing, even if it has no effect in the world, might appear to require support. The question was famously discussed by Bernard Williams in "A Critique of Utilitarianism."[25] Williams offers two examples in which a person confronts the choice about whether to perform a harmful action; if he refuses, someone else will do it, or worse. I shall focus on the first of Williams's examples, which bears more closely on the cases of interest here. George, a new chemistry PhD, is offered a job working in a lab that carries out research in chemical and biological warfare. George opposes chemical and biological warfare, but he needs a job (and jobs are hard to come by in his field), and he knows that if he refuses the position someone else will take it instead.[26] Utilitarians, Williams charges, conclude that George may take the position; they wrongly fail to consider the idea "that each of us is specially responsible for what *he* does, rather than for what other people do. This is an idea closely connected to the value of integrity."[27]

In this case, as with the New Harms, the actions George would engage in are linked only indirectly – via the acts and interventions

---

[25] Williams 1973, 97–100.
[26] In Williams's version of the example, the person waiting in the wings lacks George's scruples "and is likely to push along the research with greater zeal than George would" (1973, 98). This detail (which would give George more reason to take the job) does not apply to the cases I am interested in, and I shall ignore it.
[27] Williams 1973, 99.

of many other people, as well as other causal processes – to harmful consequences. Of course, the link is more direct in Williams's example: whereas George's research could and would be carried out by some other people (just how many it may be difficult to say, but probably no more than hundreds or a few thousand at most), the harmful consequences of buying goods made by exploited workers or using plastic bags involve hundreds of thousands or even millions of people. And the typical consumer is less responsible for the ensuing harms than George is; the sweatshop owner and/or the authority setting labor standards bear more responsibility for bad labor practices than the buyer.[28] Partly as a result of such differences, the harm done by any one individual in cases of New Harms is smaller than that done by any single person in Williams's case; correspondingly, less blameworthiness attaches to the former than the latter. But Williams's central point nevertheless applies, and helps explain the intuition that a person ought to refrain from doing harm even if her behavior makes no difference to the outcome. I am especially responsible for what *I* do, not what others do.

Yet in his interpretation of this dilemma Williams makes a deep and controversial assumption. In being responsible for what I do, am I also responsible for what I do *not* do? Williams thinks not; in attacking consequentialism, he draws a sharp line between those things "that I allow or fail to prevent" and those "that I myself, in the more everyday restricted sense, bring about."[29] It follows that – according to commonsense moral thought, in Scheffler's phrase – my duty to avoid harmful activities is stronger than my duty to engage in the equivalent quantity of "helpful" activities, and that negative duties "constitute a greater constraint on one's pursuit of one's own goals, projects, and commitments" than do positive duties.[30] The metaphor of the carbon footprint is apt: do not leave the earth worse than you found it, even if you do not leave it better.

---

[28] Who is responsible for environmental harms? In a democratic society the people are accountable, but the people's representatives, who have the opportunity to pass laws and enact policies, are more accountable.
[29] Williams 1973, 99. See also Scheffler 1995, 223.   [30] Scheffler 1995, 223.

Now one might object to this interpretation of our responsibilities, biased as it is in favor of negative duties, without embracing consequentialism – and I believe that we should. A concern with integrity, or with the expressive function of conduct, need not exclude responsibilities to make the world better. But to avoid falling down the slippery slope – at the end of which people are responsible for every evil they fail to (try to) prevent – we will have to draw a line between those things people ought to try to prevent and others for which they are not responsible or for which they are less responsible. There are a variety of ways we might draw this line, each with its own strengths and weaknesses.

One approach would treat negative and positive duties analogously. A natural way to understand the extent of our negative duties is to say that we should do *our fair share* of avoiding participation in New Harms. Ideally, I should not buy products that involve the exploitation of workers or the theft of others' rightful property; if I refrain from these activities, I am doing my share by not contributing to the harmful consequences that ensue from such behavior. In the case of climate change, one might argue that each American citizen should reduce her carbon footprint to the amount that, when multiplied by the population of the United States, would be sustainable. An analogous account might be offered in the positive case: we are not duty-bound to do everything we could do to help those in need, only our fair share, understood perhaps as the amount that, when multiplied by the population of the United States (or some other unit), would appropriately relieve need.[31] Thinking in terms of integrity, participation, complicity, and the like, a person might say: "I am not responsible for how others live their lives, only for how I live mine. And I think it would be unconscionable not to give away x percent of my income."[32] There is no reason a concern with integrity must ignore our positive responsibilities – no reason why it

---

[31] See Murphy 1993.

[32] Note that talking about "how to live" rather than "what to do" is less likely to lead to negative/positive confusion.

must draw a sharp line between what we bring about directly and what we allow or fail to prevent.

It's worth noting that a criticism of duties to aid often made in this context also applies to duties not to harm. It is sometimes said that, since many people will not do their fair share in giving aid, I ought to do more. And this kind of reasoning again raises the specter of the slippery slope toward onerous duties. Similarly, it might be said that since many people will not reduce their harmful behavior as much as they should (if at all), to compensate I ought to reduce mine even more than "my share."

For our immediate purposes it is enough to say that however we answer this criticism, there is no reason why the negative and positive cases should be treated differently.

Demandingness

Let me summarize the conclusions of this chapter so far. I have examined three possible asymmetries between negative and positive duties. First is the idea that not harming takes priority over helping. I argued that this is nearly self-evident, since in any case where suffering ought to be alleviated, one who has contributed to causing the suffering has an additional reason to alleviate it over one who has not so contributed. But having an additional reason does not imply that one who has not contributed to the harm has no reason, nor does it settle how strong that reason is.

Second is the question of the relative efficacy of avoiding harm or giving aid in the kinds of contemporary global cases we are interested in. Ironically, despite the voluminous critiques of aid, it seems plausible (although by no means certain) that a solitary individual can make more difference by giving aid than she can by avoiding participation in the kinds of activities I have included in the category of New Harms.

Third is the argument from integrity, as one might call it, which appeals to moral factors apart from efficacy as a basis of responsibility. This argument has traditionally contained a bias in favor of harm-avoidance rather than aid-giving. But there is no justification for the bias, and so we should conceive integrity in a way that is neutral between acts and omissions.

The upshot of the argument so far is something of a draw. The first point suggests that negative duties take priority, the second appears to give the edge to positive duties, the third is a tie. This is, of course, an artificial accounting. It is impossible, in theory, to say how much having created (or contributed to creating) a harm adds to one's duty to alleviate it. And there is no *general* answer to the question how much more one can help by acting than one can avoid harming by refraining from acting; the answer will depend on the details of specific cases.

The final possible asymmetry that needs examining has loomed especially large in recent philosophical discussions of positive duties, playing a central role in skepticism about their existence and extent. This is the problem of demandingness, which has arisen in previous chapters and is perhaps the driving force behind my thinking in this book. I begin the discussion here and continue it in the next chapter.

Given the enormous quantity of suffering in the world and the burdens alleviating it could create on others' freedom to live their lives as they see fit, it has seemed necessary to most moral philosophers to limit what can reasonably be demanded of ordinary human beings in the way of aid or positive duties. Warding off an onslaught of negative duties, by contrast – despite their universality, despite their seeming exceptionlessness – has not seemed pressing. Why not? The classic harms negative duties prohibit – killing, doing violence, raping, robbing, and the like – are fundamental evils that every society must forbid. Moreover, in an important sense avoiding committing these harms is easy for most people. In any case, they raise few line-drawing or slippery-slope problems. (You mean I have to avoid killing this person and that person and the other person, and all the other people too?) Positive duties have such problems built in. How much of my money, time, or effort must I expend to help all those in the world who suffer and could benefit from my help? There is no simple answer. But this feature of positive duties has been a central reason why they are controversial – why many people have thought they are at best imperfect, secondary, or even nonexistent.[33]

Is their relative undemandingness part of the *reason* only negative duties have been thought strict or perfect? In other words, is the extent of an agent's duty – negative or positive – partly a *function* of the costs of compliance with the duty? In the next chapter I investigate this question at length, arguing that demandingness *is* relevant to determining duty. At first sight, however, the answer appears to be no. Most people would agree that a cost of $10,000 lessens Emma's responsibility to aid the homeless. But even if Max will lose $10,000 if he does not kill his uncle, we do not think this lessens his duty not to kill his uncle.

Yet we can say several things about why the cases of Max and Emma are not dispositive, and may indeed be misleading. First, even in the classic cases of immediate physical harm, we do in fact acknowledge considerations of cost as relevant to determining what it is reasonable to expect the agent to do or refrain from doing. Duress and necessity are defenses that mitigate a person's guilt, even in violent crime.[34] Whatever view one takes of the relevance of demandingness to determining abstract rightness or wrongness, or personal duty, every plausible theory finds a way to justify, excuse, mitigate, or mute criticism of some conduct that falls short of morality's demands – and this is, in effect, a way of taking back with one hand what one has offered with the other.

Second, murder and mayhem are misleading examples when it comes to the relevance of demandingness to determining duty. With other kinds of harms, such as those treated in tort law – usually unintentional, like the New Harms – costs to the agent enter directly. The Hand Formula, crafted by Judge Learned Hand in *U.S. v. Carroll Towing Co.*, established the rule that the agent is liable for damage only when the burden of taking adequate precautions to

---

[33] In the last chapter I suggested that these problems can be alleviated by conceiving the duties as collective rather than individual, to be carried out by groups or institutions. I return to this point later in the book.

[34] For discussion see Lichtenberg 2009b, 118–22. Duress is an excuse; necessity is a justification. For more on the distinction see Chapter 5.

prevent it is less than the probability times the gravity of the harm to the victim.[35] These kinds of cases might be a useful model for understanding duties arising from the New Harms.[36]

Third, the classic harms reflect the fact that, for most of human history, a person could harm only those at close range. We may speculate that, as a result, humans evolved to feel revulsion at the thought of such acts – whether their own or others'. But revulsion did not extend to the New Harms, which came into existence on a grand scale only recently.[37] This is consistent with the sort of account given by Scheffler described earlier in this chapter. Absence of unease in contributing to the New Harms is of a piece with our lack of distress at the suffering of distant people whom we do not aid.

Finally, leaving aside whether people who have contributed to the New Harms or who have failed to aid distant others have done wrong or violated their duties, we might think that sometimes the language of duty and obligation is useless or even counterproductive when the duties alleged far outstrip ordinary people's motivations to comply with them. The question from this point of view is just where we should set the bar: not so high that it discourages people from taking morality seriously because they feel they have no hope of meeting its demands, but not so low that it makes no significant demands and thus defeats a (perhaps *the*) central purpose of having a morality – to motivate people to behave better than they would in the absence of its dictates. I return to this question in the next chapter.

These and earlier considerations suggest that, whatever answer we settle on with respect to the relevance to duty of demandingness per se, negative and positive duties should in this respect be symmetrical.

---

[35] *U.S. v. Carroll Towing Co.* 1947.

[36] But there are differences. Instead of the probabilistic character typical of torts (harms are more or less likely, not certain), we have the fractional contribution any individual's conduct makes to the harm.

[37] One might ask whether our psychological reactions themselves have moral significance – whether the fact that people are relatively unfazed by the distant effects of their actions must be factored into moral judgments. I think the answer is that they are relevant to judgments of blameworthiness and character but not directly to judgments of right or wrong action.

If costs to the agent count, they should count in determining both negative and positive duties; if costs do not count, they should count in determining neither.

Some further considerations about negative and positive duties

Emphasizing a sharp distinction between negative and positive duties has been central to buttressing the idea that there can be no human right to a decent minimum. It's worth amplifying some points made in earlier chapters that further undermine the distinction.

First, as we saw in Chapter 2, negative duties – i.e., duties not to harm – presuppose the existence of a baseline or counterfactual: to harm people is to make them worse off than they would have been had you not acted as you did. In the simplest cases – exemplified in criminal and tort law – such baselines are easily accessible. We can say exactly to what degree the rapist and the reckless driver leave their victims worse off than they would have been in the absence of their acts because we know how those harmed "would have been." As the past recedes, such judgments become more difficult to make and eventually become impossible, undermining the efficacy of claims about harms committed long ago, even when we have no doubt about their existence.

Unlike harm, exploitation, as I defined it in Chapter 2, does not make someone worse off than she would have been in the absence of the act in question; by hypothesis, the weaker party in an exploitative transaction is better off. So exploitation does not by itself violate a negative duty. The example I examined – a central one in our thinking about global justice and human rights – was the low wages and poor working conditions of workers employed by transnational companies in developing countries. Some deny that there is anything morally problematic with exploiting another person; even those who find it troubling may think it is less bad than harming another. And in any case it would be worse, other things being equal, were the company not to establish a factory in the developing country and instead leave the would-be workers unemployed. But other things are not equal, and this crucially affects the relevant baselines and counterfactuals. The reason the workers' wages and working conditions are so poor is not simply that this is the bargain that has been struck and could be expected to be struck given the relative strengths of the parties, but that the government and the companies have acted to prevent the workers from organizing to improve their working conditions. The government and the companies have not merely omitted to do something, they have also *acted* – and it is reasonable to think that in so acting they have violated the workers' rights.[38]

If this example even roughly represents many relationships between rich and poor individuals or institutions, then we see another reason to downgrade the distinction between negative and positive duties. The negative duty not to harm or to compensate for harm done presupposes a baseline or counterfactual. Positive duties presuppose no such baseline; we might thus consider the responsibility not to exploit "only" a positive responsibility. But what is troubling about exploitation often depends partly on accompanying harms – violations of negative duties, such as preventing workers from organizing. In the complex international world of politics and economics, such intertwinings of harmful acts with "mere omissions" are common. But that means the baseline question is no longer straightforward. What is the baseline for the exploited workers? Is it being unemployed, and thus much worse off, or is it being employed in a union, and thus better off? The question of the counterfactual or baseline, central to determining whether one agent has harmed another, is the question "Compared to what?" And in the realms we are interested in here, this question will rarely be straightforward.

Another reason for skepticism about the distinction between negative and positive duties derives from Henry Shue's arguments, discussed in the last chapter. There are two important points. First, if we take social or political guarantees to be built into any useful conception of rights, then negative rights can be costly in just the

---

[38] See, e.g., *Universal Declaration of Human Rights* 1948, art. 23 § 4: "Everyone has the right to form and to join trade unions for the protection of his interests."

same way positive rights are. Since costliness is a central reason for denying the existence of rights to a decent minimum or for downgrading them to second-class status, this point closes the gap with negative rights. Second, the assumption that positive rights means giving people things – also costly – is not sound. For a variety of reasons having to do with the importance of respect, self-respect, and independence – not merely economic cost – the best way to implement rights to a decent minimum is to ensure that people can support themselves.[39]

---

[39] See Chapter 8. For other reasons to doubt the distinction between negative and positive rights see Ashford 2009.

CHAPTER 5

Oughts and cans

Leading an ethical life is demanding. It means that we must some-times act in ways we would not otherwise choose to act – sometimes do what we would rather not do or refrain from doing what we would prefer to do. This much seems unsurprising. If leading an ethical life demanded nothing of us over and above what we would normally or naturally do, "ethics" would have no point. It would be merely descriptive – telling us how people behave, and how they judge each other – rather than prescriptive or normative. And in that case it would lack a central feature – perhaps *the* central feature – of ethics or morality. As philosophers like to put it, morality is "action-guiding."[1]

This is not to deny that description has its place. Anthropologists and journalists may describe how members of a group behave and what rules guide them without making any moral judgments, and such accounts can be interesting and informative. But if we want to know what to do, either because we are agents who have to act, or because we need to judge what standards of behavior are appropriate and right for other people as well as ourselves, we are in the realm of prescription rather than description, the normative and not simply the empirical.

So ethics makes demands on us, articulating norms for desirable conduct. It tells us that we are morally obligated not to do *this* or that

---

[1] Here I use "ethics" and "morality" interchangeably. There is something reifying about the idea of "ethics" or "morality" making demands on us or telling us what to do. I have not found a better way of talking, and assume no harm is done and that no one imagines ethics up there in the sky cracking its whip. I make some further points about uses of these terms in the last section of this chapter.

we would be less than decent if we did *that*. The broadest question is about which demands ethics ought to make. This is in essence to ask what we ought to do, how we ought to live – the fundamental ethical question. My question in this chapter is a little more modest. It has to do with the relevance of demandingness per se. Are there limits on how demanding ethics can be? Is there only so much that can be demanded of people, morally speaking? If so – if morality should not ask too much of ordinary mortals – can we hope to make serious inroads toward alleviating the terrible problems of the world? The demands I have in mind can be material or psychological; and, of course, among the most significant costs may be time and what economists call opportunity costs – other possible uses of our resources foregone.

Does morality demand what it demands?

It is not difficult to see how the problem of demandingness in its most general form arises out of the fact of global poverty. How much are we morally required to do to help people who live in dire poverty, and how much are we morally required to do to refrain from contributing to harming them? Are there any limits to what morality can demand of us?

One position, described by Samuel Scheffler, is that "morality demands what it demands, and if people find it hard to live up to those demands, that just shows that people are not, in general, morally very good."[2] There are in principle no limits to how demanding morality can be; what morality requires can be established independently of the demandingness of its requirements. Robert Goodin, who endorses this view, assumes we can decide "what people are due" and "which demands are legitimate," irrespective of considerations of demandingness. "The problem," he says, "is not that legitimate demands demand too much; the problem is instead that people find themselves able to give too little."[3]

---

[2] Scheffler 1986, 531. Scheffler is describing this position, not defending it.
[3] Goodin 2009, 2.

I reject this position, and my aim in this chapter is to show what's wrong with it. The view that Morality Demands What It Demands presupposes a conception of ethics that is purely theoretical: people's duties can be determined independent of what people are like and what sacrifices they would have to make to be morally upright.[4] Utilitarianism, to which both Singer and Goodin subscribe, lends itself to such an approach. Understood as the view that one ought to do that which maximizes the good or minimizes the bad, utilitarianism provides no principled reason why morality cannot be very demanding. It is true that for a utilitarian costs to the agent (including psychological and other nonmaterial sacrifices) must be taken into account – because pains or disutilities of any kind, to any creature who falls within the scope of moral considerations, must be taken into account. But a large cost to an individual can easily be outweighed by benefits to others. There is no cost that is per se too much to demand that an individual bear.

What can be said in favor of the view that Morality Demands What It Demands? Goodin claims that allowing consideration of "the ordinary capacities of ordinary people" to determine moral requirements would be to allow

> that bad behaviour, if sufficiently common, is self-excusing. Letting what is morally demanded of us be a function of what demands we are prepared to meet puts the cart before the horse, morally speaking. Morality's being "action-guiding" means that we should be fitting our conduct to morality's demands – not morality's demands to our conduct.[5]

These concerns are valid. Allowing consideration of "the ordinary capacities of ordinary people" to determine what morality requires could lead to a race to the bottom: if people show themselves to be morally challenged, then we should adjust moral requirements

---

[4] As Goodin puts it, the argument about "exactly what others are due and which demands are legitimate . . . should be conducted purely at the level of . . . first-order moral propositions, without recourse to any 'demandingness' side-constraint" (2009, 2).

[5] Goodin 2009, 11.

downward. Hey, let's look for depressing conclusions of studies of human benevolence, for they may let us off the hook! Relying on beliefs about human nature or psychological findings for guidance about morality's requirements could be a dangerous move.

So Goodin is right if he means that we cannot simply accept any old conception of "human beings as they are" as the standard by which to determine how people ought to act. But this is not to say that we can ignore human nature and human capacities in the way he suggests. Morality Demands What It Demands makes no moral sense insofar as it may require more of human beings than it is reasonable to ask of them. And it's also conceptually confused, insofar as it envisions ethics as more autonomous, more precise, and more divorced from the practical realm than it really is. I defend these claims in this chapter.

Can

How can we ensure that morality's demands are sensitive to human capacities without simply letting people off the hook – going too easy on them on the grounds that morality should not be too demanding? If we reject the idea that Morality Demands What It Demands, we must answer this question.

A minimum and uncontroversial condition is that morality not require people to do what is impossible. What could be more appropriate, then, than to examine a favorite slogan of philosophers, "Ought Implies Can"?[6] Ought Implies Can is usually understood to mean that you cannot be morally *required* to do something unless it is *possible* for you to do it.

Now, on its face Morality Demands What It Demands is incompatible with Ought Implies Can. But there are many meanings of "can," and correspondingly many kinds of impossibility. At a

[6] The principle was expressed by Kant in several places; for central passages and discussion of them, in addition to evaluation of the principle that Ought Implies Can, see Stern 2004, 53–61. Henry Sidgwick may have been the first to make explicit use of the principle (see Sidgwick 1907, bk. 1, ch. v, sec. 3). For the sake of appearances I omit the quotation marks around "ought" and "can" in this phrase.

minimum, Ought Implies Can means that morality cannot require you to do something that it is *logically* impossible to do, like finding a married bachelor. But of course logical impossibility does not exhaust the kinds of impossibility there are (even though it's the kind philosophers tend to focus on). Running a mile in two minutes is impossible, but not logically impossible. It seems safe to say (although who knows what the future will bring?) that it is *physically* impossible for a human being to run that fast.[7] Running a mile in four minutes is impossible for all but a small number of people in the world, and was once thought to be impossible for anyone.

Remembering a string of a hundred thousand digits is impossible for human beings. Let's call this *mental* or *psychological* impossibility.[8] For virtually all human beings, remembering a string of five hundred digits is impossible. Killing a baby may be psychologically impossible for most people – certainly for most people in most circumstances.

Not only are there different kinds of impossibility (such as logical, physical, and psychological), but impossibility is relative to a certain scope or domain. What is possible for one person may be impossible for another. Some people can run a six-minute mile, most cannot. What is possible for a person in one set of circumstances may be impossible in another. A person might, for example, be psychologically able to perform acts of violence in wartime that he would be incapable of performing under ordinary circumstances.

Technological impossibility straightforwardly illustrates the relativity of impossibility. Until quite recently in human history, it was impossible for human beings to travel faster than a few miles an hour, impossible to perform medical operations painlessly, impossible to drink a Coke.

Other questions loom about impossibility and its implications for Ought Implies Can. One is whether moral imperatives are general, or

---

[7] Metaphysicians sometimes define physical possibility in terms of consistency with "the laws of nature." But what this means is not obvious. Is a human being running a two-minute mile, or a thirty-second mile, consistent with the laws of nature?

[8] For a physicalist, presumably, mental or psychological impossibility reduces to physical impossibility. Likewise with other kinds of impossibility noted below.

whether they apply instead to particular individuals in particular circumstances. A general imperative to "Rescue people when you see them drowning" would violate Ought Implies Can because, for example, some who see drowning people cannot swim. (Leave aside that one can sometimes rescue a drowning person without knowing how to swim.) A different imperative, "Rescue people when you see them drowning if you know how to swim," would apply only to those who know how to swim. One might think that imperatives should always be conceived as applying only to particular individuals: "You – rescue people if you see them drowning" (implied: because you know how to swim). But that seems implausible, because moral teaching requires general rules that ignore individual differences, even though these differences mean that some individuals may be unable to comply with the imperative. (I return to this question near the end of the chapter.)

Another puzzle arises because some things individuals cannot do can be accomplished by groups or collective entities to which individuals belong. Suppose morality requires a more egalitarian society. This is not an achievement that any individual can bring about, although through collective action a group might be able to. What does Ought Implies Can imply in such cases? That the moral imperative applies only to the group, not the individual? But imperatives for groups must have implications for what individuals should do, because group action is parasitic on individual action.

About many things that are impossible, it is difficult to say what kind of impossible they are. It is probably impossible in the United States today to produce a socialist revolution, to reduce unemployment to zero, or to eliminate murder entirely. Claims of political, economic, and sociological impossibility seem to amount to predictions about group behavior that rely on assumptions about people's beliefs, attitudes, and motivations. Some of these beliefs, attitudes, and motivations are alterable, but as long as they remain in place there will be limits on what individuals can do to change the world.

The difficulty of characterizing types of impossibility relates to the problem of distinguishing the impossible from the merely very difficult. I know it is impossible for me to run a four-minute mile.

Is it also impossible for me to run an eight-minute mile? I have never done it, never even come close. But I also haven't tried and haven't trained. If running an eight-minute mile became important to me, I could probably do it. For a wide range of actions and achievements, the claim of impossibility rests on a variety of assumptions that are malleable rather than fixed and unchangeable. We use "impossible," and therefore "can," in ambiguous and sometimes loose ways.[9]

Let me summarize the main points of this discussion.

1. There are various kinds of possibility and impossibility: logical, physical, psychological, political, technological, etc.

2. Some kinds of possibility apply only to groups, not to individuals alone. But groups are composed of individuals, and indeed group action requires individual action. So there are conceptual complexities in sorting out the relationships between what is possible for groups and what is possible for individuals. Assuming Ought Implies Can, how we sort them out will have implications for what individuals ought to do.

3. How general are moral Oughts? The more general, the more they must allow for exceptions, which will arise in part because some people are unable to fulfill them. If, on the other hand, moral Oughts are directed at particular individuals in particular circumstances ("You ought to tell the truth in this situation"), they will be extremely varied, and more limited. Each way of conceiving Oughts has some benefits but also correlative drawbacks. The particularized approach could make Oughts virtually exceptionless. But they could not then be employed as public imperatives for teaching and guiding behavior, which is a central function of moral rules and guidelines. The general approach serves this function, but the Oughts it endorses will be full of exceptions.

4. For all these reasons, Ought Implies Can is far less clear than it may seem. What people can or cannot do is not always easily

---

[9] How loose? I may say that I am unable to meet you for lunch because I have a prior engagement. Everyone understands that I am not strictly speaking *unable* to meet you. But drawing the line even between these metaphorical usages and more literal ones is not always easy.

established, and – at least as important – is not fixed for all time. Nevertheless, a practical, action-guiding morality – that is, the right kind of morality – must take into account what is possible for ordinary human beings under given circumstances.

5. Because the line between the impossible and the difficult is not sharp, a practical morality should also take into account what it is reasonable to expect people to do. I defend this claim more fully in the rest of this chapter. Morality should not unduly test what Rawls calls the "strains of commitment," by pressing too hard on people's capacities.[10] Surprisingly, perhaps, no one has made this point better than Peter Singer himself: "An ethic for human beings must take them as they are, or as they have some chance of becoming."[11] But it is not easy to determine the limits of the possible, or to separate them from behavior deeply entrenched by custom and social norms.

Ought

Having examined the Can, I turn now to the Ought. In the most general sense we can identify the realm of Ought with the realm of value and the normative. Perhaps most basic in this realm are "states of affairs," which may be desirable or undesirable (or neutral). So, for example, dire poverty is a bad state of affairs, health (vigor, lack of disease) is a good one.[12] It is common among philosophers to use the terms "goodness" and "badness" for states of affairs, reserving "rightness" and "wrongness" for actions and policies.[13] Yet in a certain respect states of affairs are also action-oriented. They have

---

[10] Rawls 1971, secs. 25, 29.   [11] Singer 1981, 157.

[12] Perhaps we need to state these as generalizations that can be overridden in certain circumstances. For example, voluntary dire poverty is not a bad state of affairs (although we are unlikely to describe it as "dire").

[13] This is implicit in, e.g., Rawls 1971, 24–5. When theorizing, philosophers tend to emphasize the good. But the bad or evil plays a much larger role in our practical reasoning, and it is generally easier to think about how to eradicate evil than about how to create good. We might conclude that if we can eradicate evil, good will take care of itself.

Oughtness – or what I have described as moral force – built into them, because insofar as possible the good ones ought to exist and the bad ones ought not to exist. We might say, then, that good and bad states of affairs contain within themselves a presumption of action: to make the good ones exist or sustain them when they already exist, to eradicate the bad ones or prevent them from coming into being.

But this Oughtness is vague; it does not specify who should act, or how to act, to create or sustain the good or to destroy or prevent the bad.[14] As we saw in Chapter 3, philosophers (but not only philosophers) have most often understood Oughts in terms of moral obligations. But this is a mistake: "You are morally obligated to do x" is stronger than "You ought to do x," and the latter does not entail the former (although the former entails the latter).

Think again about easy rescues – the bystander who could warn the traveler of the rising flood waters or toss a life preserver to a drowning person. In Chapter 3 I mentioned students (and students are not alone) who sometimes hesitate to agree that one has a moral obligation to act even in these easy cases. One reason is that they connect moral obligation with the legitimacy of coercion. Such a connection is endorsed by H.L.A. Hart on what are perhaps at bottom terminological grounds, and for very different reasons by Elizabeth Anscombe, who believes the concept of moral obligation is law-like and requires a "God as law-giver."[15] I argued that, conceptually, the claim that one has a moral obligation to do x is separable from the claim that the state is justified in coercing one to do x or that God will punish one for not doing x, and that in fact the noncoercive meaning of "obligation" is quite standard. In that case, to say that "A

---

[14] Nor does it follow that all desirable action has only these purposes. We saw in the discussion of integrity in the last chapter that a person may sometimes have good reason to do or not to do something, even though her conduct will not bring about any good or prevent any harm.

[15] Anscombe 1958, 6. See the discussion of moral obligation in Chapter 3. As we saw there, Hart asserts that the most important characteristic of the concepts of justice, fairness, right, and obligation is that there is a "special congruity in the use of force or the threat of force" to secure the good in question – that these are the circumstances that justify coercing a person (Hart 1955, 17).

has a moral obligation to do x" is just another way of saying "It would be wrong for A not to do x."

We would expect most people to agree that one is obligated to save the endangered person in such cases once the linkage with coercion is severed. But assent depends in large part on the ease of rescue. The more costly or difficult it becomes to help a person, the less likely we are to say helping is morally obligatory.[16]

Standard theoretical approaches

Suppose we agree that other things being equal it would be a good thing, much of the time, for people to help others.[17] We might even agree on a rough ranking of courses of conduct from best to worst. But what more can we say? A central question is where to set the bar. It's natural to understand this question in terms of moral obligation: since obligation marks out the realm of clearly wrong conduct, we need to know how to locate the obligatory and to distinguish it from the optional and the supererogatory. People need to know what they must do (or not do) – what the minimum conditions of acceptable conduct are.

How do the major theoretical approaches in moral philosophy treat the bar-setting question? On the standard modern interpretation of consequentialism, a person is morally required to maximize the good. So if you will do more good on the whole by helping people than not, you are morally required to help. This assumption leads to Singer's demanding conclusion. Yet there is nothing inherent in consequentialism that entails that a person must maximize the good. Consequentialism entails only that the more good you do, the better, as John Stuart Mill asserts clearly in *Utilitarianism*:

[16] Assuming, that is, that no relational reasons of the kind outlined in Chapter 2 are in play. In general I avoid terms like "help," "aid," and "assistance" when the obligatory act in question arises from a relational responsibility such as harm or exploitation.

[17] It is not always a good thing, of course. For a discussion of the many caveats and concerns about giving aid, see Chapter 8. For a different set of objections focusing on the defects of exceptional altruism and "saintliness," see Wolf 1982.

"actions are right *in proportion* as they tend to promote happiness; wrong as they tend to produce the reverse of happiness."[18] On the other hand, the Millian interpretation still leaves us with the bar-setting question, because we need some way of expressing, for the purposes of moral education at the very least, the moral minimum, and more generally what is expected of people. Presumably consequentialists should say that the bar should be set (publicly) at whatever level is optimal, i.e., the level that will maximize the good. I return to this question shortly.

As we saw in Chapter 3, on the traditional Kantian view, the kinds of responsibilities we are concerned with here constitute "imperfect duties" of beneficence, allowing a great deal of leeway as to time, place, manner, and extent. But if the traditional consequentialist way is too demanding, this approach suffers from the opposite defect: at the very least it is unhelpful and on its face too permissive. How much must we help others? How much must we sacrifice of our own interests? We can imagine a stringent, Golden Rule-like interpretation, suggested in Kant's phrasing: we are duty-bound to help others whenever we would have wanted help if we were in their place. But this has not been the line Kantians have traditionally taken. It would, moreover, saddle them with the same questions about demandingness that have plagued consequentialists. In any case, as it is usually understood, the imperfect duties approach provides little guidance about what and how much a person ought to do.

Virtue ethics, the tradition descended from Aristotle that has become a popular alternative to consequentialism and deontology over the last few decades, focuses on persons and the character traits they ought to have and express through their behavior. Thinking in these terms often tracks more closely the way we judge others in everyday life than does the language of duty and moral obligation. Recall those who hesitate to declare (perhaps because they implicitly accept the link between obligation and coercion) that the bystander is

---

[18] Mill 1979, 7 (emphasis added). For a fuller discussion of the point that the classical utilitarians were unconcerned about the demandingness problem see Lichtenberg 1983.

morally *obligated* to save the drowning child, and who instead are inclined to describe him as a jerk, or something along those lines. (It's hard to find the right word here. "Jerk" lacks the gravity befitting someone who lets another die or suffer serious injury when he could easily intervene. Other terms – brute, cad, scoundrel – are antiquated or at least not in common use, still others not fit for print in reputable publications. Few words capture the distinctive kind of moral deficiency of the conduct in question. Adjectives seem more apt than nouns: depraved, inhuman, disgusting, awful, selfish, callous, etc.)

Virtue ethics (vice ethics might be a more apt label) averts some of the pitfalls of the moral obligation frame. It does not suggest coercion or legalism or precision. On the other hand, if "You are morally obligated to do *x*" is just another way of saying "It would be wrong not to do *x*," what is to be gained – in thinking, for example, of the ethics of rescue – by emphasizing vice or bad character? Isn't it *wrong* to be a jerk or to be callous? Or is it simply *bad*? Although philosophers generally take care to distinguish the right from the good, the wrong from the bad, the person in the street often uses these terms interchangeably. Roughly speaking, we tend to view good–bad as a continuum, while right–wrong has a more either-or character. We speak of the better and the worse, but not of the righter and the wronger. But, as I shall argue, there may be good reasons for thinking in terms of degrees of rightness and wrongness.[19]

The limits of theory

There are certain undeniable evils in the world that should not exist. You don't need industrial strength ethical theory to know that it would be better if billions of people didn't live in dire poverty. It's also clear (and will become clearer in the next chapter) that the wealthy of the world could live just as well or better with a lot less stuff. It follows that a world with less poverty and less economic

---

[19] See, e.g., Arneson 2009, 288–93. Arneson opts for talking of righter and wronger conduct.

inequality is a better world, assuming (as I shall) that these evils can be eradicated without producing worse ones.

Eradicating dire poverty, then, is a powerful moral push, an Ought. But we cannot straightforwardly draw conclusions from these premises about what morality requires of particular individuals, for a variety of reasons.

One reason is that the quest to determine moral obligation suggests a kind of precision that is often misguided. Despite their love affair with Aristotle, moral philosophers rarely heed his famous warning at the beginning of the *Nicomachean Ethics*: "Our discussion will be adequate if it has as much clearness as the subject-matter admits of, for precision is not to be sought for alike in all discussions."[20] Some obligations arise from an agent's contract, promise, act, or role; these may entail specific and well-defined duties. But absent explicit contracts, even relational duties rarely imply determinate acts or forbearances. What *exactly* are the duties implied by membership in a community, exploitation, or old harms? The answers we settle on in particular cases cannot simply be read off from the acknowledgment of a duty.

In a few cases our intuitions are firm – firmer than any theory that might be invoked to defend them. Nothing is as clear as the prohibition on direct aggression. We are morally obligated not to kill people (except in a few well-defined circumstances) or to commit physical aggression against them. Gross indifference to others' suffering – indicated by doing nothing when acting would be easy – is also an evil and a wrong and a violation of moral duty. Leaving aside explicit agreements, how do we establish moral duties beyond the clearest cases? Many philosophers believe we need an ethical theory. Consequentialism, deontology, and virtue ethics are examples of such theories – or, rather, they are types of theories whose details must be filled in. As a complete account of morality, each theory is poorly suited to determining duties. When they try, they tend to teeter in their pragmatic conclusions between the implausible and the

---

[20] Aristotle 1985, bk. 1, ch. 3.

obvious – contradicting common sense or confirming it, demanding too much of ordinary mortals or not enough.

These approaches generally present themselves as competitors for best or true moral theory. Of course, if a theory were true, the fact that its conclusions either contradicted or confirmed common sense would be irrelevant. But what could lead us to accept an ethical theory whose conclusions were so at odds with our core moral beliefs? What reason could we have to accept a view (like maximizing act-utilitarianism) that implies we ought to aid others up to the point where aiding more will make us worse off than our beneficiaries? On the other hand, a theory that simply rubber-stamps our existing beliefs is worthless.

Nothing compels us to have *a* moral theory. And no single ethical theory, I believe, justifies all our moral judgments or does justice to the whole moral landscape. Consequentialist, deontological, and virtue-based considerations each play critical roles in moral thinking, serving different purposes in different circumstances. This conclusion might sound like the easy way out, especially since it practically guarantees that ethics is an inexact nonscience. Some will argue instead that we should assume, and seek, a single foundation for morality unless we find good reason to doubt its existence. For my purposes, we already have sufficient reason for doubt. Perhaps there is some ultra-deep level at which Value is One, but for the world of ordinary human action and middle-sized objects in which practical problems arise for us, all three realms – consequences, principles, and character – are irreducible and essential components of moral judgment and evaluation.

It's tempting to describe this view as not only pluralist but particularist. Certainly, most useful moral reasoning starts close to the ground with a concrete problem and entangles itself richly with facts and circumstances. Grand theory plays no role. But particularism has a special meaning in contemporary philosophy. Jonathan Dancy describes the "core particularist doctrine" in terms of "the holism of reasons." According to this view, "a reason in one case may be no reason at all in another, or even a reason on the other side. In ethics, a feature that makes one action better can make another one worse, and make no difference at all to a third."[21] The holism of reasons is controversial. It would take us too far afield to evaluate its merits here, and I don't believe its truth or falsity matters for my purposes. Perhaps I should say I'm a particularist in practice but not necessarily in theory.

Black and white and mostly gray

At best, then, claims that one is *morally obligated* to donate x percent of one's income falsely suggest precision, and expressing these Oughts in terms of obligations is likely to mislead. So, likewise, is the claim that one is *morally obligated* to refrain from contributing to harms such as climate change by lowering the thermostat y degrees in winter. Beyond the cases of direct physical harm and easy rescue, the language of obligation is strained.

But what's wrong with these claims of obligation is not simply that they falsely suggest precision. Sometimes they are not even roughly accurate. There are at least two other reasons for thinking that duty and obligation misdescribe the moral responsibilities of individuals in these circumstances.

First, preoccupied with the realms of the obligatory on the one hand, and the saintly or heroic on the other, philosophers have neglected a large area between the two. And it is this realm that is of greatest interest to those concerned about the New Harms, the responsibility to aid, and, more generally, the moral implications of globalization.

Suppose we take the term "supererogatory" to refer to all conduct beyond what is strictly obligatory. We might then subdivide this realm into several (fuzzy) parts. At the top end are acts we describe as saintly or heroic, performed by people who do much more than most and who seem to sacrifice a great deal – the soldier who jumps on the grenade to save his buddies, the nurse who gives up all worldly possessions to care for AIDS victims in hard places. Despite what to others appears as obvious virtue far beyond the call of duty, such

[21] Dancy 2009.

people often feel that "here they stand and they can do no other"; they may even feel that they have not made great sacrifices.[22]

But in everyday life we find countless less dramatic and more common cases of "disinterested kindness and generosity" and of "going the second mile" – which, as Urmson points out, implies a difference in kind from going the first.[23] Some acts we might describe as optional but nice, sometimes very nice. Returning a lost wallet with a good deal of cash in it fits this category – whether it's just *nice* or *very nice* might depend on how much trouble it took to find the owner. And we can demarcate a level below "optional but nice": those who give or do just a little more than whatever we deem obligatory are by definition going beyond duty, but perhaps not enough to deserve commendation.[24] They might sometimes even warrant criticism for not doing more.

Of course, there is much room for disagreement about which conduct belongs where on the continuum. I believe that in general, as the costs of acting (or not acting) increase, the wrongness or reprehensibility of not acting (or acting) diminishes.[25] Direct harm to others and gross disregard for others' well-being lie at one end of the spectrum: the realm of wrongness and clear moral obligation. Aggression and violence are the obvious cases but not the only ones. A comfortable person with disposable income who does nothing to aid others in need acts wrongly. What if she donates a half a percent

[22] As J.O. Urmson puts it in his classic paper "Saints and Heroes," after describing how Francis of Assisi reproached himself for not having earlier recognized his duty to preach to the birds: "There is indeed no degree of saintliness that a suitable person may not come to consider it to be his duty to achieve" (Urmson 1958, 204). The example of the soldier is Urmson's. Urmson received the Military Cross for braving enemy fire in 1943 "to keep his battalion supplied with ammunition, ensuring that their tenuous hold on the hill of Bou Aoukaz was maintained during a crucial phase before the final assault on Tunis" – although, as befits a hero, he gives no hint of this fact in his article (*Telegraph* 2012).

[23] Urmson 1958, 207.

[24] I am grateful to David Wasserman for insight on these differences and for the "optional but nice" category.

[25] I discuss the distinctions between wrongness, reprehensibility (blameworthiness), and the appropriateness of blaming shortly.

of her income? Two percent? A person who throws trash in the street or who wastes resources in complete disregard of the environment acts wrongly. How careful does he have to be? There are no straightforward answers to these questions.

We lack words for conduct that is less than saintly or heroic but still not obligatory. "Suboptimal" is misleading insofar as it suggests that one really ought to do what is *best*, leading us back down the road to maximizing consequentialism. In ordinary life we sometimes criticize our own or others' suboptimal behavior that is not quite wrong or in violation of a duty by saying it was "not good" or even "bad."

The conditions in which a billion or more people in the world live are terrible and we have strong reasons to act to eradicate them.[26] But, on my view, describing our humanitarian responsibilities to alleviate poverty in terms of individual duties and obligations is often misleading and unhelpful. These responsibilities are better viewed as collective ones in which each individual has a small role to play, for reasons discussed here and in Chapter 3. First, they can be more effectively addressed collectively and through institutions than individually. Second, for this and several other reasons – discussed in the next chapter – individuals will be more motivated to act when others do and will then have fewer good reasons not to act. Some of these reasons, having to do with demandingness, are ones that can undermine the claim of an individual duty.

Third, I have argued that the going moral theories are unpersuasive and/or indeterminate in their claims (if any) about individuals' moral duties in this realm. Pure consequentialists may argue for a maximizing (thus very demanding) view, but there is nothing inherent in consequentialism that requires the maximizing interpretation. The Kantian view is similarly open to a wide variety of interpretations, from very strict to quite lax; contemporary contractarian theories appealing to principles it would be rational to accept or

---

[26] The conditions of many more people are also very bad. I will not try to draw the lines here, although it can be argued that the relevant group includes more than 2 billion people.

that cannot reasonably be rejected seem similarly indeterminate. Virtue approaches are no more helpful and, in asking what a good or virtuous person would do or what a bad person would fail to do, often seem to beg the question. Of course, many philosophers believe that one or another of these ethical theories is true or necessary to account for morality. As a pluralist who thinks none of these approaches gives us the whole story about ethics and as a skeptic about the value of high ethical theory, I am less patient and less optimistic. So I approach these questions differently.

On my approach, our most basic evaluative judgments are about states of affairs, which themselves exert moral force. The bad ought to be eradicated or prevented from existing. But the mere existence or possibility of an undesirable state of affairs does not in itself create a moral duty on the part of an individual to act or refrain from acting. What accounts for the slack between an undesirable state of affairs on the one hand and a moral duty or obligation on the other?

Moral obligations lie at one end of the spectrum of moral force. They express the strongest moral imperatives: the idea that one has no choice morally but to do or refrain from the act in question. Among moral obligations the very strongest are enforceable or coercible: not only is it wrong to do x or obligatory to do y but it is justifiable for the state (or sometimes nonstate actors) to force you not to do x or to do y.[27] We need some such pronouncements as guides to the moral minimum.

Beyond the obligatory (and its correlate the forbidden) lies the large area often described as supererogatory. As we have seen, this word encompasses everything from the saintly and heroic at the top end to conduct lying close to the realm of obligation and duty at the bottom, and a great deal in between. So what we have is a continuum of more and less desirable behavior, with few sharp lines outside a small, fairly well-demarcated area (comprising especially physical

---

[27] This is not quite true. Recall Thomas Nagel's point, mentioned in Chapter 3: "Sometimes it is proper to force people to do something even though it is not true that they should do it without being forced" (1975, 145).

aggression but also the grossest neglect of others' interests) that we describe in terms of duty, obligation, and wrongness.

My approach has implications for two sets of distinctions philosophers have emphasized. One is the distinction between justification and excuse; the other is between what is true, morally speaking, and what should be publicly proclaimed or (in David Enoch's phrase) "shouted from the rooftops."[28]

Justifications and excuses

In contrast to Morality Demands What It Demands, I believe that demandingness is relevant to determining people's moral obligations. If alleviating the suffering of others generally requires very significant sacrifice, that is a reason for thinking people are not morally obligated to do so.

It might be argued, however, that this view confuses justification with excuse. To *justify* an action is to show that although it might appear wrong it is not; in fact, the action is warranted. To *excuse* an action is to acknowledge its wrongness but to show that the agent is less than fully blameworthy, culpable, or responsible for performing it. To successfully plead self-defense to a charge of murder is to justify homicide; it is to say that the agent had no duty not to kill and that the killing was not wrong.[29] To successfully plead insanity or duress to a charge of murder is to excuse the act, wholly or in part, not to justify it. The killing is wrong, it should not have happened, but the agent is less than fully culpable because of certain facts about him (e.g., insanity) or about the situation in which he found himself (e.g., duress).

Similarly, it might be said that comfortable citizens of industrialized countries ought perhaps to be excused (partly or wholly) for not giving away *x* percent of their income, because of the

---

[28] Enoch, personal correspondence on file with the author, 2011.

[29] Some might argue that one has a duty to defend one's life; on this view, in cases of genuine self-defense not only is there no duty not to kill but there is a duty to kill. But this will seem implausible to many, and is not essential to the point.

burdensomeness of giving that much in a society where most others do not. If an act's demandingness gives people at least a partial excuse for not doing it, then we might blame them less for not doing more. On this view, the conduct in question is nevertheless wrong; it is excused (partly or wholly) but not justified.[30]

Let me offer two responses to this point. First, the distinction between justification and excuse gets its plausibility in realms where we have core beliefs about generally warranted and unwarranted behavior. Most people strongly believe that killing is generally wrong and that a person who kills another must explain why the killing was warranted. Most also strongly believe that killing to defend one's life is one of the few circumstances that warrant killing. By contrast, most people lack clear intuitions about what is right and wrong when it comes to aiding others beyond cases of easy rescue.

Of course, some argue on the basis of one moral theory or another that we have demanding responsibilities to help others. If that were so, the distinction between justification and excuse would apply. But I have given reasons to doubt that the truth about our humanitarian responsibilities is inscribed in the moral furniture of the universe. This is not to endorse relativism. The badness of dire poverty and human suffering more generally *is* inscribed in the moral furniture of the universe; it is clear these are terrible states of affairs and that we should move in the direction of eradicating them. (I take these truths to be self-evident, and could do little to convince someone of them who is not already convinced.) But the extent of our responsibilities is indeterminate – because of their dependence on the difficulty of acting, which itself rests on a variety of factors, and because there is no plausible theory from which determinate responsibilities follow.

There is another point to be made about the distinction between justification and excuse. In the criminal law and in ordinary life, appeals to excuses make sense where it is reasonable to expect most people to act in a certain way, but where unusual conditions

---

[30] Of course, some might argue that the conduct is neither justified nor excused. If it is not excused, then prima facie the agents in question ought to be blamed for their behavior. In the next section I discuss this issue further.

sometimes prevail or where a particular individual falls short of the general requirements. There is a standard expectation of people, a default that applies to the "reasonable person." But if the conditions that relieve people of responsibility are pervasive, if practically everyone falls short, thinking in terms of excuses makes little sense. To think this way of the forces that keep people from doing more for others than they do is to pathologize ordinary human psychology.[31]

This is not to say that we cannot or should not try to get people to act differently – that is, better. But we need to harness human psychology rather than fight it. I elaborate on this point in the following chapters.

It might be argued, however, that we need to apply a more fine-grained analysis. Perhaps we should ask questions about what is obligatory only of individuals, not about "comfortable people in general"; the answers will depend on particular facts about those individuals and their circumstances. Of course, individuals vary widely in how much they do, both absolutely and relative to their own financial and other abilities, and in how much they ought to do. Some will be justified in not doing more, some will be excused; about some we will conclude they are doing wrong and should be criticized or blamed.

Whether a person acted wrongly depends on whether it is reasonable to expect him to have acted differently. When is such an expectation reasonable? – that *is* the question. It depends partly on the prevailing moral code in the wrongdoer's society. As Richard Arneson argues, since the established moral code "exerts a massive gravitational pull on individual judgment and choice," we may often conclude that "the agent lacked a reasonable opportunity to do the right thing." But conventional morality is not decisive. "The relevant standard of blameworthiness is whether the agent had a reasonable opportunity to behave rightly."[32] In general, people with more education and greater exposure to ideas – not to mention greater wealth – are more liable to act wrongly than those with less.

[31] I owe this way of putting the point to David Luban.   [32] Arneson 2009, 291.

Public and private, appearance and reality

But even when we judge that people have done wrong, and even that they are deserving of blame, we might sometimes think they should not openly be blamed. To understand why, we need to make some further distinctions about this thing called *morality*. Let's assume that societies need some kind of public moral code or set of moral guidelines, however rough or vague or implicit, that are communicated to and accepted by their members. In addition, we can also think of morality as a decision procedure for an individual (you or me, for example) who must consider how to act and what to do. This decision procedure could be based on the public moral code or on something more personal and specific to the individual – her religion, conscience, and the like. Finally, morality might also refer to a set of truths about what's good and bad, right and wrong.[33]

It might seem that my account confuses the first with the second or third – that it confuses the optimal public moral code with the decision procedure an individual should employ in deciding how to act, or with the moral truth. On this way of thinking, it's one thing to say what the content of the public moral code should be, another to say how individuals should think about how much to help others or how much they should *really* help others.[34] Thus, it might be said that we should not demand too much of people publicly if doing so has bad effects. If the public moral code is too demanding, some people may ignore it because they feel they cannot (or will not) live up to its requirements. And that could debase the currency of morality.[35] But it might still be the case, on this view, that the very demanding

---

[33] One need not think there is a determinate truth about *all* of morality to hold this sort of view, just that there are some moral truths and that these do not necessarily coincide with the content of the optimal public moral code.

[34] The latter two might also be different from each other, of course, but I will ignore any such differences here.

[35] Urmson makes the analogy in positive law with Prohibition: "the prohibition laws asked too much of the American people and were consequently broken systematically; and as people got used to breaking the law a general lowering of respect for the law naturally followed; it no longer seemed that a law was something that everybody could be expected to obey" (Urmson 1958, 212).

standards are the right or true standards. So, for example, Singer argues that it might be right to privately accept "a very demanding morality with regard to how much we should give to relieve global poverty, while publicly advocating the more modest level that ... would maximize the total amount given ..."[36] On this view, people might really be blameworthy for not doing more than they do, but it might be counterproductive to blame them openly – to tell them, or others, that they have done wrong. So, A could hold B blameworthy, and in that sense blame her, but keep the thought entirely to himself. Or A could express blame either to B, or to others, or both. The question here is about the possible gap between the *judgment* that a person is blameworthy and the *reasons to announce it*. On this view, what's true about morality and about people's moral obligations, and what we should say publicly, are two different things.

Part of my response parallels my reply to the accusation that I have confused justification and excuse: there is no plausible ethical theory or argument for the conclusion that what *we are really morally obligated to do* is what is very demanding. But there is more to be said. Suppose it turns out that a demanding public morality stimulates people's efforts rather than depressing them – causing people to rise to the occasion, compared to a less demanding code. The idea that higher expectations elicit better outcomes is, after all, confirmed in the educational context: there is evidence that minority students perform less well in part because they are expected to perform less well.[37] If a public morality insisting on strong moral obligations to help others were effective in this way, it might seem that on my view we ought to endorse it even if it exaggerates our true moral obligations.

In reply I offer several points. First, although people may sometimes rise to higher expectations, I doubt that in rich countries today a public morality that simply announced that individuals have very

---

[36] On the assumption, that is, that asking too much is counterproductive (Singer 2009, 261). I am grateful to Singer for these and other comments about this question, raised in Lichtenberg 2009a.

[37] See, e.g., George and Aronson 2003; Ferguson 1998. Of course, we cannot simply generalize from these results to the entirely different context we are discussing here.

demanding moral obligations to help others would be effective. That doesn't mean, of course, that we should go around announcing that people do *not* have strong moral obligations, suggesting that it's perfectly fine to do little or nothing. What we ought to do is tell the truth, vividly: that there are powerful moral reasons to do more, and also that there are many things we can do – for example, act collectively – that would make doing more less demanding, giving us even stronger reasons to do more.[38] (Not to mention that it might be in our self-interest, rightly understood, to do more because, for example, it might lessen global insecurity.[39]) It's also true that, as moral codes change, what becomes obligatory can also change, for reasons I have discussed. So eventually, greater sacrifices for the welfare of others could become obligatory, even if they are not obligatory now.

But suppose for a moment we do not fight the hypothetical. Suppose a stern, demanding, finger-wagging public morality *were* effective. If the best way to alleviate global poverty were to browbeat people about their moral obligations, should we browbeat them? Yes, we should. In light of the severity of global poverty, the benefits of doing so might outweigh the costs – lying to people (since by hypothesis they do not have such stringent obligations) or manipulating them. As a pluralist, I acknowledge the inevitability of trade-offs and the lack of absolutes, and the consequences for poor people might be worth the evils of lying and manipulation. Nevertheless, the hypothetical seems to me distorted. As a guide to action and a means of motivating people, it's difficult not to believe that a more nuanced moral picture along the lines suggested in the previous paragraph would be superior.

---

[38] But not everything we can and should do to influence people's choices lies in the realm of rational persuasion and argument. We should also alter the environment within which people make choices, on the assumption that, as Richard Thaler and Cass Sunstein put it, in the choice environment there is no neutral design. See Thaler and Sunstein 2008, and Chapters 6 and 10 for further discussion.

[39] The phrase is Alexis de Tocqueville's from *Democracy in America* (1945, vol. II, sec. II, ch. VIII).

Looking more closely, we see that the question here is not just about what the content of a public morality or a moral code should be, but about what we should say "out loud," as it were, even if only to a single individual. Suppose two comfortable Americans are discussing the moral responsibilities of people like them to benefit the poor. Should A tell B that it is *wrong* not to do much more than B does – and therefore implicitly or explicitly *blame* B? Well here, one might say, if two people are talking one-on-one, one should not *tell* the other what to do; he should rather provide the other with *reasons* and *reasoning* for his conclusion. On my view, the reasons and reasoning would not primarily invoke wrongness and moral obligations but other ideas – that it is important to do more, better to do more, satisfying to do more, easier to do more if we act collectively, etc. In justifying the reason-giving approach, we can appeal to both instrumental and noninstrumental reasons. It's likely to be more effective to give reasons than to give orders or to construct false stories about why we should do more (remember that the question at issue here is whether we are justified in *exaggerating* people's true moral obligations); it is also more appropriate to treat a human being, a thinking agent, in this way. We could expand the point to the more public context, at least up to a point. If I'm right it will be more effective not to exaggerate people's moral obligations but rather to emphasize the more nuanced moral reasons for doing more, and it also treats people in a morally better way. I admit that there is a measure of idealism in this view.

These questions about whether I have confused the truth about morality's demands with what we should say about it publicly arise because to some it appears that I have conceded too much significance to appearances and effects. It doesn't follow from the fact that Singer's demands would, if publicly announced, be ineffective or counterproductive that Singer is wrong about what morality really demands. What people really ought to do and what we ought to announce that they ought to do are not necessarily identical. People may do wrong even if we judge it better not to say so, to them or others. But the gap between the two is smaller than some have imagined.

CHAPTER 6

Why people do what others do – and why that's not so bad

I have been arguing that demandingness is relevant to determining what people morally ought to do or are obligated to do, and that it is not only unrealistic but unreasonable to expect ordinary mortals to make great sacrifices for others' interests on a regular basis – to demand too much of them. Some might take this view as spelling doom for the prospect of remedying a pressing problem like global poverty, which appears too large to solve without heroic efforts on the part of mere mortals.

What this pessimistic conclusion ignores is that demandingness is not a fixed quantity. It is alterable, and we have some control over its dimensions. If that is true, we may be able to get more for less, so to speak, by making what would otherwise be demanding demands less demanding. Defending that proposition is the purpose of this chapter.

Some basic ideas

In a general sense the elasticity of demandingness can be understood in terms of the psychologist's idea of *situationism*. Over the last fifty years, hundreds of studies have confirmed that seemingly small features of the situations in which people find themselves exert enormous influence over human behavior. Psychologists and others disagree about how far we should take situationism – to what extent, in explaining behavior, we should downplay deep-seated and fixed psychological traits relative to situational factors. Radical situationists virtually eliminate the role of character and personality, which to many appears implausible.[1] But it is not controversial that "situations" play an important role in influencing what people do. Small and sometimes seemingly insignificant aspects of the situations in which people find themselves can greatly increase the likelihood that they will do A rather than B or A rather than not-A.

For example, in a famous experiment subjects who have just emerged from a phone booth encounter a woman (a confederate of the experimenter) who has dropped a sheaf of papers on the ground. Will the subject stop to help her pick up the papers? Subjects who have just found a dime in the coin return of the public phone are much more likely to help than those who did not find a dime: of those who found a dime, fourteen people helped and two did not; of those who did not find a dime, one helped and twenty-four did not.[2]

Or consider the famous experiment psychologists John Darley and Daniel Batson carried out in the 1970s. They recruited divinity students at Princeton Theological Seminary to prepare a brief sermon on the parable of the Good Samaritan, which the students were to deliver in another building.[3] Some subjects were told that they were a few minutes late, others that they were a few minutes early. On the way to the building where they were to sermonize, subjects encountered a man slumped in a doorway, motionless and with his eyes closed. As they walked by he coughed and groaned. Only 10 percent of the late Samaritans offered assistance, while 63 percent of those with a little extra time did.

Now in a sense every case that exemplifies situationism – that is, the sensitivity of behavior to small changes in the environment – shows the elasticity of demandingness. Whatever the situational factors are that cause people to do A rather than B, they mean it is easier and more probable for people to do A rather than B in certain

---

[1] For a persuasive critique of radical situationism see Luban 2003, 293–8.

[2] Isen and Levin 1972. The result was explained in terms of mood: finding a dime (not worth much even in 1972) apparently elevated a person's mood and so increased the chances she would help others. Many other experiments confirm that seemingly inconsequential situational factors can produce large effects on mood and thus on behavior. For discussion of some of them see Doris 2002, 30–9.

[3] Darley and Batson 1973.

circumstances; they do A rather than B more unthinkingly and effortlessly.

But in this chapter I explore a species of situationism that illustrates the elasticity of demandingness in a particularly robust sense. This is the extent to which people's behavior is dependent on what others around them do. People want and need things partly because others in their vicinity have them, and this is often not only rational but morally respectable. The reasons are diverse, and I explore them here.

I call this feature the relativity of well-being. The term is slightly misleading, for it is not strictly speaking a person's well-being that is relative but those factors that contribute to or determine it. What constitutes well-being, whether it can be understood in purely subjective terms – in terms of the opinions or experience of the person whose well-being it is – or whether it contains objective components, is a difficult and philosophically well-trod topic that I shall not enter into; for my purposes here the answer does not matter. Whether well-being is understood subjectively or objectively, we can think of it (even if only metaphorically) as a quantity that is subject to variation depending on its relationship to the well-being of others. That is what I mean by the relativity of well-being.

I assume it is generally a good thing for people's well-being to improve. Some people's well-being lies below an acceptable threshold, and it's urgent to get it above the threshold. Others' well-being may be sufficiently high that we deem it not worth external efforts (certainly not that of the government or other agencies) to raise it further. Occasionally we may even want to decrease a person's well-being – say, because he deserves punishment.

Relativity

Classical economic theory assumes that we increase people's well-being (welfare, utility) by increasing their absolute consumption of goods. Give them more well-being-enhancing stuff – health, education, money – and they will be better off. But this view ignores the well-established fact that some goods are positional, to use Fred

Hirsch's term: their value depends on what others have.[4] When a person's well-being depends on what others have, I speak of the relativity of well-being.

Richard Easterlin is often credited with steering modern economists to a concern with relative well-being. In a 1974 article, Easterlin found that although within a society richer people are generally happier than poorer people, happiness does not increase as a society becomes richer.[5] Thus, for example, although real per capita income quintupled in Japan between 1958 and 1987, subjective judgments of well-being did not rise.[6] The "Easterlin paradox" has been much studied and confirmed.[7] It helped give rise to a focus on the significance for a person's well-being of her position vis-à-vis others.

A striking example is a 1995 survey that asked people to choose between the following alternatives:

A: Your current yearly income is $50,000; others earn $25,000.
B: Your current yearly income is $100,000; others earn $200,000.

About half the respondents preferred the first alternative, even though their purchasing power would be *half* what it is in the second.[8] Presumably the number of people preferring this alternative would increase as the gap between the proposed incomes narrowed. The survey asked analogous questions about other goods besides income, including attractiveness, intelligence, and education (for each of these, respondents were asked about possession of the good both for themselves and for their child), praise from a supervisor, vacation time, and others. Physical attractiveness and intelligence were among the most highly positional goods, vacation time the least. In other words, it was more important to respondents to be

---

[4] Hirsch 1976.   [5] Easterlin 1974.

[6] Easterlin 1995. As Richard Layard puts it, "People in the West have got no happier in the last 50 years. They have become much richer, they work much less, they have longer holidays, they travel more, they live longer, and they are healthier. But they are no happier" (Layard 2003, 14).

[7] See, e.g., Luttmer 2005; Frank 1997. See also the work of Frank, Hirsch, Layard, and others cited elsewhere in this chapter.

[8] Solnick and Hemenway 1998. Respondents were faculty, students, and staff at the Harvard School of Public Health.

more attractive or intelligent than others than to possess a greater "absolute quantity" of these goods. The authors suggest that "positional concerns loom larger for goods that are crucial in attaining other objectives than for goods that are desirable primarily in themselves."[9]

My claim is that well-being is *largely* relative and that we often act as we do because others around us so act. There are at least two corollaries, which I express in terms of consumption. The most important one is that to the extent that people consume because others do, they could consume less if others did too, without correspondingly diminishing their well-being. It follows that doubts about how much we can reasonably demand that people sacrifice for the well-being of others are partly misplaced, for reductions in consumption, when undertaken collectively, bring with them reductions in sacrifice. For a variety of reasons we shall see, joint sacrifices are almost universally less demanding than those undertaken individually.

The other implication is moral. Critiques of consumption and acquisition often amount to indictments of human character. The idea that people consume because others do seems to imply that they are conformist, greedy, envious, materialistic, and preoccupied with status and one-upmanship. Although we should not altogether discount these traits, I shall argue that appreciating the complexities of consumption shows why it is often neither unreasonable nor disreputable for a person to consume when others do; more generally, it illuminates certain puzzles about human desires and well-being.

One further preliminary remark is important. For the purposes of the argument of this chapter I assume it would in fact benefit poor people for rich people to reduce their level of material well-being – to consume less. Some reject this proposition, arguing that giving to the poor is ineffective or even counterproductive in relieving poverty. I examine this concern and the reasons for it in Chapter 8. For the moment I adopt the assumption, common in arguments for the moral responsibility to aid the poor, that a way for the poor to have more is

[9] Solnick and Hemenway 1998, sec. 4.

for the rich to have less – that if the rich declined that latte, new sound system, or trip to Europe and transferred the savings to others in need, the latter would be better off.[10]

Even if the skeptics were right to doubt the general efficacy of the rich having less for the poor having more, certain kinds of reductions in consumption by the well-off are clearly beneficial. Climate change is the obvious example. Because its effects will harm the poorest people in poor countries most severely, reducing consumption of energy and energy-dependent goods among comfortable people would make a difference even if transfers of wealth from rich to poor were generally ineffective. So the "more for the poor means less for the rich" relationship seems clearly to hold in at least some contexts.

Infrastructure and networking effects

How are people's desires for and consumption of things dependent on what others have? We can best answer this question by considering how desires for and consumption of things are *not* dependent on what others have. It is natural to think here in terms of basic needs or minimum requirements – conditions that must be met for a person to lead a minimally decent life. The need to consume some number of calories, or to have clothing and shelter against the elements, exists independently of what others have or do. Without food we die; what others do is irrelevant.

Even biological needs, however, are not wholly acontextual. In a society where strenuous physical activity is important – because it is for some reason socially valued or because scarcity of resources

---

[10] In addition to the counter-arguments considered in Chapter 8 that transfers of wealth are ineffective or counterproductive in alleviating poverty at the demand side, there is also the view that drastic reductions in consumption would cause the domestic economy to collapse and thus would help no one. As Peter Singer argues, this is only a real worry if very significant numbers of people drastically reduce their consumption, but if changes are widespread they need not be radical, since modest reductions would be sufficient to eliminate the worst global poverty (Singer 2010, 38–9).

requires strength or speed – relative caloric intake may affect successful functioning. Whether all needs, including physical needs, are
partly relative to what others have and do is a question we need not
answer here. Two points are worth noting, however. First, much
depends on how we describe needs. Suppose, for example, we agree
that people have a basic need for enough food to survive or thrive.
Stated in this way, the need is absolute in the sense of being invariant
to context, including the behavior of others. But how much food is
enough to survive or thrive will vary depending on circumstances.
Thus, although we can describe the need in absolute terms, its
satisfaction may depend on relational facts. As Amartya Sen argues,
"the absolute satisfaction of some ... needs might depend on a
person's relative position vis-à-vis others."[11]

Second, some needs are more relative than others. The need for air
is quite nonrelative. By contrast, consider the ability to work, or even
to get around and do things (acquire food and the like) for oneself. In
many places in the United States today, it is difficult to perform these
tasks without private transportation. The need for a car is not absolute
in the sense of existing irrespective of context. The economic system
and the infrastructure could have evolved differently, so that cars
would not be indispensable. A well-functioning system of public transportation creates and perpetuates demand: the larger and finer the net it
casts (that is, the more places you can get to using it), the more people
use it; the more people use it, the greater its economies of scale; the
greater its economies of scale, the better and cheaper it gets.

In many places today, however, not having a car is more than an
inconvenience; indeed, suburban and rural families often need two
cars. A person's desire for a car, then, although dependent on what
others have and do, need not be rooted in greed, envy, or the desire
for status. This is not to deny that cars have a great deal of meaning
apart from their utility. People express themselves with and through
their cars, and cars are paradigmatic status symbols. But these
motives could be entirely absent and one might still have reason
for a car – and even a particular type of car. If enough other people

[11] Sen 1983, 155–63.

drive large, heavy sport-utility vehicles, I have a reason – safety – for driving one too.[12]

Many items once thought of as new-fangled frivolities can become entrenched, and eventually nearly indispensable, in a technologically sophisticated society: invention is the mother of necessity. Consider the myriad innovations of the twentieth and early twenty-first centuries.[13] The telephone, radio, television, computers, the Internet, not to mention the various iThings – when first introduced such items may seem like luxuries for the rich or gadget-addicted. Soon, however, their benefits become apparent; when a critical mass of users develops, *not* having the item can constitute a genuine handicap. The telephone was marketed first as a "tool of the upper class" but was quickly appropriated by farm and industrial communities for practical purposes.[14] Mobile phones, like car phones, were originally used primarily by affluent males or their chauffeurs.[15] Today those without computers and easy access to the Internet suffer serious disadvantages. We now have a term – the "digital divide" – to describe the gap between the information-rich and the information-poor, who correlate almost perfectly with the rich and poor.

You need these goods – in a straightforward sense that has nothing to do with status questions – because others have them. If you don't keep up you fall behind.

Salience and habituation

Recently my husband and I spent a semester in Jerusalem. We downsized dramatically from our house in the Washington suburbs

---

[12] For this and many other examples (not all technology-related) see Frank 1999, 9: "If I buy a custom-tailored suit for my job interview, I reduce the likelihood that others will land the same job; and in the process, I create an incentive for them to spend more than they had planned on their own interview suits."

[13] It's in the nature of this beast that what I say here will soon be obsolete. I wrote an ancestor of this chapter in the mid-1990s (before the rise of the Internet, even before mobile phones were common!), and the examples discussed there now seem to date from the stone age (Lichtenberg 1996).

[14] Hadwiger and Garard 1993.   [15] Lacohée, Wakeford, and Pearson 2003, 205.

to a small apartment. We had no car (at home we need two) and walked almost everywhere. There's no question that we missed some of our conveniences and furnishings – this is not a story about renunciation and the newfound joys of asceticism. But we marveled at how easy it was to live in much smaller quarters, wondering what we did with all that space back home. We were surprised too that it became easier, not harder, to live in the small space as time went on. Rather than feeling more and more constrained, we got used to it. Moreover, we bought very little except food. That's partly because we didn't live near stores and, without a car and with limited access to local commercial media (our Hebrew is at best negligible), we were rarely bombarded with new consumer goods.

In our zeal to find sophisticated explanations for people's hankerings after things, we have neglected the powerful effects of habituation, and of what psychologists call salience or availability, on desire. Habituation means that we get used to both negative and positive inputs: as time goes on, the bad feels less bad and the good feels less good. This kind of adaptation "may be natural selection's way of allocating scarce attention and motivation efficiently, rewarding the organism for deploying its resources to new stimuli requiring immediate attention"; it also keeps the organism motivated by preventing it from either "resting on its laurels" or becoming too depressed to act in its interests. "If the satisfaction of our last achievement never faded, there might not be a next achievement."[16] And if we never got used to chronic dis-ease, we would function poorly.

So habituation explains how easily we can get used to environments less luxurious than those to which we were previously

---

[16] Wilkinson 2007, 9. See also Frederick and Loewenstein 1999 for a survey of research on adaptation in a variety of domains – some negative (noise, incarceration, disability, bereavement), some positive (increases in income, cosmetic surgery, sexually arousing stimuli, foods). Adaptation varies from domain to domain; people adapt significantly to incarceration, for example, but not to noise. Easterlin's research (see the section on "Relativity" above), showing that increases in income do not bring increases in well-being, supports the claim that people adapt to increases in standard of living.

accustomed. A similar psychological mechanism may also explain the attraction of new goods when we do encounter them. In these matters, presence makes the heart grow fonder, and novelty stimulates desire. We are more likely to want something if we see it than if it exists for us merely as an abstract possibility. Indeed, an abstract possibility is usually unconceived, and moves us not at all.

So the fact that our friends and acquaintances have something, or that we see a new item in an ad or a store window, acts as a stimulus if the good has appeal of any kind. Advertisers and sales people have always understood this phenomenon, which can be understood in terms of what cognitive psychologists call *salience*: the physical presence of an item makes it more available to consciousness. The economist James Duesenberry describes this process in terms of what he calls the "demonstration effect":

> In given circumstances ... individuals come into contact with goods superior to the ones they use with a certain frequency. Each such contact is a demonstration of the superiority of those goods and is a threat to the existence of the current consumption pattern. It is a threat because it makes active the latent preference for these goods ... For any particular family the frequency of contact with superior goods will increase primarily as the consumption expenditures of others increase.[17]

There is nothing inherently disreputable about this desire-stimulating process, which is as plausibly attributed to human curiosity, to being alive to one's surroundings, as to greed or envy or status-seeking – the motives commonly offered by critics of consumption.

But some critics point to exactly these facts – wanting things when you see them, being moved by the consumption habits of others – as evidence for greed and envy. How can we resolve this dispute, where both sides agree about the evidence but disagree about how to interpret it? One solution is to have it both ways: to acknowledge an element that is morally neutral or even praiseworthy (curiosity,

---

[17] Duesenberry 1949, 26–7. Duesenberry describes some of the same phenomena discussed here in terms of the "interdependence of preferences." Nothing hangs on his description of the new goods as superior.

aliveness to one's surroundings) but also an element worthy of criticism (lack of self-sufficiency, overdependence on material things). Yet whether criticism is appropriate depends partly on other issues, some of which I examine in the following sections.

Nothing in these observations implies that having more things makes a person happier or better off. We may acknowledge that getting what your neighbors have enhances your welfare, without denying that everyone might be happier living more simply. This is precisely the force of the relativity of well-being. If we assume (what the ascetic would not) that the life of things enhances one's well-being in certain respects, then, beginning from the status quo of a consumption-oriented society and acquaintance with some new thing, having it may improve your welfare, even though a different bundle of experiences inconsistent with having it might improve your well-being even more. Given that your neighbors have it, you may be better off having it too.

Consumption and self-respect

Consider now the reasons that probably loom largest when people think about consumption in modern society, and that are foreshadowed in the previous sections. We think of conspicuous consumption, keeping up with the Joneses, ostentatious displays of wealth, reliance on material goods as a way of attaining status. But the contemptuous attitude revealed in these descriptions rests partly on a misunderstanding of why people want things. We have already seen two reasons for thinking so. First, because of infrastructure and networking effects, the satisfaction of needs and interests most people would agree are basic depends in part on what other people have and do. Second, acquaintance often breeds desire, and it is not necessarily a sign of greed or envy to want things when you see them.

Still, the desire to improve one's image or position vis-à-vis others plays an important part in the urge to consume. We want to have things in part to say something about ourselves to others or to get recognition from them. It is this expressive function we now need to examine more carefully.

First, it's worth noting that not all expressive consumption involves the desire to say something about one's *worth*. A person who wears a nose ring or drives a Harley Davidson may be expressing herself – we might even say she is making a statement about herself and her values – but she need not be trying to secure a place in a hierarchy.[18] Is such behavior necessarily even communicative? Terms like "self-expression" and "making a statement" suggest sending a message to others, but they can also be understood in a more private way – perhaps as an outward manifestation of inner feeling. Let's assume, however, that for most people fashion and other forms of self-expression do involve a crucial communicative component. In part, this is a practical matter: it's useful for a variety of reasons, including making contact with those who have similar interests, to let others know what you like and what you are like.

But the acquisition and display of goods is sometimes meant (not necessarily consciously) to communicate something not simply about one's interests or identity but about one's *worth*. Such status-seeking has always had a bad reputation. A long tradition of moralists advises that what other people think of us is not important and that we should not base our actions on the opinions or behavior of others. If this is true, then all consumption aimed at sending a message, especially a message about one's worth, would be disreputable as a motive. But although it's easy to imagine situations where we should not care what others think – for instance, where there is an obviously right but unpopular thing to do, and one should brave public opinion and do it – the idea that it is always disreputable to care goes too far. People wholly unconcerned with how others see them seem at best too saintly to serve as role models for the ordinary person; at worst, they may be pathologically insensitive to or contemptuous of others.

But consumption designed to send a message about one's worth masks an important ambiguity. Are you trying simply to keep up

---

[18] For a discussion of nonstatus-related expressive aspects of consumption see Strudler and Curlo 1997.

with the Joneses, or to surpass them? In *The Theory of the Leisure Class* Thorstein Veblen did much to promote the latter interpretation:

> ... the end sought by accumulation is to rank high in comparison with the rest of the community in point of pecuniary strength ... However widely, or equally, or "fairly," it may be distributed, no general increase of the community's wealth can make any approach to satiating this need, the ground of which is the desire to excel every one else in the accumulation of goods.[19]

Similarly, in an essay long but it seems wrongly attributed to John Stuart Mill, the author observes that "men do not desire merely to be *rich*, but to be *richer* than other men."[20] And Rousseau in the *Discourse on Inequality* argues that the motive for economic advancement in commercial society is "the ardent desire to raise one's relative fortune less out of genuine need than in order to place oneself above others."[21]

But although people may desire or acquire goods to show that they are *better* than others, they may also consume simply to show they are as good. Veblen, Mill (or the unknown author mistaken for him), and Rousseau fail to draw this distinction, which I believe is both morally significant and psychologically real. Let us first examine why it is acceptable and even important for people to attain some measure of perceived equality with their fellows, then ask to what extent people want not merely equality but superiority.

---

[19] Veblen, 2007, ch. 2, 26. Veblen describes the point of this kind of accumulation as "invidious comparison," although he hastens to add that "there is no intention to extol or depreciate, or to commend or deplore any of the phenomena which the word is used to characterise. The term is used in a technical sense as describing a comparison of persons with a view to rating and grading them in respect of relative worth or value" (ibid., ch. 2, 27). Whether Veblen meant to "depreciate" or "deplore" or not (we detect here the common claim among social scientists not to make "value judgments"), that is certainly how his words have been taken.

[20] Mill 1941, 49 (originally attributed to Mill but more recent scholarship [Hayek 1963] has cast doubt on this attribution; emphasis in original). The author adds: "or than certain other men," noting the importance of the reference group, discussed immediately below.

[21] Rousseau 1997, 187.

A central reason for wanting things when others have them has to do with the need for self-respect. For all but the most extraordinarily self-sufficient individuals, self-respect requires respect from one's fellows; it requires that one not be shamed before them. Self-respect and thus respect from others are fundamental human needs, as John Rawls acknowledges when he includes self-respect among the primary goods – those things one wants no matter what one's values or life plan.[22] As Veblen himself puts it, "Only individuals with an aberrant temperament can in the long run retain their self-esteem in the face of the disesteem of their fellows."[23] Satisfying the need for self-respect calls for a certain kind of equality, not superiority; it means having certain things others have, not more than others have.

No one has improved on Adam Smith's famous statement of this point in *The Wealth of Nations*:

> By necessaries I understand, not only the commodities which are indispensably necessary for the support of life, but whatever the custom of the country renders it indecent for creditable people, even the lowest order, to be without. A linen shirt, for example, is, strictly speaking, not a necessary of life. The Greeks and Romans lived, I suppose, very comfortably, though they had no linen. But in the present times, through the greater part of Europe, a creditable day-labourer would be ashamed to appear in public without a linen shirt, the want of which would be supposed to denote that disgraceful degree of poverty, which, it is presumed, no body can well fall into without extreme bad conduct. Custom, in the same manner, has rendered leather shoes a necessary of life in England. The poorest creditable person of either sex would be ashamed to appear in public without them.[24]

---

[22] Rawls 1971, sec. 67.

[23] Veblen 2007, 25. Veblen speaks of self-esteem, not self-respect. Although the terms are often used interchangeably, there are reasons for distinguishing them (see Sachs 1981). Following Sachs's main idea, I understand self-esteem to mean having a high opinion of oneself or one's accomplishments, while self-respect involves having a proper regard for one's rights, deserts, or entitlements – recognizing that one is a person of value whose interests and wishes ought to be taken seriously. Although the two concepts are related and not always easily distinguishable, what is at issue here is self-respect.

[24] Smith 1994, bk. v, ch. 2.

Marx makes a similar point in *Wage Labour and Capital*:

> A house may be large or small; as long as the neighboring houses are
> likewise small, it satisfies all social requirement for a residence. But let
> there arise next to the little house a palace, and the little house shrinks to
> a hut. The little house now makes it clear that its inmate has no social
> position at all to maintain . . .[25]

The need for self-respect – or, put negatively, the need to avoid
shame – is basic and universal. But what it takes to satisfy that need
varies from time to time and place to place. In Smith's society, self-
respect meant leather shoes. Today it means – well, whatever
example I might give may be obsolete by the time this book is in
print.

Why certain kinds of goods, such as shoes, should have the
significance Smith describes is an interesting question. It's clear that
goods functioning as status markers must be "conspicuous" – visible
and public – which explains the prominence of clothing and cars. The
inside of a person's house matters less since few people will see it.

In mass societies the opinions and respect of subgroups, rather
than the general public, assume greater importance, for at least two
reasons. First, the "general public" is a useful fiction more than
anything else. Second, it is psychologically difficult to care about
what "everybody" thinks; instead, we focus on achieving respect
from particular reference groups to which we belong. Who the
reference group is varies from person to person and context to
context.[26] Sometimes it's the people who actually live nearby, sometimes our coworkers, sometimes those who work in the same field,
sometimes the parents of our children's friends.

The path by which certain goods become "necessaries" must
involve the processes of entrenchment discussed in the previous
section. It would seem that wherever there is material progress,

---

[25] Marx 1847, ch. 6.
[26] The concept of the reference group was introduced by Robert K. Merton and
Alice Rossi in "Contributions to the Theory of Reference Group Behavior" (1968).
For a summary of reference group theory, with references, see Dawson and
Chatman 2001.

new goods will gradually assume the role of "signifying decency" that Smith describes. In less dynamic societies, the signifiers may change more slowly.

How much equality does self-respect require? Could one reasonably argue that all significant material inequalities damage the self-respect of those who have less? If so, the implausibility and impracticality of radical egalitarianism could make a *reductio ad absurdum* of the self-respect argument. But without evidence that material inequalities have a general tendency to undermine self-respect, we should make the more modest assumption that having certain limited goods is necessary for self-respect, and that it is therefore rational and reasonable for people to have those goods when others have them.

Equality or superiority?

Do people want to be merely equal to others, or do they want to be better? There are at least two reasons for thinking the difference matters. One is moral. To want to be (and to seem) as good as others seems respectable; to want to be better than or to outdo others may arouse our suspicions, at least sometimes. In Kantian terms, it is possible to will that everyone succeed in their striving for equality, but not in their striving for superiority (or, more simply, it is possible to will that everyone be equal but not that everyone be superior).[27] As American storyteller and radio personality Garrison Keillor has instructed us, all the children cannot be above average. A second reason is practical. The desire for superiority, at least in possessions, leads to arms races and prisoners' dilemmas: consumers intent on proving their superior status will induce ever-escalating spirals of acquisition. The desire for equality does not lead to the same result.

Adam Smith's own writing reflects the ambiguity between the aims of equal and superior status. In *The Theory of the Moral Sentiments* he argues that

[27] I owe this point to Thomas Pogge.

> it is chiefly from this regard to the sentiments of mankind, that we pursue
> riches and avoid poverty. For to what purpose is all the toil and bustle of
> this world? What is the end of avarice and ambition, of the pursuit of
> wealth, of power, and preheminence? Is it to supply the necessities of
> nature? The wages of the meanest laborer can supply them ... From
> whence, then, arises that emulation which runs through all the different
> ranks of men, and what are the advantages which we propose by that
> great purpose of human life which we call bettering our condition? To be
> observed, to be attended to, to be taken notice of with sympathy,
> complacency, and approbation, are all the advantages which we can
> propose to derive from it.[28]

Talk of power and "preheminence" suggests the desire to surpass
others, although the passage from *The Wealth of Nations* quoted
earlier and parts of this one are compatible with the more modest
claim.[29] Still, whatever Smith thought, the desire for superiority
certainly exists in many people.

And is there anything wrong with that? Some would insist that to
eradicate this urge is to discourage excellence and individuality.
Robert Nozick argues that "we evaluate how *well* we do something
by comparing our performance to others." Someone living in "an
isolated mountain village" may think he's good at sinking jump shots
because he makes 10 percent of them when others in his village make
only 1 percent. Then he learns about Ray Allen.[30] In this realm there
is no noncomparative standard of excellence.

There are really two questions here. One is whether excellence is
inherently comparative; the other is whether people necessarily crave
superiority over others. On the first, excellence may well contain an
inherently comparative component. Even if we could imagine a
whole community (including all the individuals in it) demonstrating
excellence in, say, musicianship, athleticism, or drawing, that judgment would imply a comparison with other communities not so good
at these things. It just can't be that *all* human beings are *excellent*
violinists or basketball players. On the desire for superiority, there is

[28] Smith 2002, pt. I, sec. 3, ch. 2, para. 1.
[29] Daniel Luban defends the more pessimistic view in Luban 2012, 2.
[30] Nozick 1974, 240. Nozick's example was Jerry West.

no doubt wide variation among people both within societies and between them.[31] Variation exists also within individuals: most people seem content to be merely as good as others in many respects even if they want to excel in some.[32] It would be foolish to deny the existence of the desire for superiority, but it is also a mistake to exaggerate its scope.

A classic study, *The American Soldier*, conducted during and after World War II, sheds light on the importance of relative achievement and deprivation.[33] In the Military Police, opportunities for promotion were poor, yet satisfaction was higher than in the Air Corps, where the chances were much better. As W.G. Runciman explains, those MPs who were not promoted tended to compare themselves with their colleagues who were also not promoted; the few who were promoted felt they had done relatively better. By contrast, in the Air Corps those who had not been promoted compared themselves to the many who were, while those who were promoted stood out less, and were thus less satisfied, for the same reason.[34]

These conclusions are borne out by casual observation. The (true) story is told of a prestigious philosophy department with nine untenured faculty members (those were the glory days). In a meeting the chair announces that the administration has given permission to tenure one of them, but only one. As they file out of the room, one young professor is heard to say "Could've been worse. He could

---

[31] Societies also differ, of course, in the goods that serve as markers of status. The Veblenesque critique of consumption can mask two different (although not mutually exclusive) complaints: that people care about status and superiority; and that these concerns manifest themselves crudely in the display of material things rather than, say, in intellectual, aesthetic, or spiritual values. Some would defend materialism on the grounds that it is less elitist and more egalitarian: everyone, after all, can enjoy material things, even if not all are equipped to appreciate what Mill calls the higher pleasures.

[32] "I don't say I'm no better than anybody else/But I'll be damned if I ain't jist as good!" ("Farmer and the Cowman," from *Oklahoma* [Rodgers and Hammerstein 1943]).

[33] Stouffer *et al.* 1949. The authors coined the now-common term "relative deprivation."

[34] Runciman 1966, 18.

have said three of us will get tenure." A person's position can seem tolerable and even acceptable as long as most other members of her reference group are in the same boat. The same line of reasoning suggests that even the desire for superiority can often be satisfied relatively – by being better than others in one's reference group. The emphasis on relative endowment contrasts with the view that human beings simply want more and more, and it implies that insofar as well-being is relative, consumption can be constrained or reduced without loss.

Still, insofar as people want superiority rather than equality we face the possibility of prisoner's-dilemma-like arms races. For that reason – as well as the intrinsic interest of the question – it is worth exploring further the distinction between the desire for equality and the desire for superiority. Is it stable? Is it clear?

Status and other goods

To think that by having or owning or showing certain goods a person can demonstrate his status is to acknowledge that such things constitute the outward signs of some nonvisible condition.[35] The economist Robert Frank calls this crucial function of consumption "ability signaling." As Frank argues, many important decisions affecting us "depend on how strangers see our talents, abilities, and other characteristics."[36] But these abilities are often unobservable, and assessing them can be difficult. To economize on the evaluation process, people take consumption goods as signals of ability.

Which goods signal which abilities varies greatly for different purposes. No one would conclude that a professor is unsuccessful because he drives an old car, but

[35] One might think instead that the possession of goods is itself tantamount to status or superiority. But I believe that the relationship is commonly taken to be an evidentiary one: possessions are thought to be a *sign* of worth. Compare the Protestant idea that emerged during the rise of capitalism that economic enterprise and wealth (although not material display) were the signs of salvation (see Weber 1958; Tawney 1980).

[36] Frank 1985, 148–9; see also Hirsch 1976.

only in a very small town where people know one another well, might it not be a mistake for an aspiring young attorney to drive such a car in the presence of his potential clients. Good lawyers generally earn a lot of money, and people with a lot of money generally drive fashionable new cars. The potential client who doesn't know better will assume that a lawyer with a battered car is not much sought after.[37]

The purely informational aspect of ability signaling performs a useful function. Reading surfaces is a shortcut, and especially in mass societies where we are usually strangers to each other, we need shortcuts. Things are not so simple, of course. I may want to fool people into thinking I have abilities I lack. I may intend the goods to communicate my interests or tastes to other like-minded people, with no status-seeking intended. Or I may just like the signifiers for their own sake (Jaguars are so beautiful!), without meaning to imply I possess what they supposedly signify.

In any case, when consumption serves to signal abilities, the distinction between consuming to show you are as good as others and consuming to show you are better, and between either of these and other purposes of having things, begins to blur. Education provides examples of these complexities – and also shows that the consumption of nonmaterial goods resembles that of material goods in important respects. What is it we hope to attain for ourselves or our children from advanced degrees, prestigious colleges, private schools, or enriched educational programs? There are three possibilities. First, we might want our child to acquire the intellectual resources to appreciate the finer things in life. The aim in this case is a nonrelative good. To attain it, having a certain kind of education is useful. In theory everyone could have that kind of education. And there is plenty of Shakespeare to go around: one person's gain involves a loss to no one else.

---

[37] Frank 1985, 148–9. Frank suggests that professors can get away with driving old cars because "earnings and the abilities that count most among research professors are not very strongly correlated" (ibid.). But it may also be because academics are thought, rightly or wrongly, to have eccentric tastes or to be less concerned with material things than other people.

Perhaps, though – instead or in addition – the good we seek through education is a better job. Better jobs are scarce, and those with more and better education have an advantage in attaining them. But better jobs can be scarce in two different ways. A job can be better because it is more interesting or rewarding (however defined) – challenging a person intellectually, for example. A better job in this sense is a nonrelative good. It is a good that happens to be scarce, however, because of certain unfortunate accidents of the world we inhabit – there's a certain amount of drudgery that must be done – and so one person's having the good excludes others from having it. There is no necessity that a person who wants a better job in this sense wants status – certainly not superiority, not necessarily even equality; status may not enter as a consideration at all. Nevertheless, if such jobs are scarce you will want to be better than others so that you rather than they get the job.

A job can be better in a different sense: it can occupy a higher position in the social hierarchy. If you want a better job in this sense, the good you seek is positional, and thus inherently scarce. Only in this case do you seek superiority, although even here there is a range of possibilities. You seek to improve your position in the hierarchy compared to some, but how high you want to rise is left open. Still, what you want in this case is to occupy a better position relative to some others than you did before. And that means that someone else must occupy a worse position.

Educational goods illustrate particularly well the instability of the distinction between the desire for equality and the desire for superiority.[38] Consider "gifted" programs in the public schools. Some parents might believe that the educational needs of their own and other children are best served by an environment that deemphasizes tracking and does not label and segregate academically talented students in special programs. But given the existence of such programs, it is rational for parents to want their children to be selected for them. For once the system is in place, if children are not labeled as

---

[38] For further discussion of these issues with respect to education see Fullinwider and Lichtenberg 2004, chs. 2–3; Lichtenberg and Luban 1997, 17.

gifted, they are thereby labeled as not gifted. Similar reasoning applies to many other phenomena. A person might prefer to live in an unfashionable neighborhood on aesthetic or sentimental grounds, but not a neighborhood so unfashionable that property values are declining. In such situations, those who fail to practice what they preach have at least a partial defense against the charge of hypocrisy. They would choose arrangement A as long as others choose it too. But, unwilling to be put at a disadvantage, they choose differently. This is just a way of expressing the central practical point of this chapter: there are many things people may be willing (or even happy) to do as long as others do them too. In the absence of collective action, competition reigns.

In such cases, the decision not to acquire more of the good in question is not simply a decision not to improve one's well-being; it is in effect a decision to lower it. (This is a primary reason why it can be difficult to distinguish the networking and infrastructure effects I discussed earlier from status questions.) When high school diplomas are a dime a dozen, employers will require college degrees; even if the extra education is not necessary for the job, it serves as a sorting device. When college degrees are a dime a dozen, employers will require advanced degrees, even though the extra education is not necessary. As Hirsch puts it, when everyone stands on tiptoe, no one sees any better.[39] But if you don't stand on tiptoe, you won't see at all. If you want to see better, you will have to get stilts. But when everyone gets stilts . . .

Some more reasons to do what others do

How much space do the relational aspects of consumption occupy in the totality of reasons for consuming? To what extent is well-being dependent on what others around you have? I doubt these questions can be answered definitively. But, as we have seen, there are many reasons to think well-being is largely relative and much empirical

---

[39] Hirsch 1976, 5.

evidence for that conclusion. There can be no question that it plays a central role.

To the extent that people's desires and reasons for wanting and having things depend on what others around them have, collective reductions in consumption will be less painful to individuals than reductions individuals take alone, even holding the absolute quantity of decrease constant. The reason is not simply that misery loves company – that it is easier for people to make personal sacrifices if they know others are doing the same. It is also that, to the extent that reasons for consumption are relative, having less does not constitute as much of a sacrifice if others also have less, for a variety of reasons we have seen – networking and infrastructure effects; adaptation and habituation; salience and availability; status, signaling, and self-respect. Furthermore, knowing that others are sacrificing to achieve the same goals, like poverty reduction, provides greater assurance that the goal will be reached and thus that the sacrifice will be efficacious.

There are further reasons why we look to others when deciding what to do or give. These reasons may not fall strictly under the rubric of what I have been calling the relativity of well-being, but they are extremely important if our aim is to increase the prevalence of behavior aimed at benefiting others. In the remainder of this chapter I discuss some social scientific findings on these matters.

Noah Goldstein, Robert Cialdini, and Vladas Griskevicius studied the efficacy of conservation efforts in a hotel.[40] Guests found one of two different signs in their rooms, each attempting to persuade guests to reuse their towels. One sign had the headline: "Help Save the Environment" with the following text: "You can show your respect for nature and help save the environment during your stay." The other sign had the headline "Join Your Fellow Citizens in Helping to Save the Environment" followed by the sentence: "Almost 75% of guests who are asked to participate in our new resource savings program do help by using their towels more than once . . ."

[40] Goldstein, Cialdini, and Griskevicius 2008.

Participation rates for those receiving the second message were 44.1 percent, compared to 35.1 percent for the other sign.[41] In other words, the belief that others were recycling their towels was more effective in producing participation than the appeal to environmental values. And the subjects were motivated to recycle even though the others who had supposedly conserved were unknown to them. Perhaps even more important, subjects had no reason to believe that anyone (except perhaps the chambermaid) would know whether they had cooperated or not.

In a second experiment, guests were presented with one of five signs designed to persuade them to recycle towels. The first said "Help Save the Environment: You can show your respect for nature and help save the environment by reusing your towels during your stay." One of the other signs began with "Join Your Fellow Guests in Helping the Save the Environment" and went on to say that 75 percent of hotel guests had recycled their towels. Another sign used the word "citizens" instead of "guests"; another broke down those who had participated by gender. But the most effective of the signs asserted that 75 percent of guests who had stayed in the same room had recycled their towels. Although all of the "descriptive norm" messages – asserting what other guests had in fact done – were more effective than the message just urging the guest to save the environment (44.5 percent versus 37.2 percent), the one that referred to other guests in the same room elicited a 49.3 percent compliance rate as against 42.8 percent for the other three descriptive norm messages combined. The study confirms that "individuals are ... more likely to be influenced by descriptive norms when the setting in which those norms are formed is comparable to the setting those individuals are currently occupying" – an interesting finding we might have reason to attend to.[42]

In the 1960s Bibb Latané and John Darley carried out a series of experiments on helping behavior, all tending to show the effects of

---

[41] The authors argue also that the results underestimate the true rate of participation, for reasons they explain (Goldstein, Cialdini, and Griskevicius 2008, 475).

[42] Goldstein, Cialdini, and Griskevicius 2008, 479.

others on people's willingness to help.[43] In one experiment, male Columbia University undergraduates were recruited to participate in what they thought was a market research survey. When a subject arrived he met a "market research representative," who brought him to the testing room and set him up with some questionnaires to fill out. The room was separated from another office by a collapsible curtain. The young woman left the room, saying she would go next door to do a few things and would return in ten or fifteen minutes. While subjects worked on the questionnaire, they heard the woman moving around next door; those who were listening carefully heard her climb up on a chair to retrieve something from a high shelf. After a few minutes, subjects "heard a loud crash and a woman's scream as the chair fell over ... She moaned and cried for about a minute longer, getting gradually more subdued and controlled ..."[44] The sounds were prerecorded, but only 6 percent of subjects expressed any suspicion later that they were not live and real.

Some subjects were alone in the waiting room when they heard the noise next door; others were in the presence of a confederate of the experimenter or of another subject. Among those who were by themselves, 70 percent offered the victim help; when a passive confederate was present, only 7 percent intervened. Even in pairs of two naïve subjects, another person's presence strongly inhibited people from helping – a result confirmed by other experiments as well.[45]

At least three explanations, not mutually exclusive, can be offered for the inhibiting effect on helping behavior of other people. One is

---

[43] Latané and Darley 1970. The experiments, previously published in psychology journals, include Latané and Darley 1968; Darley and Latané 1968; Latané and Rodin 1969.

[44] Latané and Darley 1970, 58.

[45] Latané and Darley 1970, 60–1. Altogether there were four experimental groups, run as two pairs. In the first pair, subjects were alone in the room during the emergency, or together with a confederate of the experimenter who remained passive throughout. In the second pair, two naïve subjects were in the room; in half they were strangers and in the other half friends who had been recruited together. See also the smoke experiment (ibid., ch. 6), where subjects were much less likely to report smoke emitting from a vent in the wall when other people were present.

diffusion of responsibility: in a group, each person may expect or hope that others will intervene; that belief relieves the burden on any given individual to act. The second explanation is conceptual rather than moral. We interpret situations partly in light of others' interpretations. When others in our presence act as if all is well, we are inclined to believe that all is well. Although some who depart from the standard interpretations of events turn out to be lauded as heroes and sages, at least as often we deem them crazy or strange. The third reason concerns embarrassment and self-image. Even if we feel confident that something is amiss, if everyone else is acting as if nothing is wrong, we may hesitate to act because of fears of looking foolish.[46]

For the most part, explaining why we are more likely to *act* when others act can be understood as analogous to why we are more likely *not* to act when others do not. Begin with the third reason: obviously, we will not be embarrassed or self-conscious to act as others are acting. Now the second: since we are generally influenced by others' interpretations of events, when others see the situation as one that makes helping appropriate, we are likely to agree.

The first reason – diffusion of responsibility – requires some revision in the case of action rather than inaction. With inaction, the hypothesis is that we feel less responsibility in the presence of others who could act. But why do we? Is it because we think others also have the *responsibility* to act, or because we think they are more *likely* to act? Each belief may play a part. Similarly, two responsibility-related reasons could explain why others' action might impel us to act. One is a Kantian thought of universalizability: "They're doing their part; I'm no different, so I should help too." The second involves the imagining of the joint effects of many people's action, which might spur us on in a way that thinking only of my own little contribution might not: "Look, if we all pitch in we can really solve this problem and do more than put drops in the bucket."[47]

---

[46] These factors are discussed at various places in the articles and book by Latané and Darley and in Ross and Nisbett 2011.

[47] I have discussed this point in Lichtenberg 2004, 92–4.

These explanations of the ways people are influenced by others'
behavior are buttressed by a line of research among psychologists and
economists on "cascades" – i.e., bandwagon or snowball effects.
"Informational cascades" occur when people "start attaching credi-
bility to a proposition P ... merely because other people seem to
accept P."[48] Informational cascades correspond to the idea that we
look to others to interpret events. If no one is helping that man lying
on the sidewalk, then perhaps, appearances to the contrary notwithstanding, he doesn't need help after all. "Reputational cascades"
occur when people conform not because they are committed to a
belief or an action but in order to look good among their peers. In
bystander situations, the point may be to avoid looking foolish rather
than to gain positive approval. But the desire to be thought upright or
generous – or in any case at least as good as the next guy – no doubt
plays a part in motivating people to give more, especially if facts
about giving are publicly known. Publishing the names of benefac-
tors in alumni magazines and symphony programs capitalizes on such
desires, and we can imagine creative additions: lists of the Top 100
Pro Bono Law Firms or the Most Altruistic Companies.

Experiments conducted by Elizabeth Hoffman and her colleagues
confirm the significance people attach to their reputations.[49] In these
"dictator game" experiments, a subject is asked to divide $10 between
himself and an anonymous counterpart in another room. The subject
can divide the money however he chooses and the counterpart must
accept the decision. The experiments vary in how much anonymity
and social isolation they provide the subject – that is, whether or to
what extent others will know what he decides. Not surprisingly, when
no one, including the experimenter, knows how the subject has divided
the money, he is likely to give less to the counterpart than if his
decision is known. In general, the less anonymity and social isolation
provided the subject, the more she is likely to give the other person.

---

[48] Kuran and Sunstein 1998, 721.
[49] Hoffman, McCabe, and Smith 1996, 653–60. For further discussion, see the
examination of the respect of one's peers as a motive for acting in the section on
"Encouraging collective action" in Chapter 10.

Informational and reputational cascades together are part of what Timur Kuran and Cass Sunstein call "availability cascades," in which the availability or prominence of a kind of behavior or a belief triggers like responses among individuals.[50] As more people act in a certain way or show they believe a certain proposition, the behavior or belief is more "available" and its effects on others more powerful. These are further reasons for thinking we often shape our beliefs and behavior around our perceptions of the perceptions and behavior of others.

---

[50] For a discussion (directed to a different subject – risk perception and regulation) and further references see Kuran and Sunstein 1998.

CHAPTER 7

Whose poor?/who's poor?: deprivation within and across borders

The arguments of the last chapter show that collective action by comfortable people in affluent societies could greatly diminish the demands benefiting the poor would make on them as individuals, and not simply because individuals might then be responsible only for their fractional contribution of the total amount redistributed. To the extent that people do things because others around them do – that is, to a great extent, as I have been arguing – having less constitutes a much smaller sacrifice if others also have less, for a variety of reasons we have seen. Thus, if people act together, we do not have to expect individuals to be saints or heroes to make huge inroads into alleviating poverty. And so we are forced neither to acknowledge onerous individual duties nor to minimize our moral responsibilities.

But these arguments about the significance of relative deprivation give rise to several puzzles. First, if well-being is so dependent on what others around you have, and assuming an equal distribution of goods is impossible, then the poor will always be with us. No matter what we do, there will be people at the bottom of the ladder, so what's the point of attempting to eradicate poverty? Second, why should we benefit the global poor rather than the poor of our own (affluent) societies – who are, after all, "around us" in a way the faraway poor are not? On the other hand – third – even the poorest people in developed societies are rich by global standards. Does that mean they are not in fact really poor?

Absolute and relative

Part of the answer to these questions is easy, and part is complicated. Let's begin with the easy part. No sensible person would argue that well-being is entirely relative. The need for food, clean water, and other basic conditions is partly given by our circumstances as physical beings, and the absence of these conditions prevents people from having a decent life. Everyone needs a minimum caloric intake, clean water and sanitation, shelter, and protection against infectious disease; the value of these goods does not depend on what others have.

The world's poorest people lack these essential requirements. The World Bank estimates that about 1.29 billion people – about a quarter of the people living in developing countries – live below the international poverty line of $1.25 a day.[1] They "consume on average slightly less than 1400 calories a day," about half what the Indian government recommends for a man engaging in moderate activity or a woman in heavy activity.[2] One in six children in the developing world is underweight.[3] In parts of sub-Saharan Africa such as Sierra Leone, life expectancy is 45 years or less; the main cause is the death of children, about 30 percent of whom die before the age of five, of preventable causes like malaria, diarrhea, and respiratory infections.[4] A higher standard of living – more and better food, shelter, sanitation, and other health interventions – undoubtedly improves people's well-being when they are below a certain minimum.

It's easy to get confused here. As I argued in the last chapter, it's not really a person's well-being that is relative – we can think of well-being in absolute terms. But a person's well-being is partly determined by what others have and do; the worth of certain goods, like money and what it buys, varies accordingly. Conceiving of well-

---

[1] World Bank 2012b. The poverty line was raised in 2005 from $1 to $1.25 a day. It "is based on 89 national poverty lines taken from poverty assessments by the World Bank between 1990 and 2005. National poverty lines are typically set with some version of the 'cost of basic needs' method. First, a food poverty line is established by pricing a food bundle that provides a minimum calorie intake. To this is added an allowance for nonfood spending, typically obtained from data on the nonfood spending of people near the food poverty line" (World Bank 2008). The term "developing countries" masks great differences among countries and the poorest people within them; the majority of the poorest people are in sub-Saharan Africa and South Asia.

[2] Banerjee and Duflo 2007, 149. [3] World Health Organization 2012.

[4] Marmot 2004, 64.

being in terms of capabilities – what people can be and do – Amartya
Sen puts the point this way: "relative deprivation in terms of incomes
can yield absolute deprivation in terms of capabilities."[5] So it can be
important to know people's relative standing in order to judge their
absolute well-being. Inhabitants of one society with an absolutely
larger bundle of goods can have lower well-being than others in a
different society with a smaller bundle. For example, African
Americans are materially rich by global standards, but their life
expectancy (71.4) is far lower than that of people in much poorer
countries such as Costa Rica (77.9) and Cuba (76.5).[6] Clearly,
possession of income or material goods does not correlate perfectly
with well-being.

Nevertheless, there is a strong presumption that those lacking the
most basic necessities should be at the top of the list when it comes to
remedying poverty. We will return to reassess this claim at the end of
the chapter, after exploring some of the complexities raised by the
concept of relative deprivation. But consider also that in addition to
the 1.29 billion people below the $1.25 a day poverty line, another
billion or more live below a second poverty line of $2 a day. Is their
situation comparable with that of poor people in affluent countries? In
2011, 46.2 million people in the United States – 15 percent of
Americans – lived below the poverty line (about $23,000 for a family
of four).[7] Is there a useful way to decide which group is in greater
need of assistance? How should a comfortable person in a rich
country who wants to allocate resources to poor people, based solely
on their need, choose whom to benefit? In what follows I try to make
some inroads into answering these questions.

Comparisons

Comparing the well-being of poor people in affluent societies with
poor people in developing countries is difficult, and anyone who

[5] Sen 1999, 89.   [6] Marmot 2004, 66. See also Sen 1999, 21–4, 96–7.
[7] United States Census Bureau 2012a. See Gapminder 2005, pt. 2 on regional development trends, showing that there are no extremely poor people in OECD countries.

pretends it can be done with scientific rigor is probably a fool or a fraud. Consider an analogous problem, comparisons not across countries but across time periods within a single country. Would you rather be a rich Briton in 1900 or a poor one in 2000? In 1900, the mortality rate for infants under twelve months among the "servant-keeping class" in York, England was almost 10 percent. Admittedly, this was far better than the rate of 25 percent for the poorest people in York.[8] But infant mortality among the poor in England today is less than 1 percent – a tenth the rate among the rich a hundred years ago.[9] So who would you rather be? Of course, to answer this question you would want to know more about other differences in well-being between rich and poor, then and now. You would have to factor in the superb inventions of the twentieth century like anesthesia and indoor plumbing, which are generally available to the poor in contemporary developed societies. Nevertheless, although losing a child is one of the worst things that can happen to a person, it would not be surprising if many people would prefer to be rich in 1900 than poor in 2000.

When contemporary people think of the suffering that earlier generations of parents routinely endured as a result of high child mortality – or that many poor people in developing countries still endure today – they may imagine that adaptation and expectations make a difference: that in societies where parents habitually lose several children in infancy or childhood, they are more prepared for such tragedies and adjust to them better than do people in societies where this is a rare occurrence. It's a dangerous thought: Oh yes, the deaths of their children don't hurt them as much; they're used to it. Yet insofar as well-being is determined partly by what is normal in your environment and by what others around you have and do, adaptation and expectations seem inevitably to play a role.[10]

Just as it is difficult to make comparisons across history, comparing poor people in developing countries with those in developed countries is not easy. Consider the arresting fact that the poorest 5 percent

[8] Rowntree 1902, 206.   [9] Marmot 2004, 63–4.
[10] See Chapter 6 for further discussion of habituation.

of Americans are "at the 68th percentile of the world income distribution."[11] Of course, one cannot straightforwardly draw conclusions from statistical data. Income levels tell only part of the story, and even more sophisticated understandings of wealth and poverty, such as the United Nations Development Programme's Human Development Index (HDI), which takes into account health and education, don't tell us everything we need to know.[12] In addition to intrinsic difficulties with the comparisons, which I shall discuss shortly, the data are aggregate data about countries as a whole, which do not tell us about how wealth and poverty are distributed among individuals. And those studies that focus on poverty may not distinguish clearly between the situations of the extremely poor (under $1.25 a day) and the poor (under $2 a day).

The limitations of our statistical knowledge might lead us, in trying to compare the situation of poor strangers with that of poor compatriots, to construct models or paradigms – an imaginary or real poor Indian and an imaginary or real poor American, say. Such ideal comparisons would inevitably be artificial and even question-begging; after all, deciding which individuals are the relevant ones to compare is part of what we need to know. Constructing such ideal types also involves risky stereotyping.

Do we really need to compare? Whom are we trying to convince, and of what? Do those who focus on global poverty doubt that poor Americans are poor? Perhaps not. But they may argue that even the poorest Americans are not as badly off as poor sub-Saharan Africans, for example, and thus should have lower priority for assistance. Do those concerned about poverty in the United States doubt that the poor in sub-Saharan Africa are really poor? Almost certainly not. But they may think people have special duties to compatriots, even if they are better off than noncompatriots, or they may think that the

[11] Milanovic 2011, 116.
[12] United Nations Development Programme 2010. The authors of the report are fully cognizant of the limitations of the HDI. See the section on "Some abstract illustrations" below for further discussion.

importance of relative well-being makes poor Americans poorer than they look – perhaps comparable to the poor in poor countries.

So there is reason to attempt some comparisons, even though they will inevitably be rough and not fully decisive. In what follows I examine several issues. First, I explain why it is reasonable to consider the poor in developed countries poor despite the fact that they possess many modern amenities. Since the poor in developed countries seem to be absolutely well-off compared to the poor in developing countries, their problems must derive partly from inequalities in their societies; we need to understand the significance of those inequalities. I also examine the moral argument that people have special duties to their compatriots, thus justifying giving poor compatriots priority over poor strangers. The philosophical debate has centered almost exclusively on this question. But at least as compelling, I believe, is understanding how relative deprivation figures in appropriate judgments about who is poor and why, and thus in comparisons between different groups.

Lives of the poor in rich countries

It is commonplace in popular discourse to speak of poverty and economic inequality in the same breath or even interchangeably. To identify the two can be a way of emphasizing, perhaps sometimes unconsciously, the relativity of well-being. But the identification can be misleading. In theory, poverty and economic inequality are easily distinguished: we can imagine a society of people who are all poor but equal, and also an unequal society in which no one is poor. (Philosophers are adept at constructing such possibilities.) Conservative critics of egalitarianism object that there is nothing wrong with economic inequality per se: it must be shown at the very least that inequality results in deprivation of some vital good. The critics imply that egalitarians want equality for its own sake, demonstrating rigid ideological commitments (communism!) or a fetishistic focus on the magical properties of equality.

It is not hard to see how one might conclude that the least well-off Americans are less in need of benefits than poor people in developing countries, even those who are not the poorest. Almost no one in the United States today lives without a television (except by choice), indoor plumbing, and enough food. The title of a 2011 report from the Heritage Foundation sums up the skeptical view: "Air Conditioning, Cable TV, and an Xbox: What Is Poverty in the United States Today?" More than three quarters of poor households have some form of air conditioning; a majority have a DVD player; more than a third have a computer (38.2 percent, compared to 68 percent for all US households).[13] Almost no one goes hungry.

But this doesn't mean the poor in developed countries are not poor. The reason is pretty obvious: income or material goods alone are not an adequate measure of well-being, and it is well-being we ultimately care about.

Why are material goods and income inadequate measures? One reason is that people can have bad fortune in love or health that seriously undermines their well-being and that money or material things cannot compensate for. Let's leave this factor aside, on the assumption that there is little that can be done about it at the level of public policy or even moral endeavor. More relevant is that some of the most important determinants of well-being are not material, even though they are partly determined by material conditions: safety, security, peace, privacy, stability, freedom, participation in one's community, employment, recognition, respect, and self-respect. Poor people in the United States and other developed countries often find these goods in short supply.

For example, poor people in urban settings often live in noisy, crowded, unsafe environments. The cheapest, most easily available foods are processed and unhealthy; fresh fruits and vegetables may be hard to come by in neighborhood "convenience" stores, and better grocery stores are often far away and inaccessible to people without cars. The problem, as we have all become aware, is not sufficient calories but the content of those calories. Where neighborhoods are

---

[13] Rector and Sheffield 2011. Figures cited in the report come from the US Department of Energy, Residential Energy Consumption Survey 2005. The report, and Fox News's story about it, are brilliantly parodied by Stephen Colbert (2011).

unsafe, children and adults stay indoors; gyms are unaffordable, parks distant, so people get little exercise. Poor people are less healthy than rich people.

Poor people experience high rates of unemployment and under-employment, and the effects of these conditions can be devastating for economic and psychological well-being. These days especially it is not only the poor who find themselves unemployed, of course. The vivid descriptions of suffering caused by unemployment now com-monplace in the mass media may jolt us into recognizing the toll it has always taken on poor people with limited employment oppor-tunities. "Poverty is a domineering context" that can deplete "mental resources, such as attention, planning, problem solving, and self-control."[14] Evening shift work and the stress associated with poverty and unemployment have negative effects on sleep and parenting behavior. Why do poor people buy DVD players instead of more useful things? As it happens, DVD players are pretty cheap, and their cost-to-gratification ratio may be high. The poorest people in poor countries also spend some of their very limited resources on festivals, alcohol, and tobacco. The desire to spend on entertainment "appears to be a strongly felt need."[15]

Yet in describing how and why poor people often lack these crucial contributors to well-being, it is difficult to avoid talking in comparative terms. Take health, which we can assume is one of the central factors in well-being. Poor people today live longer than rich people a century ago, so in what sense, it may be asked, is their health bad? It's bad compared to richer people in their society. Health and longevity are directly correlated with socioeconomic status at every level.[16] In the United States, health disadvantages are "particularly

---

[14] Mullainathan and Shafir 2013, 291–2. See also Tierney 2011, about the effects of "decision fatigue" on poor people: "Because their financial situation forces them to make so many trade-offs, [poor people] have less willpower to devote to school, work and other activities that might get them into the middle class."

[15] Banerjee and Duflo 2007, 5, 21.

[16] Deaton 2003a; Marmot 2004; Wilkinson 1996. This is the main thesis of both Marmot's and Wilkinson's books.

pronounced at the lower end of the income hierarchy."[17] Poor
African Americans in Washington, DC live on average twenty
years less than rich white people in Montgomery County,
Maryland, a nearby suburb.[18] Life expectancy among poor African
Americans, then, is not very different from life expectancy in many
poor countries. Since 1977, life expectancy among male workers who
retire at 65 has risen "6 years in the top half of the income distribution
but only 1.3 years in the bottom half"; the differences between
higher- and lower-income people have widened radically since the
mid-twentieth century.[19]

Poor people in developed countries rarely die of malaria or diarrhea.
But they have much higher rates of obesity, heart disease, diabetes,
asthma, HIV/AIDS, and almost every other illness than more affluent
people in their society.[20] Twice as many poor people report experiencing depression as do people who are not poor (30.9 percent versus 15.8
percent).[21] The diseases poor people get result partly from differences
in environmental factors and behavior, as we have seen: stress, danger,
higher rates of smoking, and the relative scarcity of nutritious food and
possibilities for exercise. But over and above these factors, health is
correlated with inequality per se: being of inferior social status is
associated with greater susceptibility to disease.[22]

But to the extent that this is so – that poorer people have worse
health than richer people – we seem to be left with the question with

---

[17] McDonough et al. 1997, 1480.   [18] Marmot 2004, 2, citing Murray et al. 1998.
[19] Krugman 2010, citing Waldron 2007. More specifically, "male Social Security-
covered workers born in 1941 who had average relative earnings in the top half of
the earnings distribution and who lived to age 60 would be expected to live 5.8
more years than their counterparts in the bottom half. In contrast, among male
Social Security-covered workers born in 1912 who survived to age 60, those in the
top half of the earnings distribution would be expected to live only 1.2 years more
than those in the bottom half" (Waldron 2007, 1).
[20] See, e.g., Levine 2011, 267 ("Counties with poverty rates of >35% have obesity
rates 145% greater than wealthy counties"); Jones et al. 2009 (including sources on
the relationship between low socioeconomic status and cardiovascular morbidity
and mortality); Marmot 2004, passim; Wilkinson 1996, passim.
[21] Brown 2012.
[22] Marmot 2004; Wilkinson 1996. Angus Deaton (2003b) argues that *income* inequality is not a health risk, but does not deny that other forms of inequality may be.

which we began: is being poor in a rich country all that bad, or is it only bad compared to being richer in the same country?

Some abstract illustrations

We can better understand the puzzles about the significance of relative deprivation abstractly, by imagining two societies, each containing two unequal groups. Suppose a person in the better-off group in a developed country, Erewhon I, has disposable income and is trying to decide whether she should help her own poor compatriots or the poor people in a developing country, Erewhon II (see Table 1). Her only concern is to help the worse-off group – the one in greater need. Whom should she help?

The answer is pretty obvious: it is impossible to know on the basis of the information given which group – the poor in Erewhon I or the poor in Erewhon II – is in greater need, because for reasons we have seen income and other material goods are not a sufficient indicator of people's well-being, and it is well-being we are interested in. So suppose we posit that, instead of income, the numbers in question stand for well-being, whether understood in terms of subjective happiness, human flourishing, human development, capabilities, or some other quality (see Table 2).

Table 1. *Income*

	Erewhon I	Erewhon II
Rich	600 farthings	400 farthings
Poor	300 farthings	200 farthings

Table 2. *Well-being*

	Erewhon I	Erewhon II
Rich	600 hedons	600 hedons
Poor	300 hedons	200 hedons

If we represent matters this way, it seems clear that – thinking simply in terms of greater need, and leaving aside any special duties to compatriots – the rich in Erewhon I should benefit the poor of Erewhon II, who are clearly worse off than the poor of Erewhon I. But that clarity comes at the cost of usefulness, for we cannot gauge well-being directly, nor can hedons be transferred. And one important question is how well-being is affected by relative deprivation.

Of course, we do have better measures of well-being than the farthings represented in Table 1. Income alone (even taken as a proxy for living standards) is an inadequate measure, so suppose we add two other important indicators that follow the United Nations Development Programme's HDI: health, as measured by life expectancy at birth, and educational attainment.[23] Clearly health and education are important contributors to an adequate conception of well-being (see Table 3).

Table 3. *HDI*

	Erewhon I	Erewhon II
Rich	600 HDI	400 HDI
Poor	300 HDI	200 HDI

Here we have better evidence than in Table 1 that the poor in Erewhon II are absolutely worse off than the poor in Erewhon I.

Still, these indicators make no room for the significance, if any, of relative deprivation within a society for people's well-being. To see how relative deprivation can make a difference, consider each of the HDI's indicators mentioned in the previous table: education and life expectancy (see Tables 4 and 5).[24]

It is reasonable to assume that gains in life expectancy bring absolute gains in well-being, irrespective of the longevity of others in one's

[23] United Nations Development Programme 2010, 12–13. Since the last report the indicators have been modified somewhat, but not in any way that affects the point here.

[24] Here as elsewhere in these tables the numbers given are imaginary and somewhat arbitrary. I assume it makes no difference for my purposes here, as long as the poor in each society have less than the rich in that society and the poor in Erewhon II have a lower index than the poor in Erewhon I.

Table 4. *Life expectancy*

	Erewhon I	Erewhon II
Rich	75 years	65 years
Poor	65 years	55 years

Table 5. *Years of education*

	Erewhon I	Erewhon II
Rich	15 years	12 years
Poor	10 years	6 years

society. By contrast, the benefits of increased education cannot be wholly determined without reference to the education of others. As we saw in the last chapter, some of education's benefits are "absolute" – developing one's skills and understanding, and learning to better appreciate some of the finer things in life, like art, philosophy, and literature – but some are relative or positional. To compete for higher-paying, more rewarding jobs, for instance, a person may need more education than her competitors, irrespective of its intrinsic benefits. An educational arms race can ensue, with more advanced degrees required for jobs that do not really need them and that in the past would have gone to people with lesser educational attainments. That extra education may be expensive and involves opportunity costs. The main point here is that in such cases part of the increase in educational attainment represented in Table 5 (and in the HDI) might not really represent an increase in well-being. To the extent that a person needs more education because others have more, the poor in Erewhon I, represented in Table 5, will not be better off than the poor in Erewhon II.

Inequality and well-being

So relative deprivation affects well-being to the extent that the value of a particular good, like education, depends on how much of it others have. In such cases absolute gains of the good are not necessarily absolute gains. A central question, then, is how extensive the reach of relative deprivation is – to what extent having less than others of measurable things produces absolute losses in well-being. If socioeconomic inequalities within a society – or something highly correlated with inequalities – have such an effect, that would explain why, even controlling for environmental and behavioral factors, socioeconomic status is correlated with health at every level up and down the spectrum.[25] And it would also explain why overall increases in a society's wealth do not bring increases in happiness (once a certain level of affluence has been reached), while at the same time within a society richer people are happier than poorer people.[26]

How, more specifically, would we account for the correlation of health and happiness with socioeconomic status? A plausible answer is that people may be deprived of certain essential nonmaterial goods when they are poorer than – unequal to – others in their society, even if they have higher income, more education, and better health than people in other societies.

Among the most important goods of this kind are recognition and self-respect. As we saw in the last chapter, thinkers from Adam Smith to Karl Marx to John Rawls have understood these goods as essential to well-being. In Smith's day, "a creditable day-labourer would be ashamed to appear in public without a linen shirt." Not having one would "denote that disgraceful degree of poverty, which, it is presumed, no body can well fall into without extreme bad conduct."[27] Poor people in industrialized countries may be similarly deprived of self-respect and recognition in ways that significantly reduce their well-being, making it comparable to that of some poor

---

[25] Marmot 2004.

[26] Easterlin 1974; Easterlin 1995; Frank 1997; Layard 2003; Luttmer 2005. See also Frank 1999, 111 for references.

[27] Smith 1994, bk. v, ch. 2. A related phenomenon is "loss of face." Citing research by Martin Daly and Margo Wilson, Richard Wilkinson argues that loss of face – that is, "loss of pride, humiliation or loss of prestige in the eyes of others" – is the most common reason people engage in violent behavior (1996, 168). Daly, Wilson, and Vasdev 2001 contend that in Canada and the United States inequality is a stronger predictor of lethal violence than the average level of material well-being.

people in developing countries. Being functionally illiterate, paying for groceries at the store with food stamps, having your children come to school early for a free breakfast, not being able to afford to go to the dentist, losing your house to foreclosure – such experiences can undermine a person's self-respect and the esteem of others. These conditions are humiliating.[28] In American society, lack of self-respect and the respect of others results in part from the high degree and conspicuous display of materialism prevalent there, as well as the special insult of living insecurely and without protection from illness and other calamities in a culture of wealth and excess. Clearly, as Smith saw, exactly which deprivations undermine self-respect and the esteem of others is partly convention-dependent: it varies according to the customs and standards of particular societies. ("Necessaries" are *"whatever the custom of the country* renders it indecent for creditable people ... to be without."[29]) Moreover, we cannot entirely disentangle loss of self-respect from other, more concrete losses: having crooked and discolored teeth puts one at a disadvantage, in love and work at the very least, in a society where most people's teeth look pretty good; the personal costs of illiteracy go without saying. But over and above such harms, there is an expressive aspect to such deprivations – they *say something* about and to poor people in rich societies – that turns insult into injury.[30]

Of course, something similar might be said of global poverty today: part of what makes it unacceptable is the coexistence in one world, the jarring contrast, of deprivation and excess. I agree, and it's one of the main motivations for this book. But there is a difference between the relationship of a rich person in a developed country to poor people in her own country and her relationship to poor people in other countries. I am not referring to any special duties or associative

---

[28] In *The Decent Society*, Avishai Margalit suggests (following Sidney Morgenbesser, as Margalit explains in the preface) that having a decent society is more urgent than having a just society, and that a decent society is one "which does not humiliate" (1996, ix–x).

[29] Smith 1994, bk. v, ch. 2 (emphasis added).

[30] The subject of expressive harms has received a lot of attention from philosophers in recent years. See, e.g., Anderson and Pildes 2000.

obligations people may have to their compatriots; I shall discuss this question shortly. Here, I mean to highlight something else, which might be called psychological proximity. The psychological proximity of people within a society – the awareness by the poor of the rich and by the rich of the poor – makes questions of recognition, self-respect, honor, humiliation, and loss of face more salient than they are across borders. (So I disagree with philosophers who argue that distance is morally irrelevant to our responsibilities.) The poor may be continually confronted with those who have more – on the street, in stores, and (despite much income-based educational segregation) in schools – just as the better-off are confronted by those who have less.

There are other essential goods the least well-off people in developed societies may be deprived of that render them genuinely poor. One is inclusion. "People are poor if they cannot afford the patterns of activity of the society in which they live."[31] Another is control over their lives, which might also be described in terms of autonomy or freedom or capability – the ability to carry out one's desires and aspirations. A third is power, meaning power to affect social or political institutions. Political power, it seems, is zero-sum: more for some necessarily means less for others, so it is nearly tautological to say that the poor have less power than the rich. Neither inclusion nor control over one's life is inherently zero-sum, but being less well-off commonly correlates with being more isolated and less in control. Lack of control is not simply a matter of insufficient income but also of domination, in the workplace and elsewhere. People in the lowest-status jobs generally have the least ability to make decisions and exert control over what they do.[32] In addition to having work that is often monotonous and unchallenging, they tend to be subjected to a high degree of direct domination by others. In this respect, some poor

---

[31] Stern, Dethier, and Rogers 2005, 6. The authors suggest this explanation as part of an account of poverty in developed countries – one that is in part relative.

[32] Marmot suggests that less control among poorer people and those lower in the social hierarchy partly explains the health gradient (Marmot 2004, ch. 5).

people in developing countries, many of whom are of necessity entrepreneurs, may be more free.[33]

In addition to lack of self-respect and recognition, then, exclusion from normal patterns of activity, lack of control over their lives, and domination by others affect the well-being of the least well-off in developed societies but may not show up in the usual statistical measures.

Magnitudes of inequality

These considerations support the commonsense view that the least well-off people in developed countries, especially those with high degrees of economic inequality, are genuinely poor. An appreciation of the importance of relative deprivation for absolute well-being helps explain why.

Yet conservative critics argue that inequality is an indelible feature of human societies and that the attempt to eradicate it is the death of excellence, innovation, human betterment (even for the worst-off, because the rising tide lifts all boats), and freedom. I shall not attempt a full-scale analysis of these claims here. But an important part of the response is that we must distinguish among magnitudes of inequality. Some inequality may be inevitable or desirable, but extreme inequalities are neither. Yet the distribution of wealth in many developed countries is extremely unequal and becoming more so. In the United States, earnings inequality decreased substantially from 1939 to 1949 and remained stable for around two decades; in the 1970s and especially the 1980s it greatly increased.[34] The top 1 percent of workers in the United States got about 9 percent of total income in 1976; by 2008 their share was 21 percent.[35] In the late 1970s, pay for CEOs was about 30 times the typical worker's pay; today it's around 200 times the typical worker's pay.[36] Wealth inequality is even more skewed than income inequality.[37]

---

[33] Banerjee and Duflo 2007, 20.   [34] Kopczuk, Saez, and Song 2010, 92.
[35] Inequality.org 2012a.
[36] Economic Policy Institute 2012. See this site for other arresting statistics.
[37] Economic Policy Institute 2012.

Yes, absent complete equality some people must be at the bottom
of the hierarchy: if not all the children can be above average, then
unless everyone is equal some must be below average. But that truth
is compatible with smaller differentials between bottom and top than
those becoming increasingly common.

Moreover, decreasing the gap is not just the desire of a left-leaning
minority. In a 2005 survey by Michael Norton and Dan Ariely, more
than 5,500 nationally representative respondents saw three unlabeled
pie charts showing wealth distributions among the five quintiles of
the population.[38] One pie chart was perfectly equal: each quintile had
20 percent of the wealth. The second reflected the distribution of
wealth in the United States (although respondents were not told this
fact), where the top quintile has 84 percent of the wealth and the
bottom two quintiles together have 0.3 percent. The third pie chart,
which was supposed to reflect Sweden's economy (also unbeknownst
to respondents), showed an intermediate state, in which the top
quintile had 36 percent of the wealth. Respondents were asked both
to estimate the degree of wealth inequality in the United States and to
construct ideal distributions. On average respondents greatly under-
estimated US inequality: they thought the richest quintile had 59
percent rather than 84 percent. And on average they expressed a
desire that the richest have 32 percent. The intermediate, "Swedish"
distribution was preferred to the US distribution by 92 percent of
respondents.

So most Americans – presumably more hostile than most national
groups to economic equality – greatly underestimate inequality in the
United States and would prefer a much more egalitarian distribution.
This finding about people's values is important in itself. But the
question remains how far, realistically, inequality can be diminished.

Criticizing Norton and Ariely's study, Mark Gimein notes that the
intermediate chart does not represent the wealth distribution in
Sweden but rather its *income* distribution (as the authors admit, albeit
obscurely). The distribution of wealth in Sweden, although significantly more equal than in the United States (the top quintile has 73

[38] Norton and Ariely 2011, 9–12.

percent), is still highly unequal.[39] Felix Salmon asserts that this will always be the case: "A huge part of the population of just about every country is going to have zero wealth – if you live paycheck to paycheck, for instance, or if you're young and haven't been earning money for long, or if you just spend a lot. That doesn't mean you're poor."[40] And so, both Gimein and Salmon believe, Norton and Ariely's findings are less significant than they appear.

Naturally, in morally judging inequality it's appropriate to leave out spendthrifts, as well as the young who have not been working for long. But simply to assume a class of people who live paycheck to paycheck is a textbook case of begging the question. Is the existence of such a group an inevitable fact of life? Living paycheck to paycheck *does* mean you're poor if you have nothing saved for medical or other emergencies. Since Swedes do not have to worry about healthcare and, as Gimein acknowledges, have "a strong social safety net and pension plans," they don't need savings in the way Americans do.

No society is completely egalitarian, but societies differ significantly in the degree of substantive inequality they permit. And the degree of inequality matters for well-being. The degree of income inequality correlates with the incidence of disease and mortality in a society. Once a certain level of development has been reached, the most egalitarian societies, not the richest, have the best health.[41] The degree of inequality also affects the crime rate: "the impact of inequality on violent crime is large, even after controlling for the effects of poverty, race, and family composition."[42]

The idea that smaller inequalities would damage well-being less than larger inequalities is intuitively plausible. Imagine two workers

---

[39] Gimein 2011.   [40] Salmon 2011.
[41] Wilkinson 1996, 75. Wilkinson's explanation is that the least unequal societies are the most socially cohesive, with a strong community life and a thriving public arena. Social cohesion is no doubt affected by some of the qualities I discussed earlier, such as recognition, self-respect, and inclusion. For the positive correlation between inequality and infant mortality see Inequality.org 2012b. The exception is Singapore, which has the greatest inequality but the lowest infant mortality.
[42] Kelly 2000, 537.

in the same organization. A is a mid-level employee, B is her boss, several steps up the corporate ladder. A recognizes that B has more responsibility than A and that B's job requires greater education and skills than A's. She may well accept that B should have a higher salary than A. But how much higher? Double? Four times higher? Eight? The arguments for economic inequality justify differentials, but not the massive ones that are increasingly common in industrialized societies and that foster humiliation and exclusion.

Nor, in the workplace, is it simply a matter of income. Insofar as control and freedom are essential to well-being, we can enhance people's well-being by fostering more autonomy. In the Whitehall studies, which followed the health of British civil servants over many years, Marmot and his colleagues found that workers "at the same level in the occupational hierarchy with differing amounts of control had markedly different rates of disease."[43]

Even if inequality is inevitable, then, its magnitude can be reduced. And smaller inequalities would make the poor less poor.

Special duties to compatriots?

I have been examining a putatively empirical question: how to compare the well-being of poor people in rich societies and poor people in developing societies, in order to decide who is worse off. By contrast, most philosophical discussions concerned with comparing the local and global poor ask a moral question: do we (people in developed countries, or any country for that matter) have special or "associative" duties to compatriots that we do not have to strangers? If so, it is morally permissible or even required to benefit the poor in our own country rather than, or at least prior to, benefiting poor people elsewhere.

Why think people have special duties to their compatriots? The idea is that we stand in certain relationships with our fellow country-men that give rise to obligations. The paradigm of a special relation-ship is the kind we have with family members. I have special duties to

---

[43] Marmot 2004, 124, citing earlier studies he co-authored.

my parents, my children, and my husband that I do not have to other people. These duties are not necessarily all assimilable to a single source.[44] After all, I entered into a relationship with my husband voluntarily, and likewise I chose to have children, but I did not choose to be born. Duties to my spouse and children can be understood to arise partly from my choices and voluntary actions, but duties to my parents cannot be. Still, even duties to spouse and children cannot be fully understood in contractual terms without begging the question by assuming that whatever our duties are, they arise from implicit agreements. In fact, these special ties probably cannot be fully understood in terms of *duties* at all. As Bernard Williams famously observed, to think you should rescue your wife rather than a stranger from a burning building because you have a *duty* to rescue your wife is to have "one thought too many."[45] Nor is it likely that my duties to my parents can be cashed out simply in terms of gratitude or reciprocity: I cannot determine exactly what I owe them by knowing exactly what they did for me.

Some have attempted to ground special duties in their beneficial consequences. The world works better if people take care of their own children and families rather than spreading their efforts more broadly. But, as with the other explanations just mentioned, the consequentialist account seems to leave a remainder. We don't think people have special duties to their children simply because that's a useful means of promoting the general welfare. All such explanations – contractual, gratitude- or reciprocity-based, and consequentialist – omit something important. To fill the gap, some philosophers argue that these special responsibilities rest on "features internal to a relationship: either the non-instrumental importance of the relationship itself or its non-instrumental importance for the participants in the relationship."[46]

---

[44] In writing this section I have benefited from discussion with Nate Olson and from reading his dissertation (Olson 2012).

[45] Williams 1981, 18. In Chapter 3 I offered other reasons for questioning duty-talk. I ignore those reasons here and employ the term for the sake of clarity.

[46] Olson 2012, 44.

Explaining exactly how these features give rise to special responsibilities becomes even more difficult when we move from the
paradigm of intimate relationships to relationships among members
of religious, ethnic, cultural, or national groups, where the assumption that there is something noninstrumentally important in the
relationships themselves is more strained and the "one thought too
many" objection less plausible. This is not to say the case cannot be
made. I acknowledge that among the four possible grounds – contractual, gratitude- or reciprocity-based, consequentialist, and the
noninstrumental or intrinsic account – there is almost certainly
some truth in the claim that we have special duties to fellow members.
Here I focus on special duties among members of a society or state,
since that has been the main subject of philosophical debate.

Even if we do have special duties to compatriots, however, we may
also have humanitarian or cosmopolitan duties to strangers. How do
we weigh them against each other? Several considerations are relevant. For one thing, presumably we have humanitarian or cosmopolitan duties to our compatriots *in addition* to any special duties we
have, since our compatriots are also human beings. If so, one might
think that the humanitarian or cosmopolitan duties to each group
cancel each other out, and the special duties prevail. But even if
people have special duties to compatriots, it does not follow that such
duties take absolute priority over duties to strangers. It makes more
sense to think that any such special duties have a certain weight but
that other factors, such as the degree of need of strangers, or any
harm we have done to them, also have to be taken into account. We
might conclude that other things being equal, a person's duty to
compatriots is greater than her duty to strangers, while recognizing
that other things are rarely equal.

Thomas Nagel makes the compatriot/stranger distinction in terms
of duties of justice and duties of charity. (I discussed that distinction
in Chapter 3.) He argues that "justice is something we owe through
our shared institutions only to those with whom we stand in a strong
political relation," i.e., a state.[47] Nagel acknowledges minimal

---

[47] Nagel 2005, 121.

humanitarian duties to noncompatriots. But according to Nagel's "associative view" of justice, relationships of justice obtain only among members of a state, because members are "both putative joint authors of the coercively imposed system, and subject to its norms" – both subjects, and "those in whose name ... [the state's] authority is exercised."

Yet Nagel admits that the facts of global poverty and inequality "are so grim that justice may be a side issue."[48] Here we find an odd reversal of the usual priorities: if we have to choose, he implies, charity may sometimes trump justice. Moreover, Nagel acknowledges that even on his conception, "some conditions of justice do not depend on associative obligations."[49] All people everywhere have certain justice-based negative rights – Nagel mentions bodily inviolability, freedom of expression, and freedom of religion – and it is wrong to violate them. The question is how far such negative rights extend. As we saw in Chapter 2, depending on how such a principle is interpreted, it could give rise to far-reaching duties to compensate poor people in developing countries for harms done to them – as Thomas Pogge, Richard Miller, and others have argued the harm principle does – and these would then come under the heading of justice. So just as we may have humanitarian duties to compatriots, we may have justice-based duties, such as duties not to harm, to strangers.

A different slant on these questions emerges if we conceive of the category of "duties to compatriots" not in terms of individual-to-individual relationships – what does person A owe her poor compatriot, person B? – but rather in terms of duties to members on the part of the collective, which for short we may call "the state." Thus, for example, one might argue that "the whole point ... of having a government is for the government to do something more for us than it does for anybody – not because of any special 'relationship' of a touchy-feely kind, but simply because that's what the government is *for*."[50] If we put a label on this argument, we could call it

[48] Nagel 2005, 118. [49] Nagel 2005, 126.
[50] Claudia Mills, personal correspondence on file with the author, 2012.

consequentialist (and thus not touchy-feely): the world works better when identifiable agents and institutions are assigned responsibility to meet people's needs. That is why governments are thought to be the primary duty-bearers of human rights, as we saw in Chapter 3. The problem, of course, is that governments are not always willing or able to do their duty. So yes, a US citizen may legitimately expect disaster aid from her government rather than from Venezuela.[51] But what is a citizen of Sierra Leone to do?

Even if we believe that for one reason or another people have some special responsibilities to ensure the well-being of their compatriots, then, it in no way follows that they have no significant duties to those outside their society. If defenders of special duties to compatriots believe people in rich countries can ignore the global poor, they need to explain why.

Comparing the global and local poor

My purpose in this chapter has been to compare the situations of three (roughly delineated) groups of poor people: the 1.3 billion people in poor countries who live below the World Bank's $1.25 a day poverty line; those in poor countries who are above that poverty line but still live on less than $2 a day, another World Bank benchmark; and people classified as poor in developed countries. Let's call these groups the VPPC (the very poor in poor countries), the PPC (the poor in poor countries), and the PRC (the poor in rich countries). Earlier I stated a presumption that the claims of the VPPC take priority, and I believe it still stands. People below an absolute threshold of adequate nutrition, sanitation, and basic health measures have stronger claims to benefits than members of other poor groups. Even those who believe we have special duties to compatriots might

[51] In 2005 Hugo Chavez, the late President of Venezuela, started sending millions of dollars of aid to the South Bronx through Citgo Petroleum, the American subsidiary owned by the Venezuelan state oil company. One beneficiary noted: "It's a sore point because it took what most people would consider a third world nation to help the U.S. Which is kind of a slap in the face because we're supposed to be one of the superpowers; why can't we help our own?" (Barnard 2007).

agree – thinking, as it appears Nagel does, that the claims of the absolutely poor may override such special duties.

Comparing the claims of the PPC and the PRC is more difficult, for reasons that should by now be clear. In essence, deciding how poor the PRC really are, especially for purposes of comparison with the PPC, depends a great deal on how much weight we put on nonphysical and nonmaterial aspects of well-being. If respect, self-respect, inclusion, autonomy, and power matter a lot, then the PRC are likely to be poorer than the usual indicators suggest. Of course, these nonmaterial factors must be incorporated into well-being assessments of the PPC as well. My hunch is that doing so would not affect their well-being negatively as much as it does the PRC – because, ironically, the greater proportion of poor people in poor countries makes poverty less shameful and isolating there; because, as we saw earlier, the PPC are more likely to be entrepreneurial than the PRC; and perhaps because material goods are less salient in poor countries.

These are only speculations, and in general the comparisons I have attempted in this chapter are rough and "unscientific." (But I have not seen better – or even any – attempts to make such comparisons.) Still, I think they suggest that a person has good reason to allocate resources to benefit the poor in her own (rich) society rather than the PPC.

Just how strong the reasons are will depend partly, of course, on our conception of special moral duties to compatriots. I do not believe these special responsibilities as usually understood play a large role, and moreover I doubt that the "weighing" can lead to any precise conclusions. The factors I have focused on – which, I believe, have been almost completely neglected in the philosophical literature – have to do with relative deprivation: how and to what extent deprivations compared to others contribute to losses in well-being that render people, as we could say, poorer than they might seem.

Some might argue that these factors are themselves a ground for special responsibilities to compatriots. It seems to me more appropriate to view them as criteria for determining poverty rather than responsibility, even though it so happens that the deprivations in question are often relative to others in one's society. In other words, if relative deprivation increases our responsibilities to poor compatriots, it's not so much because we have greater responsibility to them per se, but that they fare worse than it might seem and thus have stronger claims to be benefited. Or perhaps we should split the difference and say we have special responsibilities to those in our society because we are typically more visible, salient, or palpable to each other than we are to those far away.

Two worries, and responses

Let me respond to two objections these conclusions might prompt. First, suppose that Marie, a citizen of a rich country, spends a significant proportion of her resources working to improve the situation of the poor in her own country. Marie donates more than 10 percent of her income to organizations aiding and defending the poor; she engages in political activity supporting unionization efforts and in other ways joins forces with people at the bottom of the economic ladder; after disasters like Hurricanes Katrina and Sandy she uses her vacation time to help build and rebuild houses. But she does nothing for the VPPC. Is it my view that Marie is doing wrong, or that she should be criticized? That might seem to follow from the claim that the VPPC have priority over both the PPC and the PRC. But it flies in the face of what I would expect is the common view: that Marie and her actions are admirable.

To this challenge several responses are appropriate. We might begin by asking whether Marie has ever considered the lives of the VPPC. If not, that demonstrates a certain narrowness of vision that should be criticized. To be so oblivious, these days especially, is a flaw. And one might think that in becoming nonoblivious, Marie would feel compelled to contribute something to benefit the VPPC simply on the grounds that they are human beings who deserve recognition and respect.

Yet perhaps Marie has thought of the VPPC but has concluded that her responsibilities to compatriots are more weighty, or that she can be more effective alleviating poverty in her own society than outside it. Although I have doubted the existence of strong special duties to compatriots, I would not fault a person who really took such duties seriously, rather than simply using them as an excuse to do nothing for the global poor while not helping poor compatriots either. It's also not obvious that it's easier to improve the situation of the PRC than the PPC and VPPC, but it's understandable that someone might think it was, and it might sometimes be true.[52]

In Chapter 9 I argue that, as far as making moral judgments goes, we should distinguish persons and motives on the one hand, and actions and behavior on the other. So one might think that the solution is to say that Marie is a good or admirable person because she is altruistically motivated, even though what she does is wrong. But that seems an inadequate response here. Two other facts are more to the point. One is that Marie does so much more than most people do for the poor, whether in rich or poor countries, that it is difficult to fault her conduct. This judgment is in keeping with my general view (defended especially in Chapter 5) that we cannot judge human behavior without taking into account prevailing norms. The other fact is that, even if Marie is not doing the "rightest" thing she could be doing, she's still doing something that is morally very important. (I also defended this sliding scale view of rightness in Chapter 5.) Think what she might be doing instead with her time and money.

Another concern is that the conclusions of this chapter might seem overwhelming. I have been arguing that, among all the people in the world who can be considered poor, the claims of the bottom 1.3 billion or so should take priority, but that the claims of the somewhat less poor also have a great deal of merit. That could seem almost a joke – sure, let's end poverty for more than a billion people . . . and

---

[52] At the very least, for a given price one can generally help more people in poor countries than in rich countries. To take an example provided by the organization Giving What We Can, suppose your goal is to help blind people. It costs about $50,000 to train one guide dog. For the same cost, "we could completely cure enough people of Trachoma-induced blindness – a disease affecting people in poor countries – to prevent a total of 2,600 years of blindness" (Giving What We Can 2013, Myths About Aid: Myth 7).

then do even more! But this is to fall prey to the individualistic bias that I have been arguing we should avoid. Acting collectively, ending extreme poverty does not demand a great deal of comfortable people. In 2005 economist Jeffrey Sachs, director of Columbia University's Earth Institute and author of *The End of Poverty*, estimated that to end it would require of rich countries a commitment of between $135 and $195 billion between 2005 and 2015 – "significantly less than the 0.7 percent of GNP promised in ODA."[53] Jim Yong Kim, president of the World Bank, recently set 2030 as the target for ending global poverty, and many experts think this is a plausible aspiration.[54] The amounts required of comfortable people and rich countries would make little or no difference to their well-being.

And to the extent that the arguments I have been making are convincing, we could reduce domestic poverty too, by decreasing the magnitude of inequality – probably the prime cause of poverty in rich countries – without rendering the better-off significantly worse off.

[53] Sachs 2005, 299.
[54] Lowrey 2013. It's now expected that by 2015 "the global poverty rate will fall below 15 percent, well below the 23 per cent target" (UN Millennium Campaign 2013). One reason for this optimism, however, is that the bar is set low; many people above this poverty line are genuinely poor. To end poverty for these people as well (the PPCs, in my terminology) would be somewhat more demanding. But not excessively so, I believe, especially when these goals are assumed collectively. For further discussion see Sachs 2005, ch. 15; Singer 2010, 160–8; and Chapter 10.

CHAPTER 8

Hopefully helping: the perils of giving

The previous chapters have focused on the nature and extent of our moral responsibilities to benefit others, and on how to make such responsibilities less demanding. But we must now consider whether the assumption that we *can* solve some of the problems created by global poverty – or, more generally, by the unmet needs of others – is a reasonable one. If it is not *possible* to help people, then on the assumption that Ought Implies Can we have no responsibility to do so.

Why might one doubt that it's possible to aid others? Some of the reasons are more or less inherent in the very notions of giving and receiving; others are tied to the specific conditions and circumstances surrounding programs and policies designed to aid poor people in developing countries, and sometimes also in developed countries. I begin by examining the nature of giving and receiving in very general terms, and then look at aid in the economic, social, and political contexts most relevant to poverty today.

Describing what ought to be done

The seeds of some of the difficulties are contained in the very words we choose to describe what ought to be done when one person is in need and another is in a position to help him. First, the natural implication of words like *help, aid, assistance, charity*, and *beneficence* (the last primarily a philosopher's word) is that the would-be aider has had no part in bringing about, reinforcing, or maintaining the situation that makes aid necessary. The aider is in this sense a bystander to suffering – with the adjective *innocent* lurking just beneath the surface. So one reason some critics conclude there is something wrong with giving is that it contains this implication. They believe instead that poverty results from actions and decisions taken by states, corporations, individuals, and others, and that those who might help – in particular comfortable people in developed countries – are not altogether innocent of responsibility for these conditions. So the critics want to reject these terms.

Two responses are possible. One is to deny that terms like *aid*, *assistance*, and *charity* contain these implications. Haggling about what exactly words do or do not imply or suggest is not a very fruitful activity, and of course straightforward answers to such questions are not always available. Still, I believe that for the most part these words do imply that the would-be aider is a bystander to suffering who has not had a role in producing or maintaining it. The word *benefit* is more neutral, and I sometimes use it to avoid begging any questions about causal role.[1]

The other response is that however much poverty, global or local, results from institutional and systemic factors that people have had a role in producing or maintaining, there are still many cases when one person is in need and another who is unambiguously a bystander might benefit her. Moreover, even if A *has* harmed B and owes B compensation on that ground, there might in addition be other reasons for A to benefit B – just because B is in need and A can help without undue sacrifice to her own interests. These cases have been a central concern of this book: what responsibilities do we have to meet others' serious needs simply because they have such needs and we can do something to remedy them?

But if it is important to address these questions – and to be clear about how they differ from questions of responsibility that rest on harm, exploitation, or prior relationships – we are still left to determine how, if at all, they can be framed in a way not fraught with problematic associations. And there are reasons to think these terms *are* fraught, even aside from the suggestion that the would-be aider is

[1] The term was suggested to me by *On Benefits*, by the Roman Stoic Seneca (1935). What I say about all these words applies to both the noun and verb forms.

a mere bystander or is causally innocent. These reasons, at least some of which are illustrated in the following story, account for some of the pitfalls of giving.

Dissecting a small act of aid

Imagine a student who encounters a fellow traveler in the airport – a well-dressed businessman (as he appears) rushing to catch a plane, who has hurt his back picking up his luggage. She volunteers to carry his suitcase to the gate. Here is a small act of charity of the kind many people perform regularly and without thinking twice. It does not involve heroic self-sacrifice; it does not save a life. But examining conduct of this kind may shed light on some features of acts we would typically describe as charitable, and help show what is essential to them and what is not.

Carrying his suitcase is not something the student owes the man as compensation for harm she has done him. His injury was not her fault. It was, we may suppose, nobody's fault. He has been a victim of misfortune, not injustice. Nor is she entwined in any relationship with him – personal, professional, political, or economic – that might require her to act to protect his welfare or improve his good.

Do the negative associations often pinned on "helping" and "charity" attach to this act? That depends largely, if not entirely, on the psychological states of the parties themselves. Apart from the inherent situational "superiority" of the helper – she has something (the ability to carry a heavy object) that the other lacks, and needs – no chronic inequality between them exists; indeed, as I have described the example, his status dominates hers. She probably expects nothing from him except thanks. If he shows no gratitude, she may be annoyed or angry and might even regret having helped him. What about him? Gratitude, if he feels it, may be tinged with other emotions. As I have told the story, a woman aids a man, and in our culture (and most others) men do not like to depend on women for heavy lifting.

The attitudes of donor and recipient might differ if the person helped were lower in socioeconomic status than the helper. But predictions here are iffy. A person accustomed to the lower-status position might not chafe at the aid; on the other hand she might be more sensitive to class and inequality. The higher-status person might be uncomfortable to be in the unusual position (as he sees it) of recipient of aid; on the other hand he might be less sensitive and mind less. At least as important as socioeconomic status is the degree to which a person's need for help reflects enduring features of her situation. Compare the following cases: (a) an able-bodied person carrying the luggage of a person with a temporarily strained back; (b) an able-bodied person carrying the luggage of a permanently disabled person; (c) a person giving money to a stranded traveler who has had his wallet stolen; (d) a rich person giving a poor person money for food. The recipients' enduring conditions in the second and fourth examples are more likely to give rise to pity on the part of donors or resentment on the part of recipients than the situations described in the first and third, which do not reflect chronic dependence.

Giving and indebtedness

For one person to aid another implies an inequality from the start: one person *has*, the other *has not*, and *needs*. Well, one might say, so be it: that is, after all, how things are; if have-nots had what they needed, giving would be unnecessary.

The transfer from donor to recipient that occurs when one assists the other paradoxically compounds the difference between the two. Although the recipient, who began with less, now has more and is in that respect more equal to the donor, that is because he has been given something by the donor. A long line of anthropological, sociological, and psychological research shows that gifts are not free and that they come with strings attached. As Marcel Mauss argues in his seminal work *The Gift*, although in theory presents and gifts are voluntary, "in reality they are given and reciprocated obligatorily."[2] The common experience of feeling indebted to others

[2] Mauss 1990.

by unrequited gifts or invitations shows we already know this. At issue is what sociologist Alvin Gouldner calls the "norm of reciprocity" and what social psychologist Robert Cialdini calls "the rule of reciprocation" – the idea that "we should try to repay, in kind, what another person has provided us."[3] Gouldner argues that this norm is "no less universal and important an element of culture than the incest taboo."[4] Reciprocity is both a psychological fact and a moral norm. Yes, moochers, schnorrers, sponges, free riders, freeloaders, and parasites exist. (It's interesting that we have so many words for such people.) But much more common is the experience of indebtedness when a person receives something – whether gifts, favors, or assistance – from others.

The feeling often coexists with gratitude, which is typically understood to be a positive emotion. Certainly its opposite, ingratitude, is almost universally regarded as a serious character flaw, even if Hume overstates the case in insisting that "Of all crimes that human creatures are capable of committing, the most horrid and unnatural is ingratitude."[5] Yet the feeling of indebtedness inherent in gratitude is distinct from it, because one can feel indebted but not grateful. As Cialdini confirms, giving unwanted gifts is a primary strategy among sales people and others trying to extract money or commitments from other people.[6] It explains why, even though you may be hungry, you may refuse the free sample in the supermarket if you don't want to buy the product. Indebtedness, whether coexisting with gratitude or not, generally involves a certain discomfort or unease. Indeed, this discomfort is central in motivating the desire to repay what has been given.

[3] Gouldner 1960, 171; Cialdini 2001, 20. See also Schwartz 1967.
[4] Gouldner 1960, 171. Gouldner cites Edward Westermarck: "To requite a benefit, or to be grateful to him who bestows it, is probably everywhere, at least under certain circumstances, regarded as a duty" (Westermarck 1908, vol. 2, 154).
[5] Hume 1978, bk. iii, pt. i, sec. i. Seneca claims that "among all our many and great vices, none is so common as ingratitude" (1935, bk. i, sec. i). Seneca continues: "He who receives a benefit with gratitude repays the first installment on his debt" (ibid., bk. ii, sec. xxii).
[6] Cialdini 2001, 31–3.

Building on the work of anthropologists like Mauss and Bronislaw Malinowski, Cialdini argues that the "web of indebtedness" that accompanies acts of giving and receiving is "a unique adaptive mechanism of human beings, allowing for the division of labor, the exchange of diverse forms of goods and different services, and the creation of interdependencies that bind individuals together into highly efficient units."[7] Feelings of obligation combine to form a social glue. Even so, such feelings are complex and ambiguous, as many have noticed. Mark Twain quips that "if you pick up a starving dog and make him prosperous, he will not bite you. This is the principal difference between a dog and a man."[8] Emerson sounds the same theme: "It is not the office of a man to receive gifts. How dare you give them? We wish to be self-sustained. We do not quite forgive a giver. The hand that feeds us is in some danger of being bitten."[9]

Does it matter if donors put no conditions on their gifts? Perhaps not very much. Even if they expect nothing in return, recipients may feel beholden and experience the need to reciprocate. When donors do expect a return, they more explicitly put recipients in their debt. What kind of return can recipients give? If they are poor, it may not be a material one. They have given donors some kind of power over them, acknowledged their superiority, left the ledger unbalanced.

Seneca notes these psychological complexities of giving and receiving, although his own solution is questionable. Seneca defends "a binding rule" that the donor should immediately forget the gift was given, while the recipient "should never forget that it was received." "Repeated reference to our services wounds and crushes the spirit of the other."[10] But if that is so, we may ask, will silence be enough to sustain the recipient's self-respect?

---

[7] Cialdini 2001, 20–1.   [8] Twain 1894, 214.   [9] Emerson 1876, 155–6.
[10] Seneca 1935, bk. II, sec. x. Seneca's concern is largely with demonstrations of virtue and vice; thus, he says, "I owe nothing to you if you saved me in order that you might have someone to exhibit" (ibid.). I believe questions about the value of motives and the like are distinct from, although easily confused with, the questions considered here; I take them up in the next chapter.

Such undertones help explain the problematic nature of the word *charity*. I long thought of the subject of this book in terms of charity, but discovered in describing my interests to others that landmines lurked beneath the surface. We often describe the kinds of acts I focus on in this book as acts of charity; we speak of charitable donations and describe organizations aimed at helping others as charities. You might think of an act of charity, as I did, as one aimed at benefiting another, where the benefit cannot be understood either as compensation or reparation for previous harm done by the donor to the recipient, or as deriving from a special relationship between donor and recipient.[11] But there is also in the idea of charity a suggestion of personal merit or the supererogatory – of people giving to others even though they are not morally obligated to do so, and thus exhibiting virtue. And in that case, gratitude is clearly called for.

As we saw in Chapter 3, there is nothing inherent in the idea of acts benefiting another not based on prior relationships that precludes them from being obligatory. Depending on how much context is described, they may even be perfect duties – that is, duties corresponding to rights on the part of recipients. The bystander who could warn the traveler of the rising waters (Macaulay's case), or who could save the drowning child when it's easy and she is the only one who can (Singer's case), are examples. But there is that whiff in *charity* of the gift, freely given. Perhaps this suggestion connects partly to the word's origin in the Latin *caritas*, which means love; "philanthropy" means love of humankind. Love is a feeling that cannot be commanded, so one might infer that it must be freely given.[12] But we should interpret charity here as we might interpret the commandment to love your neighbor. You can't command people to feel a certain

---

[11] Is it not possible to perform acts of charity toward people with whom one has a special relationship? Our responsibilities to benefit parents, children, friends, and the like are not usually framed in these terms. I suppose they could be – one might say that a person should be *especially* charitable to her loved ones – but this is not standard usage. I don't think much hangs on the question.

[12] Of course, we don't have direct control over our feelings, so it may be a fallacy to think of them as free in any case.

way, but you can command them to act *as if* they loved their neighbor. In this sense charity could be obligatory.

Some people are in need and others may be able to benefit them. The degree of moral force – how strong the responsibility, if any, for would-be donors to benefit recipients – varies greatly depending on the particular circumstances, of course. But are there ways to mitigate the problems of hierarchy and indebtedness – problems that almost inevitably threaten in such situations? Here I offer some antidotes.

First antidote: we are all indebted

The first response is to recognize that all people – including those who have fared well in life and seem not to need others' help – are indebted to many others past and present for what they have and have achieved. Americans are particularly suffused with the myth of hyper-individualism and self-sufficiency: American society encourages the idea that people can make it on their own and therefore deserve what they get (one way or the other). Even though people routinely thank their parents, spouses, and friends for their successes (think of Academy Awards night!), the myth survives in common defenses of wealth and property rights. The CEO's salary and benefits are deserved: he worked hard, made the company profitable, and is morally entitled to whatever benefits he can command.

But the "I don't owe nobody nothin'" view is not merely overstated; it is false through and through. It is not simply that we are indebted to those closest to us – family, friends, teachers – who have directly helped us become what we are and do what we do. We owe a debt also to those many invisible and anonymous others who have over time improved the world, who together are responsible for medical, technological, and economic advances that make our lives better. The point has been made by a bevy of Nobel Prize-winning economists, including George Akerlof, Joseph Stiglitz, Douglass North, and Herbert Simon, who argues that

> if we are very generous with ourselves, I suppose we might claim that we "earned" as much as one fifth of [our income]. The rest is the patrimony

associated with being a member of an enormously productive social system, which has accumulated a vast store of physical capital, and an even larger store of intellectual capital – including knowledge, skills, and organizational know-how held by all of us – so that interaction with our equally talented fellow citizens rubs off on us both much of this knowledge and this generous allotment of unearned income.[13]

The point has also been made by scholars such as Richard Posner, Robert Dahl, and Thorstein Veblen; by scientists from Isaac Newton ("I have stood on the shoulders of giants") to Albert Einstein; and by entrepreneurs like Warren Buffett, who asserts that "society is responsible for a very significant percentage of what I've earned."[14] The most inventive inventors and entrepreneurial entrepreneurs could not do what they do without the labors of multitudes of people before them and around them.

So dependence on others is inevitable. If more people recognized that such interconnections and interdependence are the common human condition, the burden on the psyche of admitting that one needs assistance would diminish.[15] And words like "help" and "aid" might shed the connotations I believe they now almost inevitably have – the suggestion that the model human being is *not* dependent.

Second antidote: anonymity and privacy

Two important – and related – antidotes are suggested by the example we have just been examining. We rarely feel burdened by indebtedness, even on those occasions when we recognize that our enjoyments and achievements rest on what others, past and present, have done. That is at least partly because the acts and achievements

[13] Simon 2012. Simon refers here to income, but much the same can be said about wealth and standard of living. For citations to the views of the others cited in these paragraphs see Alperovitz and Daly 2008, ch. 7 and passim.

[14] Quoted in Collins, Lapham, and Klinger 2004, 17. Buffett's public invitations to the government to raise tax rates on him and others like him follow naturally from this claim.

[15] For the inevitability of dependence in human relationships see Kittay 1999.

on which the comforts of our lives depend are collective products that cannot be tied to identifiable individuals whom we know or who know us. The collectivity and anonymity of gifts makes indebtedness easier to endure.[16]

The eleventh-century rabbi, physician, and philosopher Maimonides noted the benefits of anonymity in "Laws on Gifts for the Poor," in the seventh volume of the *Mishneh Torah*, his encyclopedic guide to Jewish law. Maimonides's famous "eight degrees of charity" delineates eight steps, in descending order of goodness, that can characterize the relationship between donor and recipient. Best is to assist someone by

> providing him with a gift or a loan or by accepting him into a business partnership or by helping him find employment – in a word, by putting him where he can dispense with other people's aid.

The next three steps require anonymity, preferably on both sides but at least on one:

> A step below this stands the one who gives alms to the needy in such manner that the giver knows not to whom he gives and the recipient knows not from whom it is that he takes.
>   One step lower is that in which the giver knows to whom he gives but the poor person knows not from whom he receives.
>   A step lower is that in which the poor person knows from whom he is taking but the giver knows not to whom he is giving.[17]

Maimonides ought to say (and probably means) that even the first step should be carried out anonymously where possible. Obviously one cannot accept someone into a business partnership anonymously, but gifts, loans, or assistance with employment can be done in this way. When neither donor nor recipient knows the other's identity, the possibility of smugness and condescension on the one side, and of humiliation and resentment on the other, decreases. If only partial anonymity is possible, better for the recipient not to know the donor than vice versa – presumably because the dangers of dependence or

---

[16] Collectivity generally implies anonymity, although the converse does not hold.
[17] Maimonides 2003, ch. 10, 7–14.

humiliation on the part of the recipient outweigh the risks of the donor's condescension.

These considerations apply most directly to cases of one-on-one aid between individuals: helping one's neighbor or coworker or employee, or a stranger on the street or in a shop. And, as I argued earlier, psychological experiences will no doubt vary depending on the particulars of the situation, such as the age and social standing of the parties to the interactions. Giving aid one-on-one requires sensitivity if it is not to humiliate the recipient.

But the problem can arise even where donors and recipients are members of groups. Imagine a group of destitute villagers who receive a significant donation of food aid from a philanthropic organization. The inhabitants do not know the identity of the individuals who have contributed to the organization and the contributors do not know the identity of the villagers. The chances of humiliation and the bad kind of indebtedness are less, it seems, than if they did know each other. But this view may depend partly on the supposition that everyone in the village needs assistance, so that aid does not make one person stand out. Compare the welfare system in a developed society. Here again aid is given collectively, so that the welfare recipient is not indebted to any particular individual, and those whose taxes fund welfare payments are unlikely to be acquainted with specific recipients. Still, the welfare recipient may feel humiliated when he hands his food stamps to the store employee, or is seen by others at the social services office. These others are not necessarily those who have donated to him, although insofar as they are taxpayers and the social services come from taxes they will be participants. But the example demonstrates a certain ambiguity between *anonymity* and *publicity*. A may know that B gave to him, and B may know that A is the recipient of his donation. On the Maimonidean view I have been endorsing, this is itself problematic; it would be better if B did not know A's identity and better still if A did not know B's. But the psychological perils associated with being the recipient of aid result only partly from indebtedness to the donors; partly they result from being, and being seen as, the recipient of *anyone's* aid.

Third antidote: rights

Probably the strongest antidote to the dangers of indebtedness when one person or group benefits another derives from the concept of rights – more specifically, human rights. If the recipient of a benefit has a *right* to it, then indebtedness is inappropriate. To have a right to something is to be entitled to it, and not to be required to thank anyone or be grateful for getting it.

Some might regard this response as question-begging. Surely it cannot be sufficient reason for thinking people have a right to a decent minimum that otherwise they would have to thank their beneficiaries or that it would be demeaning for them not to have such a right! It's true: the drawbacks of indebtedness do not suffice to show that people have rights, since rights in any meaningful sense have strings attached – they entail duties or obligations on the parts of other people. Establishing the warrant for such strings is difficult for at least two reasons. One is demandingness: we need to know what it is reasonable to insist that one person do for another. The other concerns identification: how can we know which people are attached at the other end of the strings to those who have rights? Were it not for these two problems, we could let a million rights bloom, at least on the assumption, which I take to be uncontroversial, that satisfying people's basic needs is of fundamental importance.

Much of the argument of this book has been devoted to showing that the two problems are related and should be approached together. In Chapter 3 I argued that the identification problem would be greatly minimized by viewing the responsibilities to benefit those in need as collective responsibilities, and that there are other good reasons for so viewing them. Collectives such as countries are easier to identify than individuals, and there are many fewer of them. Global poverty results from structural and institutional factors and features, and from the collective behavior of individuals, and thus needs to be addressed in a concerted fashion. Finally, as I argued at length in Chapter 6, the demands on individuals are greatly reduced when they do as others do – and one way to do as others do is to act together *with* them.

So the case for expressing the claims of poor people to a decent minimum in terms of rights is not *simply* that they will thereby be better able to maintain their self-respect. But this is in itself an excellent reason, if we can remove the other stumbling blocks – concerning demandingness and identification – to taking rights seriously. And I believe we can.

International aid

So far I have been considering some very general features that cast a shadow over acts of assistance and the experience of receiving aid. But the contemporary critique of aid zeroes in on more concrete difficulties and impediments that attach to efforts to aid poor people in developing countries. Beginning in the 1990s a flood of books, some receiving a great deal of attention, have charged that aid is at best ineffective and at worst damaging and counterproductive. Here are some revealing titles.

> *The Road to Hell: The Ravaging Effects of Foreign Aid and International Charity*
>
> *Lords of Poverty: The Power, Prestige, and Corruption of the International Aid Business*
>
> *Famine Crimes: Politics and the Disaster Relief Industry in Africa*
>
> *A Bed for the Night: Humanitarianism in Crisis*
>
> *The White Man's Burden: Why the West's Efforts to Aid the Rest Have Done So Much Ill and So Little Good*
>
> *The Dark Sides of Virtue: Reassessing International Humanitarianism*
>
> *Dead Aid: Why Aid Is Not Working and How There Is a Better Way for Africa*[18]

If the apparent conclusions of these books are right, we should not work to improve the lives of people in great need because we will inevitably fail. In that case, the very premise of this book founders.

---

[18] Maren 1997; Hancock 1994; de Waal 2009; Rieff 2002; Easterly 2006; Kennedy 2005; Moyo 2010.

The first thing to say about this view is that believing it would be convenient. I do not think the critics of aid are in fact generally motivated by a self-interested desire to get themselves or comfortable people or countries off the hook. Many of them have worked in the fields of international aid and development; they are experienced and knowledgeable and have good reasons to be skeptical of aid's effectiveness. Still, whatever their motives, their message is one some people would be all too happy to hear, whether for self-interested or ideological reasons, or both: no need to worry about others' hardship because there's nothing you can do about it; God helps those who help themselves, so just mind your own business and cultivate your own garden. We have reason to be suspicious, then, and to examine these claims closely.

The second thing to say is that despite the titles of these books and the sound bites that accompany them, their authors almost invariably have suggestions about what can be done to alleviate global poverty, including ideas about what affluent people and countries should do. For example, William Easterly, whose 2006 book *The White Man's Burden* stands as one of the hallmarks of the anti-aid movement, acknowledges that "maybe aid even works on average in some sectors, such as health, education, and water and sanitation."[19] Health, education, water, and sanitation! Not exactly trivial matters when it comes to alleviating poverty.

So in fact when you look closely you see that the critics' objections may be more about the *what* and the *how* than the *whether*. We'll look at specific examples shortly, but here it is worth formulating the point in more general and forceful terms. I have been concerned about the drawbacks of words like *aid*, with their common implications that the would-be aider has played no causal role in bringing about or perpetuating the situation for which aid is needed; that the aider is virtuous, going above and beyond the call of duty; or that gratitude from the recipient is called for. Yet another common implication is that aid equals cash transfers or in-kind donations of food, clothing, and other basic necessities. Dispensing such items is the image we may have of

---

[19] Easterly 2006, 178.

what "charities" do. And of course this image is sometimes accurate. Disasters – fires, hurricanes, tsunamis, earthquakes – happen, and when they do people need immediate supplies of hard goods.

Yet consider this remark by Raymond Offenheiser, president of Oxfam America, one of the premier charitable organizations fighting poverty:

> The long-term answer is never food aid . . . Farmer-led innovations . . . that produce more crops using fewer resources hold promise. But fighting hunger also means urging governments and companies to make smarter investments in agriculture and climate preparedness . . . It means taking steps to protect growers' access to natural resources like water and land. It means creating long-term, equitable solutions to the climate crisis . . . Oxfam's work . . . is about building the resilience of local communities over the long haul.[20]

Eliminating chronic poverty, Offenheiser asserts, requires changing political and economic structures and institutions. This is also what many of aid's critics insist must take place. Yet they suggest that institutional approaches are not *aid*; aid, their objections imply, necessarily means cash transfers or in-kind assistance.

So the controversy between defenders and critics of aid reveals a confusion between two senses of "aid" – a broad one and a narrow one. The moral and philosophical question implicit in the broad sense of "aid" is whether affluent people and countries have a moral responsibility to do *something* to alleviate poverty in developing countries. I have spent much of this book arguing that they do. Suppose you agree – whether on humanitarian grounds or because you believe that rich people and countries have caused or contributed to the existence of poverty in developing countries or have benefited from it by, for example, exploiting their superior bargaining position. It is then a further question *what* exactly those who have these responsibilities ought to do. Leaving aside the matter of how far these responsibilities extend (a question I have attempted to transmute by collectivizing it), we need to know *what* sorts of actions and policies are appropriate. But unless *nothing* done by such agents can

---

[20] Offenheiser 2011.

be effective, the responsibility to act remains; the question is what to do. I return to this point below.

Still, some of the critics imply the strong thesis that nothing outsiders can do is effective, and that much of it is counterproductive. As Dambisa Moyo, a former consultant to the World Bank, puts it: "The problem is that aid is not benign – it's malignant . . . aid *is* the problem."[21] But here too we find ambiguity in the use of the term *aid*. Moyo's target is almost exclusively what she calls "systematic aid – that is, aid payments made directly to governments." This is either bilateral aid, in which one government transfers funds or goods to another government, or multilateral aid given by institutions like the World Bank. Moyo is not challenging the work of "charity-based aid . . . disbursed by charitable organizations to institutions or people on the ground."[22] Of course, some critics of aid, like Maren, do include charity-based aid organizations among their targets. And in any case the ambiguity helps sell books and sensationalize the issue. Since individuals are most likely to be able to direct their efforts by donating to charitable organizations, the broad-brush panning of aid could be very damaging to these efforts.

Why do so many critics think aid is at best ineffective and at worst damaging? They have a variety of reasons. Here I outline the main ones.[23]

---

[21] Moyo 2010, 47. See also Hancock: "Aid is not bad . . . because it is sometimes misused, corrupt, or crass; rather, it is *inherently* bad, bad to the bone, and utterly beyond reform . . ." (1994, 183).

[22] Moyo 2010, 7–8. Hancock concedes that although there are problems with the "long-term development work of almost all" the NGOs, most of their efforts are well-motivated and worthwhile. "The same, however, cannot be said for official aid agencies" (1994, xiii).

[23] The discussion that follows owes a great deal to chs. 6 and 7 of Singer 2010, and to ch. 3 of Cullity 2004. Cullity rebuts critics who argue that aid is at best ineffective and at worst counterproductive. But he is sympathetic to their concerns and often puts their points at least as eloquently as (and certainly more concisely than) they do. See also Wenar 2011 for an excellent (although somewhat pessimistic) analysis; I unfortunately learned of it too late to be able to incorporate its insights fully into this chapter.

- Most generally, the critics point to the misguided optimism, ignorance, and arrogance of the many individuals and institutions who over the years have assumed that Western know-how could from above and afar deliver universal, top-down, one-size-fits-all solutions to poor people in developing countries without an adequate understanding of local conditions and of the differences between the circumstances and causes of poverty in different places.
- A more concrete manifestation of these failures is the "damaging fantasy that comes from simplistically conceiving of the problems of the poor as a need for rescue – a need to be plucked away from a situation of threat by a single beneficent action, like the plucking of a child from a pond." This way of thinking "infantilizes the poor, treating them as victims to be acted upon" and conceiving "poverty-related need and suffering as an act of god, rather than a political problem which needs to be met by political action."[24]
- Aid encourages its recipients – whether individual poor people or the governments and policymakers who negotiate for aid – to be dependent on others, by removing incentives for them to look for better ways to reduce poverty.[25]
- Aid has bad effects on local economies. For example, sending food aid can depress local food prices. Aid can give rise to "Dutch disease": a strengthening of a country's currency that makes its products uncompetitive in the international market.[26]
- Aid has bad political effects. It props up corrupt rulers in those countries that receive aid, providing them with funds and making them less dependent on internal support.[27] Even when rulers do

---

[24] Cullity 2004, 35.   [25] Maren 1997, ch. 9 and passim; Moyo 2010, 66.
[26] Moyo 2010, 62–4. Dutch disease is one common explanation given for the "resource curse" – the fact that the poorest countries are often rich in natural resources. "The resource exports cause the country's currency to rise in value against other currencies. This makes the country's other export activities uncompetitive. Yet these other activities might have been the best vehicles for technological progress" (Collier 2007, 39). Not only natural resources but anything that causes a large inflow of income, including foreign assistance, can lead to Dutch disease (Ebrahim-zadeh 2003).
[27] Moyo 2010, 49; Bauer 1981, 93–5; Sogge 2002, 8, 101–2, and passim.

not actually take the money intended for poor people, they control it and the people who receive it. Aid can therefore undermine incentives for real political change.

- The motives and purposes of those who give aid – foreign governments, multilateral organizations, and NGOs – are often troubling or even pernicious. As Cullity puts it, "the aid business is propelled by the same mixture of naivety, racist condescension, and callous or hypocritical self-interest that governed the Third World's colonial past, and created its current problems." At its worst, then, the purpose of aid is to "open up developing countries for Western businesses, and to supervise the transfer of resources from poor to rich."[28]
- Aid organizations are part of an industry that may sacrifice "its intended beneficiaries in order that it may survive and grow," relying on TV and other media to make things look as bad as possible.[29] Describing Somalia in the 1990s, Maren argues that "famine and horror became a commodity. The worse it looked the better it sold."[30] Realistic portrayals are less telegenic; the more effective ones humiliate those to be helped.

Some responses to the criticisms

These criticisms are often overlapping and interrelated. Let me begin with the last two. First, although it may be true that some aid organizations capitalize on pity and demean the people whom they are supposed to be helping, many do not. A cursory look at the public information of a variety of aid organizations – available on their websites and in published communications – shows that many portray poor people in developing countries with dignity and respect. (This is, of course, an empirical question, and the reader is invited to judge for herself.) And these organizations should not be blamed for faults that should be ascribed to the tabloid media.

A second point is that motives are irrelevant. What matters for our purposes here is whether there are good reasons for people to act as

[28] Cullity 2004, 41.   [29] Maren 1997, 11.   [30] Maren 1997, 213.

they do, not what their actual motives are. If a person is in danger there is good reason for another to rescue him. Perhaps the rescuer acts because she hopes to go to heaven, or to impress her friends. That would affect our judgment of her character, but not our judgment of the rightness of what she does. It's easy, in thinking about aid and charity, to be confused on these matters, and I investigate them further in the next chapter.

Let's consider now what I believe are the more central criticisms. As Cullity argues, they seem to amount to the claim that aid is either ineffective – it altogether fails to help those it is supposed to help – or counterproductive. The charge that aid is counterproductive could mean that it actually leaves those individuals it is designed to help worse off. Or it could mean (and, I believe, more commonly does mean) that even though it might help those individuals, it inhibits the kind of economic and political change that would lift whole groups of people out of poverty by enacting long-term, structural change.

To the charge that aid does not help those it is designed to help, or even makes them worse off, there are numerous counterexamples. Some forms of aid are effective, and some are not. Many of the most prominent examples of successful aid involve improvements in health. The World Health Organization (WHO) wiped out small-pox, which had been killing 2 million people a year, in twelve years.[31] Deaths from malaria have declined by more than 25 percent in the last decade.[32] WHO has eradicated river blindness in parts of West Africa.[33] Many other examples can be given:

> A vaccination campaign in southern Africa virtually eliminated measles as a killer of children ... A national campaign in Egypt to make parents aware of the use of oral rehydration therapy from 1982 to 1989 cut childhood deaths from diarrhea by 82 percent over that period. A regional program to eliminate polio in Latin America after 1985 has eliminated it as a public health threat in the Americas. The leading preventable cause of blindness, trachoma, has been cut by 90 percent in children under age ten in Morocco since 1987 ... Sri Lanka's commitment to preventing maternal deaths during childbirth has cut the rate of

[31] Singer 2010, 85.   [32] McNeil 2011.   [33] Lancaster 1999, 51.

maternal mortality from 486 to 24 deaths per 100,000 births over the last four decades.[34]

What is as remarkable as these facts and figures is that they come from William Easterly, best known for his scorching criticisms of aid. The truth is that Easterly acknowledges "the ability of aid agencies to be effective when they have narrow, monitorable objectives that coincide with the poor's needs and with political support in the rich countries for an uncontroversial objective like saving lives."[35] Let's not be misled by the word: these objectives are "narrow" in the sense of being well-defined, but they are of the greatest moment.

In light of these examples, how should we understand the claim that aid does not help people, or even harms them? Think first of the concern that aid produces dependence. Either the charge has no application in this context, or we should say instead that we are all dependent. The Westerner vaccinated against smallpox, polio, and measles and shielded against other diseases by public health measures has no more lifted himself up by his own bootstraps than he has flown with his own wings. As I argued earlier, all people are dependent on the acts of others for the benefits they enjoy; this is reason for humility but not humiliation.

Assuming, then, that most people would prefer to live rather than die and to be free from debilitating diseases, even if their lives remain very difficult, it is clear that vaccination programs and other public health measures have often benefited them, have made them better off by their own lights. So what could it mean to say that aid is ineffective or counterproductive? It could mean that although some kinds of programs, such as these, are worthwhile, others are not. And it certainly seems undeniable that of all the possible kinds of aid, some will be beneficial and others ineffective or even harmful, and that we

[34] Easterly 2006, 241.
[35] Easterly 2006, 241. Perhaps some will disagree that saving lives is an uncontroversial objective, citing racism against people of color or fears of population growth as reasons Westerners would not mind seeing more poor people in developing countries die. But other critics may argue that the West wants more consumers for its products and so has reason to want such people to live.

should engage in the former and avoid the latter. Knowing which is which is often difficult, and no one would deny that there has been a lot of waste over the years. But over the last decade many scholars, policymakers, and activists have devoted a great deal of attention to distinguishing the wheat from the chaff.[36]

To say that aid is ineffective or counterproductive, in the face of the kinds of radical health improvements just described, seems to mean instead that these benefits are outweighed by other costs. One such cost often mentioned is overpopulation: if death rates decline radically as the result of medical advances and health interventions, then the planet will eventually be too crowded to feed everyone.

The appropriate responses to this Malthusian argument are of two kinds. One rests on the finding, made widely known by Amartya Sen, that hunger and starvation result not primarily from absolute short-ages of food, even within poor countries, but rather from the political and economic structures that determine food entitlements.[37] But there is also the fact that much of the food that *is* grown does not go to feeding human beings. As Singer explains, some of it – 100 million tons of corn a year – becomes biofuel for American gas tanks.[38] And a huge quantity – 756 million tons of grain in 2007 – is fed to nonhuman animals, which convert the crops into meat and other animal products. It takes thirteen pounds of grain to produce one pound of beef, six pounds of grain to produce one pound of pork. The total amount of grain fed to cows and pigs raised for slaughter is twice what is needed to feed all the 1.3 billion extremely poor people in the world.[39]

This is not to deny that there is a limit to how many people the planet can support. Global population cannot increase indefinitely. But the most effective way to slow it – and this is the second response to the Malthusian argument – is not by letting people die of

[36] See, e.g., Banerjee and Duflo 2011 and Karlan and Appel 2011 for descriptions of important work done by them and many others. I consider some of their findings below.

[37] Sen 1981; see also Cullity 2004, 6–8.   [38] Singer 2010, 121.

[39] Singer 2010, 121, citing the United Nations Food and Agriculture Organization and other sources.

preventable diseases but by reducing poverty, increasing education, and providing opportunities for better healthcare. It is well known that birth rates decline as people's standard of living rises. In poor rural environments the benefits of children who can work "outweigh the cost of feeding an extra mouth ... And when you can no longer work in the fields, your children will be the only ones to look after you."[40] So in these environments people have strong incentives to have large families. Fertility falls as societies become less agrarian and less poor. Lower birth rates are also strongly correlated with female education, at least in part because educated women are more likely to work. "Recent data from many countries have shown that women with at least a secondary-level education eventually give birth to one-third to one-half as many children as women with no formal education."[41] High birth rates are also partly the result of unplanned pregnancies; a 2002 study "estimated that as many as a quarter of all pregnancies in developing countries in the 1990s were unintended."[42] So the availability of information about family planning, and contraception for those who want it, are central to reducing birth rates.

More responses

Some aid does not save people's lives (and thus does not trigger the overpopulation objection); it simply improves their well-being in fundamental ways. Singer describes several compelling examples. One is eye surgery to prevent blindness and other serious eye diseases. A foundation established by an Australian ophthalmologist had by 2003 "restored sight to a million people, at a cost of roughly $50 per person." Another is a hospital in Ethiopia whose two physicians treat women with obstetric fistulas, a condition resulting from childbirth in physically immature or malnourished women. Fistulas cause urine and feces to trickle through the vagina,

---

[40] *Economist* 2009; the article includes sources for the data. Singer gives a good summary of these matters in Singer 2010, 123.
[41] Population Reference Bureau 2007.   [42] *Economist* 2009.

producing a foul smell that renders the woman an outcast. It can be easily cured, at a cost of somewhere between $100 and $400.[43]

How could anyone object to such projects? Perhaps the answer is that although these projects have proved successful, many others have not. No one doubts that saving lives and reducing disease, suffering, and ignorance are good things; the question is whether we know how to achieve these goals and whether the many projects undertaken, and the billions of dollars spent, are on balance successful or are instead wasteful and ineffective. When put this way, we can see that the question is ill-formed. It suggests that we should evaluate aid wholesale. But even if more aid projects failed than succeeded, even if more money was wasted than was well-spent, that would only show that we need a more fine-grained analysis of what works where and when.

The critics may be right that some have labored under the illusion that there are universal, top-down solutions that can simply be applied to poor countries with miraculous results. That way of thinking is becoming obsolete, no doubt partly as a result of the failures of aid and the successes of its critics, and is being replaced by the realization that we must "step out of the office and look more carefully at the world."[44] One way to analyze successes and failures is through the use of randomized control trials (RCTs), an approach pioneered at the Abdul Latif Jameel Poverty Action Lab (J-PAL) at MIT. RCTs apply the methods familiar in medicine to evaluate the benefits of drugs, separating people randomly into different "treatments" and then seeing which treatment group fares better. For example, some pregnant women who came to public health clinics in western Kenya for prenatal care were given bed nets, which are extremely effective in reducing the incidence of malaria, while others

---

[43] Singer 2010, 100–3; see Singer's full chapter (6) for other examples.

[44] Banerjee and Duflo 2011, 14. A similar revolution has taken place over the last few decades in moral philosophy. Thinking about practical moral problems is not a matter of "applying" a few simple universal principles (thus the problematic character of the common term "applied philosophy"). You have to immerse yourself in the particulars to arrive at plausible approaches to moral and all other problems.

were sold the bed nets (at varying prices). The experiments established that, contrary to the view of Easterly and others that people value things more when they pay for them than when they get them free, "increasing the price from zero to seventy-five cents (which was the going rate for a discounted net from Population Services International) would drive off three-quarters of customers."[45]

RCTs have also been used to find ways to improve school attendance in developing countries; achieving universal primary education is among the top UN Millennium Development Goals (MDGs). Experiments in western Kenya showed that giving uniforms to students who didn't have them cut school absenteeism by more than a third.[46] In Mexico's Progresa program, a government-sponsored initiative paid poor mothers whose children's attendance at school was at least 85 percent. The program is costly and the government wanted to know how effective it was. Experiments showed that students receiving these "conditional cash transfers" "were significantly less likely to drop out."[47]

A striking set of school attendance experiments concern deworming. Worms infect a quarter of people worldwide. They can cause severe symptoms but are often associated with "a general and persistent malaise." One deworming pill destroys about 99 percent of worms in the body and protects a person for about four months; its total cost is about twenty cents. In an experiment originally carried out in western Kenya that gave deworming pills to students in primary schools, the absentee rate fell by about 20 percent. The results were replicated in India.[48] In Kenya, children who got the deworming pills for two years "went to school longer and earned, as

---

[45] Karlan and Appel 2011, 245; see also Banerjee and Duflo 2011, 6–8, 49–50. The authors of both books are associated with J-PAL.

[46] Karlan and Appel 2011, 199–200.

[47] Karlan and Appel 2011, 201–2, and Banerjee and Duflo 2011, 78–9. Later experiments in Malawi found that conditionality was not always important: school attendance might increase when people were given financial aid even if the aid was not made contingent on school attendance (Banerjee and Duflo 2011, 80). The conclusion we can draw: it's complicated!

[48] Karlan and Appel 2011, 206–9.

young adults, 20 percent more than children in comparable schools who received deworming for just one year."[49]

Of course, RCTs are not possible or practical in all cases. Administering RCTs is itself expensive, and "some aid projects may bring benefits that cannot be quantified."[50] Singer describes several such projects, including two supported by Oxfam. One organized Indian ragpickers – women who sift through garbage dumps to find items that can be recycled – so that they could demand higher prices and be protected from harassment. Another helped women in Mozambique get much-needed legal protection. Until recently, girls could be married at fourteen, and were completely under their husbands' control. The new law, passed by the Mozambique parliament in 2003 and spurred by the project, raises the marriage age to eighteen, allows women to head families, and grants them "rights over the couple's property after one year of living together in a customary marriage."[51] Other successful projects include funding of elections and election monitors by the US Agency for International Development (USAID), which "has helped ensure relatively free and fair electoral outcomes" in Africa, and its program in South Africa between 1986 and 1993, which helped build black leadership and strengthened community institutions.[52]

These projects exemplify one of the important counter-arguments, to which I have already alluded, that must be made to those who vilify aid. Aid is not necessarily a matter of giving people stuff – even stuff like vaccines and medicines – but of helping them to alter oppressive political and legal structures. The hackneyed proverb is "Give a man a fish and he will eat for a day. Teach a man to fish and he will eat for a lifetime." It's hackneyed partly because, as critics point out, it's unlikely that outsiders will know more about fishing than the locals. But the claim that there is nothing anyone but the locals themselves can ever do to improve their environment does not stand up to scrutiny. Although self-help is an important value,

---

[49] Banerjee and Duflo 2011, 31.
[50] Singer 2010, 94. For other criticisms of RCTs see Deaton 2010.
[51] Singer 2010, 94–7.   [52] Lancaster 1999, 97.

complete self-sufficiency is not possible. As I have argued, no one is nearly as self-sufficient as the propaganda implies some of us are or anyone can be.

Further ruminations

So the unflashy truth seems to be that "Sometimes aid works, and sometimes it does not."[53] Aid could fail to work in either of two basic ways. It could simply fail to achieve what it sets out to achieve, and thus be a waste of time and money. Or it could make things worse. There are, no doubt, many examples of the former. And it may be inevitable that aid fails in this way a good deal of the time: things are complicated, consequences are unpredictable, we know less than we should. Even successful projects are not always replicable in new circumstances.

But suppose that for every $100 you gave to alleviate poverty only $60 achieved a benefit – did what it was intended to do. Does that mean you should only give $60? If that $60 achieved the same results as the previous $100 then (other things being equal) the answer would be yes. Take the rest and go out to dinner. But that's probably not how these things work. If you gave $60, it might be that only $36 would be effective. If things are complicated, consequences are unpredictable, and we know less than we should, then we might have to build these inefficiencies into our calculations about how much to give. Of course, waste is undesirable. Thus, many committed scholars and policymakers work hard to better understand how to improve the odds that aid can do what it sets out to do. But the mere fact that some efforts fail cannot be reason enough to stop giving or even to give less unless we know how to distinguish successful from unsuccessful projects.

The fact that aid often fails would only be a reason to stop giving it altogether if giving it was actually counterproductive, if it made things worse than they were before. This seems to be the view of Hancock, who says that aid "is *inherently* bad," and Moyo, who insists

---

[53] Karlan and Appel 2011, 5.

that aid *"is* the problem."[54] We saw earlier that the plausibility of these claims rests largely on conceiving of aid too narrowly – in terms of in-kind goods or cash infusions – or of limiting the field of inquiry to assistance from governments or institutions like the World Bank. So we should restate the question in a way that eliminates the ambiguity. The question, then, is whether there is anything outsiders (mainly comfortable people in developed countries) can do to improve conditions for poor people in developing countries.

Only those seduced by rags-to-riches stories could conclude that the answer is no, and that poor people can only raise themselves up by their own bootstraps. Yes, there is a lot of room for reasonable disagreement about what works. And there are many levels at which things can work or not. We have seen examples of projects in health and education that can bring benefits to individuals.

Critics sometimes dismiss individual successes on the grounds that they do not produce structural, long-term institutional change – which, it is widely agreed, is necessary for economic development. The critics sometimes imply that these small-scale or individually oriented projects could even inhibit structural – i.e., institutional – change.[55]

How could genuine improvements in health and education *inhibit* institutional change? Perhaps the thought is that in such cases people will be less discontent and therefore more likely to accept the status quo. This argument is problematic on at least two grounds. The first is the implicit assumption that we should sacrifice the well-being of present people for the uncertain prospect of gains to future people. Admittedly, the tradeoffs in such cases are very difficult. Think of Jessica McClure, the eighteen-month-old girl who in 1987 fell into a well in Texas, attracting worldwide media attention. Enormous resources were spent to rescue Jessica (it took two and a half days), even though the money and effort could have instead been invested in preventive measures designed to avoid accidents to many more

[54] Hancock 1994, 183; Moyo 2010, 47.
[55] For discussion of the institutional turn, see, e.g., Hoff and Stiglitz 2001 and Evans 2005.

people. Yet when confronted with terrible accidents to real and identifiable human beings, few people are willing to bite the bullet and insist that we should forego rescue and invest only in prevention instead.[56]

Moreover, there is historical support for the view that people are more likely to rise up against unjust institutions when their prospects have improved, rather than when they are most downtrodden. According to this view – "the revolution of rising expectations," often attributed to Alexis de Tocqueville – better social conditions do not inhibit social and political change but hasten it.[57] So at the very least there is no incompatibility between improving people's health and education, or protecting their basic human rights, and producing structural change; at best, the first could increase the odds of the second.

Few people today would argue that outsiders can solve the problems of the poorest societies, which result in significant part from bad governance and bad policies. As Paul Collier puts it, "The societies of the bottom billion can only be rescued from within."[58] But that doesn't mean outsiders can do nothing to make improvements more likely or to make the lives of individual people in those societies better. I have discussed a sampling of successful projects, and there are many others. Some are directly concerned with improving basic goods such as health and education. Others focus on improving agricultural productivity in developing countries.[59] Some organizations, like Amnesty International and Human Rights Watch, work to protect rights against violence or to freedom of expression, and to expose those responsible for looting their country or harming its

---

[56] Kennedy 1987. See Jenni and Loewenstein 1997 for discussion of the "identifiable victim effect." Donations from sympathetic strangers, estimated at the time to amount to between $700,000 and $1,000,000, were put into a trust fund for Jessica, which she received when she turned twenty-five (Celizic 2007).

[57] Tocqueville 2011, pt. III, chs. 4 and 5; Brinton 1965.   [58] Collier 2007, 96.

[59] For example, the Gates Foundation supports research to develop varieties of crops that can better withstand environmental and soil stresses and provide better nutrients (Bill and Melinda Gates Foundation 2013). USAID works with African farmers to develop new crops that are drought-resistant, and to build small silos that reduce spoilage (Kristof 2012).

citizens. Some address injustices in the terms of international trade, for example by lobbying governments for the elimination of agricultural subsidies in rich countries. Some attempt to reform intellectual property laws and policies in order to facilitate the delivery of life-saving and life-altering drugs to poor people in developing countries.[60] Some focus on "illicit financial flows," which deprive developing countries of a trillion dollars a year "through corruption, smuggling, money laundering, and corporate tax evasion."[61] Some work to slow climate change, which will harm poor people in poor countries the most. Such efforts could make huge differences to the well-being of millions of people.

[60] For an example see the work of the Health Impact Fund 2012.
[61] Academics Stand Against Poverty 2013.

CHAPTER 9

On motives and morality

Alleviating global poverty is a morally pressing concern. I have been more or less taking that proposition for granted, and have focused my energies on showing that, although it is not only unrealistic but also unreasonable to expect ordinary human beings to make large sacrifices for the well-being of strangers (much less to insist that they are duty-bound to do so), we might nevertheless effect changes in their behavior that would reduce poverty without demanding too much of them.

To some this strategy will seem misguided. They believe the moral value of acting to benefit others – as by reducing their suffering – depends partly or wholly on the motive or reason from which a person acts. If so, advocating changes in behavior that altogether bypass what we typically think of as "moral" motives or reasons misses something crucial. The arguments of this book raise other questions as well about the nature of human motivation and its role in moral argument. How important is it that people act from moral rather than self-interested motives? To what extent can we count on such motives? I attempt to answer some of these questions in this chapter.

Motives and outcomes

The short answer to the immediate challenge that my approach undermines what is important about morality is that it rests on a confusion between two different interests we have in morality. Roughly, these two interests correspond to the outer realm of consequences and outcomes on the one hand, and the inner realm of character, motives, and reasons on the other. I take it for granted that poverty and disease are bad things that ought to be eliminated or reduced insofar as we can do so without sacrificing other important values.[1] At the same time, we care, and I shall argue should care, about people's motives intrinsically, and not simply because they correlate with behavior we want to encourage. These are two separate tracks.

Let me contrast my approach with two others. The obvious contrast is with the view I shall call Kantian. In the *Foundations of the Metaphysics of Morals* Kant asserts that "Nothing in the world . . . can possibly be conceived which could be called good without qualification except a good will."[2] A good will is one that wills according to certain motives or reasons. In the *Critique of Practical Reason* Kant makes explicit that good outcomes cannot be determined independently of the good will but only by means of it: "The concept of good and evil must not be determined before the moral law (for which, as it would seem, this concept would have to be made the basis) but only (as was done here) after it and by means of it."[3]

Kant famously (or, depending on your view, notoriously) goes further, asserting not only that it is the motive that matters morally but that "to have genuine moral worth, an action must be done from duty." Clearly it is not sufficient to act *in accordance* with duty – to do what duty demands. But nor is it enough to act with the aim of furthering another person's legitimate interests. One must do one's duty because one recognizes it *as* one's duty.[4]

Some who might agree with Kant about the centrality of motive will differ on this point, believing that good motives matter – even, perhaps, that they are all that matter – but that acting out of love or

---

[1] This sounds much like Peter Singer's principle that "If it is in your power to prevent something bad from happening, without sacrificing anything nearly as important, it is wrong not to do so" (Singer 2010, 15). As is obvious from the argument of this book, however, I have been trying to avoid the hard choices Singer's formulation forces upon us. Nothing in the discussion here hangs on my disagreements with Singer, and I do not mean to beg any questions about what other values are important and when they should be sacrificed.

[2] Kant 1997, Ak. 4, 393. [3] Kant 1996, Ak. 5, 63. [4] Kant 1997, Ak. 4, 397–8.

empathy or concern for others counts as a good motive. We will return to this disagreement later in the chapter. For the moment it is enough to highlight the view that the only morally important thing is the character of a person's motives, leaving aside for now the precise nature of praiseworthy motives.

At the other end of the spectrum is the pure consequentialist perspective. On this view, people's motives can possess two kinds of worth: they can be intrinsically valuable loci of whatever is, according to the particular consequentialist theory, the ultimate good, such as pleasure or happiness; or they can be instrumentally valuable means to producing pleasure or happiness.[5] Motives can be intrinsically good insofar as they are pleasurable to the agents whose motives they are, but more commonly their value will be instrumental. So the consequentialist cares about people's motives mainly as engines of good outcomes. We should value and encourage acting from benevolent or altruistic motives insofar as they lead to greater good and less suffering. Still, there is nothing *intrinsically* valuable about them, except when they embody pleasurable states.

So at one end of the spectrum we find the view that only motives matter morally, and at the other end that they matter barely at all – for the most part only instrumentally. Both these positions seem to me mistaken. We care about outcomes (such as that people do not live in poverty or suffer from disease), but we also care about the motives from which people act. And each of these matters intrinsically, not simply as means to other ends. That we care about outcomes intrinsically may seem more obvious (Kant to the contrary notwithstanding): that suffering is bad seems to go without saying. But what about motives? It may well be that our valuing of certain motives or traits of character is utilitarian in origin. (In the current fashion we might emphasize their evolutionary advantages.) If concern for other people tends toward the general good, then altruistic

---

[5] Here I take pleasure and pain as the relevant states; we could replace these with happiness and unhappiness, well-being and ill-being, or some other pair. The point is that some such states will be intrinsically valuable on a consequentialist conception.

motives will be instrumentally valuable. But that is compatible with our now valuing them for their own sake. Consider an analogy: sex may have evolved because of its evolutionary advantages, but that doesn't mean that people have or value sex only for reproductive purposes.[6] Judgments about people's motives play, and should play, an important role in our thinking – it's hard to make sense of our conceptions of justice and desert, and of religious conceptions of the afterlife, without them – and are not simply instrumental judgments about how likely it is that particular motives will produce valuable outcomes.

Of course, this does not settle the question of which motives we do or should value, or which kinds of human character are desirable. As we saw, Kant believed that the only morally valuable motive is acting from duty. It's more common to think that benevolent *feelings* such as love, empathy, or caring are also praiseworthy. And, of course, some people deny that any such altruistic motives are desirable. Ayn Rand and other libertarians extol the "virtue of selfishness" and denigrate altruism.[7]

My purpose has not been to decide exactly which motives are morally desirable but simply to establish that some are, not only because they lead to good outcomes but because they reflect our inherent concern with character. Recall the challenge to which I am responding: put most simply, that making it easier for people to benefit others robs these actions of their moral value. The assumption underlying this challenge must be that the moral value of benefiting others lies *exclusively* in its motive. I deny that. There is intrinsic value in good motives, but there is also intrinsic value in reducing undeserved suffering.

How do we compare the value of the two? It is probably non-sensical to imagine that there could be a single metric to compare them. Still, I believe that in general reducing suffering is more important than the existence of good motives. Suppose we have to choose between the following alternatives (recognizing at the same time the slight absurdity of the comparison). We can eliminate A's

[6] See de Waal 2010.   [7] Rand 1964.

malnutrition, disease, and ignorance without requiring that B act from good motives. Or, on the other hand, B has the best will in the world, exerting herself greatly to alleviate A's suffering, but, as Kant so strikingly puts it, "by a particularly unfortunate fate or by the niggardly provision of a step-motherly nature, this will should be wholly lacking in power to accomplish its purpose"[8] – and so A's malnutrition, disease, and ignorance remain. If these are our only alternatives, we should choose the former.

But one reason the comparison may strike us as silly is that in the world as we know it there is no real danger of crowding out virtue and heroism, no matter how much easier we make it for people to benefit others. We can facilitate people's doing good without fearing that there will be no good left to do. What remains is the province in which we can judge motives and character.

We may suspect there is more to be said about these matters. And in a book about the ethics and psychology of benefiting others, it is important to consider whether and to what extent people *can* act altruistically, and how such motives can or should supplement or replace the less purely moral ones I have discussed, most prominently in Chapter 6. I turn now to these questions.

Is altruism possible?

Let's begin with the question that seems to lurk in the minds of all undergraduate ethics students, and many others as well: do people *ever* act altruistically?

Looking at the world commonsensically, it's hard to doubt the existence of altruism. Examples large and small seem to abound of people attempting to help others with no prospect of reward. Consider two spectacular examples from the recent past. Shortly after the new year in 2007, Wesley Autrey, a man standing with his two young daughters on a New York City subway platform, jumped down onto the tracks as a train was approaching to save another man who had suffered a seizure and fallen. Autrey lay on top

[8] Kant 1997, Ak. 4, 394.

of the other man between the tracks as the train passed over them. His desperate action succeeded, and neither man was hurt.[9] Just a few months later, an engineering professor at Virginia Tech, Liviu Librescu, blocked the door to his classroom so his students could escape when Seung-Hui Cho, a gunman who was in the process of killing thirty-two of his classmates, attempted to enter. The students jumped to safety from the classroom window; Professor Librescu died from Cho's gunshots.[10]

If these acts do not count as altruistic, then what in the world, we may wonder, could altruism be? But anyone who has considered these questions knows that doubting altruism is easy. Yes, it's undeniable that people sometimes act in ways that benefit others, and that they may do so at what appears to be significant cost to themselves. Yet it may seem that when people act to aid others they expect something in return – at the very least, the satisfaction of having their desire to help fulfilled. For some it's a small step to the conclusion that achieving their own satisfaction is always people's dominant or even their only motive. Genuine altruism, it seems to follow, is an illusion. To those caught in its web the apparent logic of these steps may seem inexorable.

Philosophers and college sophomores are not alone in asking how altruism is possible. Evolutionary theory also makes the question compelling. At first glance it appears that evolution has no place for altruism, since organisms that put others' interests above their own would not survive to reproduce their kind. This is the crude but popular picture of evolution as "survival of the fittest." Yet we seem to observe examples of altruism in nature, and evolutionary theory must explain how they are possible.

Two accounts of biological altruism have been prominent. One is *reciprocal altruism*, first set out in a 1971 article by Robert L. Trivers.[11] Reciprocal altruism elevates "I scratch your back, you scratch mine" to a theory. Organisms sometimes sacrifice their good to the good of others, but they do so, according to this view, in the expectation that the favor will be returned. Reciprocal altruism requires that

---

[9] Buckley 2007.   [10] Downey 2007.   [11] Trivers 1971.

organisms interact more than once and that they are capable of recognizing each other, otherwise returning the favor would be impossible. An example of reciprocal altruism is the vampire bat, which dies if it goes without food for more than a few days. Individuals donate blood, by regurgitation, to other group members who fail to feed on a given night.

The other leading biological theory of altruism is *kin selection*, also known as inclusive fitness. Where reciprocal altruism focuses on the individual organism as the unit of selection, kin selection centers on the gene. This is the famous "selfish gene" theory made popular by Richard Dawkins, although the idea was developed originally by William Hamilton in 1964.[12] On this view, an individual who behaves altruistically to others sharing its genes will tend to reproduce those genes; the likelihood that the genes will be passed on depends on how closely related the individuals are. Parents share half their genes with offspring; likewise among siblings; first cousins share an eighth. The kin selection theory is supported by the observation that individuals tend to behave altruistically toward close relatives.

A third evolutionary approach departs both from reciprocal altruism's focus on the individual organism and kin selection's focus on the gene. *Group selection* takes groups of organisms as the evolutionary unit. First proposed by Darwin himself, the theory eventually fell out of favor, but has recently been revived by Elliot Sober and David Sloan Wilson.[13] The idea is that groups containing altruists possess survival advantages over those that do not. A clan in which members work for the good of all rather than their individual good will prosper against enemies.[14] Under plausible assumptions, individual group members will be more likely to survive and reproduce their (partly altruistic) kind.

---

[12] Hamilton 1964; Dawkins 1976.   [13] Sober and Wilson 1998.

[14] The weakness in this view is that groups of altruists seem to be subject to "subversion from within," as Dawkins calls it in *The Selfish Gene*. "Free riders" who behave selfishly will possess advantages within the group, and altruists, it seems, will eventually die out. For a useful summary of the controversy see Okasha 2009.

But although contemporary discussions of altruism quickly turn to evolutionary explanations, the connection between the latter and the commonsense meaning of altruism is questionable. Consider reciprocity in the commonsense understanding of altruism. If a person acts to benefit another in the expectation that the favor will be returned, the natural response is: "That's not altruism!" Genuine altruism, we think, requires a person to sacrifice her own interests for another without consideration of personal gain. Calculating what's in it for me is the very opposite of what we have in mind. Reciprocal altruism seems at best to amount to enlightened self-interest. Kin selection also falls short, by failing to explain why people sometimes behave altruistically toward nonrelatives.

But there's a more fundamental reason why evolutionary altruism does not amount to altruism in the ordinary meaning of the term. When we ask whether people have acted altruistically, we are interested in their *motives* or *intentions*: we want to know whether they *intended* to benefit another person (recognizing the cost to themselves) or whether their *reason* for acting was to benefit another (without regard to personal gain). Whether people act altruistically, then, depends on their psychological state, on what is going on, or not going on, in their minds when they act.

Biological altruism, on the other hand, is defined in terms of "reproductive fitness": an organism behaves altruistically when it tends to increase another organism's ability to survive and reproduce while decreasing its own. Biological altruism implies nothing about mental states; birds and bats and even bees are capable of it. As Sober and Wilson put it, "An organism need not have a mind for it to be an evolutionary altruist."[15]

So in a certain sense evolutionary and psychological altruism have nothing to do with each other, since the commonsense psychological variety has everything to do with motives and the evolutionary variety has nothing to do with them. Indeed, as Okasha notes, thinking of most biological organisms as selfish is just as wrong-

[15] Sober and Wilson 1998, 202.

headed as thinking of them as altruistic: selfishness, like altruism, is about motives and intentions.[16]

Of course, biological and psychological altruism can coexist: a person who intentionally sacrifices her interests for another will, other things being equal, decrease her reproductive fitness. If she sacrifices her life, her genes will not be carried on (unless she sacrifices her life for a close relative who procreates, as kin selection would predict). Still, the existence of evolutionary altruism is not *sufficient* for psychological altruism, our commonsense understanding of the concept, which has to do with motives and intentions. Nor is evolutionary altruism *necessary* for psychological altruism. Behavior is not determined solely by genes and evolution; environment, culture, and choice also play a role. Even if we found no examples of evolutionary altruism, psychological altruism would still be possible.

There is, furthermore, an irony in the relationship between biological and psychological altruism. The leading accounts of biological altruism present a dark side in terms of our usual understanding of unselfish behavior. Individuals who favor their genetic relatives, members of their own group, or others similar to them almost by definition lack these inclinations toward those who are not so related. Altruism, from this point of view, is relative, and correlates with the division between in-groups and out-groups. If our hope is for altruism to enlarge empathy for other human beings and lessen hostility or indifference, the biological account may disappoint, because it inevitably implies an "us" and a "them." Still, biology is only part of the story.

The lures of psychological egoism

Our question is whether people ever act altruistically, in the ordinary, psychological sense of that term. According to the view philosophers call psychological egoism, people never intentionally act to benefit others except to obtain some good for themselves.

---

[16] Okasha 2009.

A few words about the term "psychological egoism" to help avert misunderstanding. Psychological egoism is a descriptive thesis about what actually motivates behavior. By contrast, ethical egoism is the normative view that people *ought* only to act in their own self-interest. In what follows I shall be talking about psychological rather than ethical egoism; I will generally speak just of egoism.

Psychological egoism is a stronger view than might be supposed. It says that people never act to benefit others except to obtain some good for themselves. So understood, if you are suffering and I could relieve your suffering with no cost to myself, I wouldn't do it unless I expected to gain from helping you. On this view, we are completely indifferent to others' suffering except insofar as it affects us. A weaker view that might still be called egoism is this: people always choose to benefit themselves over others. On this understanding, although I would not incur even a slight cost to relieve your suffering, if I could relieve it with no cost I might do it. This view allows that even though people are essentially self-interested they are not necessarily completely indifferent to the suffering of others. The difference between the two views might seem trivial, given that benefiting others usually involves some cost to the agent. But it's not trivial, because (a) sometimes benefiting others does not involve any real cost to the agent; (b) the strong version of egoism expresses a harsher picture of human emotion and motivation than the weaker, and is, I believe, implausible; and (c) the weaker version opens the door to questions we want answers to if we reject egoism (as I argue in what follows we should). How much does it cost a person to relieve the suffering of others? And the follow-up normative question: how much cost is it reasonable to expect a person to incur?

So according to psychological egoism, altruistic behavior always has an ulterior motive. Altruism (that is, psychological rather than biological altruism) is the denial of egoism, so if ever in the history of the world one person acted intentionally to benefit another, but not as a means to his own well-being, egoism would be refuted. In this sense, altruism is a very weak doctrine: by itself it says nothing about the *extent* of selfless behavior; it asserts only that there is at least a little bit of it in the world. We have some ultimate (intrinsic, non-instrumental) interests in the well-being of other people.

Egoism possesses a powerful lure over our thinking. It has, I believe, two sources. One is logical, deriving from philosophical puzzles and difficulties encountered in thinking about these questions. The other is psychological: it rests on thinking about our own motives and intentions.

Consider first the psychological. One reason people feel pushed to deny the existence of altruism is that, looking inward, they doubt the purity of their own motives. We recognize that even when we appear to act altruistically, other reasons for our behavior can often be unearthed: the prospect of a future favor, the boost to our reputation, or simply the good feeling (or warm glow, as economists like to call it) that comes from appearing to act unselfishly. As Kant and Freud understood, people's true motives may be hidden, even (or perhaps especially) from themselves: even if we think we are acting solely to further another person's good, that might not be the real reason. Perhaps there is no single "real reason" – actions can have multiple motives. To decide whether an altruistic motive is dominant or decisive requires a counterfactual test: would you still have performed the action had you not benefited in some way? But even if the question is theoretically answerable, we are rarely if ever in a position to answer it.

So the lure of egoism as a theory of human action is partly explained by a certain wisdom, humility, or skepticism people have about their own or others' motives. We know that we are not as selfless as we would like to be or even as we might appear. But there is also a less flattering reason for our attraction to egoism: it provides a convenient excuse for selfish behavior. If "everybody is like that" – if everybody *must* be like that – we need not feel guilty about our own self-interested behavior or try to change it.[17]

But although these observations give us reason to be cautious in attributing altruistic motives to ourselves or others, they do not

---

[17] Sober and Wilson (1998, 273–4) make a related point, citing studies showing that economists, who tend to believe in psychological egoism, cooperate and help others less than noneconomists, and that this does not simply result from self-selection. For one such study see Frank, Gilovich, and Regan 1993, 159–71.

license the conclusion that no one ever acts altruistically. Generally, that inference is aided and abetted by consideration of some logical puzzles surrounding altruism and egoism.

One of egoism's traps is that it seems impossible to disprove. No matter how altruistic a person appears to be – take Wesley Autrey or Liviu Librescu or your favorite do-gooder as an example – it is possible to conceive of their motive in egoistic terms. If Autrey had ignored the man on the tracks, he would have suffered such guilt or remorse that risking his life was worth it to him to avoid that pain. The person who gives up a comfortable life to care for AIDS patients in a remote and hard place *does what she wants to do*, it seems, and therefore gets satisfaction from what appears to be self-sacrifice. So, it appears, altruism is simply self-interest of a subtle kind.

The impossibility of disproving egoism may sound like a virtue, but it's really a fatal drawback, as anyone who has studied a little philosophy of science knows. An empirical theory that purports to tell us something about the world – as egoism, which claims to describe the nature of human motivation, does – should be falsifiable. Not false, of course, but capable of being tested and thus proved false. If every state of affairs is compatible with egoism, then egoism does not tell us anything distinctive about how things are in the world.

Is egoism a genuine scientific theory about human motivation that is in principle falsifiable? It's not clear. In a series of sophisticated experiments, Daniel Batson and his colleagues tested the hypothesis that people always act egoistically. They considered three types of egoistic explanation, the most common being "the aversive-arousal reduction hypothesis." According to this theory, "becoming empathically aroused by witnessing someone in need is aversive and evokes motivation to reduce this aversive arousal."[18] In other words, observing others' suffering causes us pain, but we help others to relieve our distress, not theirs. The alternative explanation – that

---

[18] Batson 1991, 109. The other two theories are the "empathy-specific punishment" theory, according to which we help others to avoid experiencing social or self-censure; and the "empathy-specific reward" theory, which says that we help others in order to get certain social or self-rewards – generally, mood enhancements. To test each theory Batson and his colleagues carried out a number of experiments.

our motive in helping is ultimately to relieve the *other's* pain – Batson calls the "empathy-altruism hypothesis."

In one experiment, subjects view a videotape of a woman ("Elaine," a confederate of the experimenters) who they believe is receiving painful electric shocks. After witnessing two shocks, the subjects are told they can substitute for Elaine, receiving the shocks themselves. Subjects in the "easy-escape" treatment have been told at the beginning that they can quit the experiment after witnessing two shocks; those in the "difficult-escape" treatment are told they will have to watch Elaine endure ten shocks. Batson assumes that those who feel more empathy for others are more likely to help than those who feel less; the experimenters manipulate the degree of empathy subjects feel by leading them to believe they have a lot, or not very much, in common with her. (In other experiments empathy is manipulated by different means.)

According to Batson, both the egoistic and the altruistic hypotheses predict that low-empathy subjects will be likely to refuse to take Elaine's shocks when escape is easy. For high-empathy subjects, when escape is difficult "both hypotheses predict a relatively high rate [of helping] because helping is the best way to reach either goal" – reduction of the subject's distress (as the aversive-arousal hypothesis predicts) or reduction of Elaine's distress (as the altruistic hypothesis predicts).[19] The hypotheses differ only in their predictions about what high-empathy subjects will do when escape is easy: the egoistic view predicts they will choose to escape, thereby avoiding the aversive feelings produced by seeing Elaine receive shocks; the altruistic view predicts subjects will agree to take the shocks.

The results of this experiment confirm the altruistic hypothesis. But (not surprisingly) they do not conclusively disprove egoism. Perhaps high-empathy subjects realize they will experience guilt or unpleasant memories of the shock victim afterwards and choose not to escape for that reason. Batson and his colleagues devised an experiment to test this version of egoism as well.[20] Its results also disconfirm it. Still, other egoistic explanations can be found for the

[19] Batson 1991, 110.   [20] Batson 1991, 167–8.

results. The experiments tested a good number of them and found them wanting, and so we may be justified for the time being in assuming that egoism is false. As Sober and Wilson note, however, because sophisticated forms of egoism appeal to the internal rewards of helping others – rather than money, for example – it's always possible that a more subtle psychological reward lurks that the experiments have not detected.[21] Whether or to what extent we should be concerned about this possibility is a question to which I shall return.

Desire and the satisfaction of desire

Another logical puzzle that makes the debate between altruism and egoism hard to resolve has to do with ambiguity in the concepts of desire and the satisfaction of desire. If people possess altruistic motives, then they will sometimes act to benefit others without the prospect of benefit to themselves. In other words, they will choose the good of others ultimately or intrinsically or for its own sake – not simply as a means to their own satisfaction. We can suppose that Professor Librescu desired that his students, whose lives were in danger, not die; he acted accordingly to save them. Since his act was successful, his desire was satisfied. It does not follow, however, that *he* was satisfied – in fact, since he died he experienced no satisfaction. The fact that a person's desire is satisfied implies nothing about any effect on his mental state or well-being.

Nevertheless, when a person's desire is satisfied he normally experiences satisfaction. (Not always: a person may be perverse in the sense that the satisfaction of a desire brings no satisfaction to him.) In that case, the satisfaction of even an apparently altruistic desire will bring the agent some sense of well-being. We normally feel good when we do good. But it does not follow that we do good *only in order* to feel good. Indeed, it may seem that acting altruistically could succeed in making us feel good only if we already possessed an independent desire for the good of others.

---

[21] Sober and Wilson 1998, 273.

Bishop Joseph Butler made an argument of this kind in the eighteenth century, and it has been thought by many to refute egoism:

> That all particular appetites and passions are towards *external things themselves*, distinct from the *pleasure arising from them*, is manifested from hence, that there could not be this pleasure, were it not for that prior suitableness between the object and the passion: There could be no enjoyment or delight for one thing more than another, from eating food more than from swallowing a stone, if there were not an affection or appetite to one thing more than another.[22]

In our own time Thomas Nagel echoes this argument, focusing on pain rather than pleasure. Responding to the claim that what motivates altruistic behavior is the desire to avoid feeling guilty for acting selfishly, Nagel argues that guilt cannot explain altruism, "because guilt is precisely the pained recognition that one is acting or has acted contrary to a reason which the claims, rights, or interests of others provide – a reason which must therefore be antecedently acknowledged."[23]

Sober and Wilson believe this alleged refutation of egoism is fallacious. The problem, they argue, is with the major premise of Butler's argument: "When people experience pleasure, this is because they had a desire for some external thing, and that desire was satisfied."[24] The premise is false, they believe. Some sensations are intrinsically pleasurable (the smell of violets, the taste of sugar) and others intrinsically painful (headaches), and one need not have a desire – a cognitive attitude – to experience them as pleasurable or painful.

Sober and Wilson argue not only that the premise is not true but that it fails to license the conclusion that egoism is false. Butler, they say, confuses "two quite different items – the *pleasure* that results from a desire's being satisfied and the *desire for pleasure*."[25] If one

---

[22] Butler 1969, Sermon XI, para. 6 (emphasis in original).   [23] Nagel 1970, 80, n. 1.

[24] Sober and Wilson 1998, 278.

[25] Sober and Wilson 1998, 279. Sober and Wilson here speak of hedonism, probably the most common species of egoism. I think the point applies to other forms of egoism as well.

desires food and eats, the result will be pleasure. But if egoism is true, then the desire for pleasure could cause the desire for food. As Joshua May puts it, "Even if the *experience* of pleasure always presupposes a desire for the pleasurable object," it is possible that the desire for that object itself "is merely instrumental to a *desire* for pleasure."[26] If egoism is correct, the desire for pleasure is the only ultimate desire.

I myself am not certain whether these points dispose of Butler's supposed refutation of egoism. I will not pursue that question here, because Sober and Wilson's arguments strike me as less significant than they look. Butler may well not have *refuted* egoism; in fact, it's difficult to imagine refuting in one fell swoop a theory with such a powerful hold on so many people's imaginations, and if we thought that's what Butler did we should think again. What Butler did show, however, is that egoism is not *inescapable*. And it's the apparent inescapability of the egoist's conclusion – from the premise that satisfying even apparently altruistic desires normally produces pleasure in the agent to the inference that all we ever want is pleasure for ourselves – that has exerted the vice-like grip on so many people, causing them to embrace egoism. To untie the link between these two propositions is enough for our purposes.

Egoism and altruism on the ground

Suppose that psychological egoism is in fact a nonempty, empirical theory that has not been conclusively shown to be false; or suppose for a moment even that it is true. What difference would that fact make to our attitudes toward living human beings and to our practices in the real world – to our moral judgments and the way we raise and teach our children, for example?

I believe it would make no difference at all. The reason is precisely analogous (or perhaps even identical, as I shall explain shortly) to P.F. Strawson's reasons for thinking the age-old philosophical debate about determinism and free will is irrelevant to our interpersonal

---

[26] May 2011, section entitled "Butler's Stone: Presupposition & By-Products" (emphasis in original).

relationships and to our moral practices of judging, praising, blaming, and more generally responding humanly to other people. Strawson's central idea is that we human beings could not have the interpersonal relationships we do have in the absence of the "reactive attitudes," which respond "to the quality of others' wills towards us, as manifested in their behaviour: to their good or ill will or indifference or lack of concern."[27] Speaking of determinism, Strawson argues:

> The human commitment to participation in ordinary inter-personal relationships is, I think, too thoroughgoing and deeply rooted for us to take seriously the thought that a general theoretical conviction might so change our world that, in it, there were no longer any such things as inter-personal relationships as we normally understand them; and being involved in inter-personal relationships as we normally understand them precisely is being exposed to the range of reactive attitudes and feelings that is in question.[28]

Strawson's idea has exerted a powerful influence in contemporary philosophy, but as far as I know no one has noted its relevance to the debate about egoism and altruism, where I believe it applies just as it does to determinism and free will. Since psychological egoism claims that *ultimately* (an important word in these discussions) human beings have no good will toward others, that they lack concern for others, the doctrine cannot make a difference to the way we think about our relationships with other people and how we lead our lives.[29]

---

[27] Strawson 1962, sec. 5.   [28] Strawson 1962, sec. 4.

[29] In fact, the core idea goes back to Hume, who in the Appendix on Self-Love in *An Enquiry Concerning the Principles of Morals* asserts: "I esteem the man, whose self-love, by whatever means, is so directed as to give him a concern for others, and render him serviceable to society: As I hate or despise him, who has no regard to any thing beyond his own gratifications and enjoyments. In vain would you suggest, that these characters, though seemingly opposite, are, at bottom, the same, and that a very inconsiderable turn of thought forms the whole difference between them . . . And I find not in this, more than in other subjects, that the natural sentiments, arising from the general appearances of things, are easily destroyed by subtle reflections concerning the minute origin of these appearances. Does not the lively, cheerful colour of a countenance inspire me with complacency and pleasure;

It can plausibly be argued that psychological egoism, conceived as the view that the desire for pleasure causes all human action, just *is* a particular manifestation of determinism. But the Strawsonian point clearly applies whether or not this is so. It is impossible to imagine "ordinary interpersonal relationships" in the absence of reactive attitudes about other people's "indifference" to or "lack of concern" for others. Such attitudes are for all practical purposes equivalent to judgments about the extent to which people are ultimately moved only to benefit themselves, or whether their motives include non-instrumental concern for the well-being of others. We commonly praise and criticize both people's particular actions, and their characters more generally, in terms of such assessments; indeed, it's hard to think of traits more commonly noticed or valued than "the quality of others' wills toward us," their relative concern or self-absorption.

Perhaps the theoretical debate is important and there are good reasons to care about it. But it cannot have any effect on our day-to-day attitudes and practices. If we believe that actions directed at benefiting others are morally or socially valuable, we will want to encourage them; we will think those inclined to behave altruistically are morally praiseworthy and those who ignore the interests of others are morally criticizable.[30]

But how, it might be asked, given the difficulties of detecting people's true motives, *do* we distinguish egoistically from altruistically motivated behavior? Indeed, in light of the foregoing discussion of Batson's experiments, what do we mean by "true" motives if not those deep ones that even sophisticated experiments cannot detect?

even though I learn from philosophy that all difference of complexion arises from the most minute differences of thickness, in the most minute parts of the skin . . .?" (Hume 1998, Appendix II, para. 4). Thanks to Andreas Schmidt for directing me to this passage.

[30] I do not mean to imply that self-interested motives are always morally problematic – surely they are not – or to deny that altruistic motivations can sometimes reflect troubling qualities. Jean Hampton argues that altruism can reflect lack of self-respect (1993). For the view that heroic deeds (such as those performed by people who rescued victims of the Nazis) can involve imposing unjustified risk on others (such as the rescuers' families), or involve a lack of moral perspective and understanding, see Galston 1993.

We may feel inclined to answer as Justice Potter Stewart did when asked how he knew what pornography was: we know it when we see it.[31] And often we do; I surmise that within a group of friends or acquaintances we would find fairly wide agreement about who among them is at the self-interested and who at the other-directed end of the spectrum.

But this response takes us only so far, because of course we don't always know egoism (or altruism) when we see it. Any single bit of behavior can plausibly be explained by a variety of motives, some more egoistic than others and others not egoistic at all. And most people have been fooled some of the time by behavior they thought was caring when it was self-interested (and perhaps sometimes the other way round).

Harry meets James at a party, and the two soon become friends. Shortly thereafter, James, who lives alone, becomes ill. Harry goes out of his way to be solicitous of James's welfare, running errands for him and generally making his life easier. James's family runs a business, and Harry needs a job. Eventually Harry is hired by the family company.

This skeletal story is compatible with a variety of interpretations about Harry's motives. Did Harry befriend James with an eye to getting the job? Did the need for a job influence his behavior when James got sick? Or was Harry's getting hired an event (perhaps partly a consequence of James's gratitude to Harry) that Harry neither considered nor worked to bring about? It is impossible to answer these questions from the few facts provided. But that doesn't mean that knowledge of what drives Harry is necessarily unattainable. To find out we would need to know more about what Harry knew and when he knew it. And we would want to see how Harry behaves over the long term, as well as how he acts toward other people and in other contexts. Of course, even apparently other-directed behavior over the long term toward James and his family would not be decisive if Harry's employment security depended on his remaining in their good graces.

[31] *Jacobellis v. Ohio* 1964.

If from the very beginning, or even from the time James became ill, Harry calculated to land the job, we would think him selfish, and also devious. (Since openly self-interested behavior is often self-defeating, deviousness goes with the territory.) We can imagine information that would confirm this hypothesis; just as criminals leave evidence of their deeds, so do more minor moral miscreants, and others are often good at detecting the signs. But knowledge of someone's motives, and even our own, can be difficult to come by.

Treating someone well (as if altruistically) with the aim of getting a job is a paradigm of egoistic behavior, which is marked by both the goal of material gain and the use of explicit calculation. Consider first material gain. Why is treating others well for this purpose widely frowned upon? It can't be simply that material advancement is thought to be a crass goal, since in American society, for one, it is perfectly (and perhaps all too) respectable. One reason may be that, especially in conjunction with conscious calculation (which only the agent herself may have knowledge of), the explicitly instrumental and self-interested character of the motive is too transparent for our taste, raised as most of us are to value other-directed action. Material gain is fine, but using someone so crassly to achieve it is not. Perhaps more important, a person whose motives are purely material cannot be trusted if those incentives disappear.

Consider a different motive. Suppose Harry helps James from the thought that he might someday need James's help. This motive might be less plausible as I have described the example but makes sense of common varieties of neighborliness. You agree to water your neighbor's plants when he is away, thinking somewhere in the back of your mind (or even in the front) that he may feed your cat when you take off for the weekend. This is not, of course, the Golden Rule – "Do unto others as you would have them do unto you" – but rather "Do unto others so that they may be more likely to do unto you." Although in theory the distinction seems sharp, in practice it is less so: people may often act on the latter maxim even if they appear (to others or themselves) to be acting on the former, or they may act from both at once. In this sense reciprocal altruism, one of the evolutionary accounts I rejected as true altruism earlier in this chapter, no doubt plays a prominent role whether we are aware of it or not.

Do we typically disapprove of such motives? Not, I believe, in the way we disapprove of helping others with an eye toward direct material gain. Why not? One reason, perhaps, is that it is less nakedly self-serving – after all, the decision to help is based only on a probabilistic estimate that one *might* need benefits reciprocated in the future. Another is that this motive may be confused or conjoined, in the mind of either agent or beneficiary, with the more purely altruistic Golden Rule justification. In fact, I believe that such mixed motives are common. Of course, if we found evidence showing that Harry helped only because he foresaw his own future need, that would influence our judgment of the kind of person he is.

Finally, suppose Harry helps James because it makes him feel good to help. He might get the "warm glow" because James and others approve of and like him for what he does. The glow would then result from "reputational effects," as economists call them, which might lead to future benefits for Harry.[32] If in helping Harry had in mind some specific benefit, his motive would be explicitly self-serving and materialistic in the way described above, and we would, if we knew, accordingly downgrade our opinion of the moral worth of his actions. If his behavior were not calculating in this way, there are still a variety of possibilities. Harry might simply

---

[32] In "dictator experiments" carried out by psychologists and economists (described briefly at the end of Chapter 6), a subject is given money to divide however he chooses between himself and another purported subject. The experimenters vary the amount of "social distance" – i.e., anonymity – between the subject and others (including the experimenters), hypothesizing that the greater the social distance the less likely that the subject will share the money. With less social distance, the prospect of reciprocal benefits as well as reputational effects for the subject could motivate him to share (see, e.g., Hoffman, McCabe, and Smith 1996). In general, the experiments confirm the hypothesis that greater anonymity correlates with less sharing. But even in double-blind treatments with full anonymity, some subjects give the other "a considerable amount of money." The authors acknowledge that this behavior could reflect true other-regarding preferences, although they note that the subjects "may be suspicious of our procedures to guarantee anonymity" (ibid., 658).

enjoy being liked; since helping (we are assuming) makes him popular, he tends to continue in this vein. But nice guys don't always finish first, and Harry's behavior might not increase his popularity. Perhaps helping others makes him feel good anyway; because of his upbringing, for example, he is content knowing he has done the right thing whether or not other benefits follow. He is wired to feel good when he does good.

In the examples of this paragraph we see what I believe most people would agree are increasingly praiseworthy motives. And yet it may seem we have come back to where we left off in examining Batson's experiments and the paradox of desire and the satisfaction of desire. Leaving aside that it is usually difficult or even impossible to know others' motives, haven't I simply reopened the can of worms I was trying to close – the possibility that all motives are in the end self-interested?

Good people

The answer is no, not in the sense that matters for our purposes – the purposes and forms of life of which Strawson reminds us. What differentiates these examples most importantly is the degree to which the agent explicitly calculates to achieve a self-interested end. To the extent that the agent thinks to herself "I am helping the other in order to benefit myself (in this or that way)," to that extent we locate her behavior and motives at the self-interested end of the spectrum. Now of course if psychological egoism is right, all of us are always acting only to benefit ourselves. But it would be absurd to think that we are always *explicitly calculating* for our own benefit.[33] Does this mean that what we call altruism is merely self-deception (and the deception of others) – behavior that, while not characterized by explicit calculation, is nevertheless motivated deep down, beyond our powers to perceive, by the desire to benefit oneself?

---

[33] See Sober and Wilson 1998, ch. 10. I take it that Sober and Wilson's arguments for the inefficiency of purely egoistic motivations from an evolutionary standpoint would include the inefficiency of constant calculation.

One reason to think the answer is no brings us back to Butler's argument: just because making others happy makes me happy does not mean I make others happy only in order to make myself happy, and without an independent desire for others' happiness my own would not follow as a consequence. Although as we saw earlier Sober and Wilson think the case has not been made for an independent desire for others' well-being, the case has not been made against it either, as I have argued. And without further evidence for egoism, it's only an unshakable faith in its truth that would lead us to doubt the existence of such desires.

Still, it cannot be denied that in many people who act altruistically there is a close connection between their own subjectively experienced good and the good of others. And is there anything wrong with that? It's probably the commonsense view that this state of affairs is just as it ought to be. And the view has a distinguished pedigree going back to Aristotle. Asserting that "virtue of character is concerned with pleasures and pains," Aristotle explains:

> For it is pleasure that causes us to do base actions, and pain that causes us to abstain from fine ones. Hence we need to have had the appropriate upbringing – right from early youth, as Plato says – to make us find enjoyment or pain in the right things; for this is the correct education.[34]

The sorts of altruistically inclined people we admire tend to take pleasure in the well-being of others and in furthering it. Parents' typical feelings for their children represent the paradigm of this kind of "wiring" linking the good of the agent to the good of the beneficiary, and to some extent can serve as a model. Of course, it's rare to find the good of agent and beneficiary so closely tied as in the case of parents and children. In fact, the link there is so close we may wonder whether it is best described as altruism, insofar as the parent's concern for the child's welfare verges on identification. (In the extreme case – well, not *that* extreme – we find parents "living through" their children and getting ego-gratification from their accomplishments.) It would in any case be unrealistic to hold the

---

[34] Aristotle 1985, bk. ii, ch. 3.

parent–child model as one onto which we can graft, wholesale, less personal other-directed actions and relationships. It might even be incoherent or objectionable, insofar as agents will always have to choose among possible beneficiaries, with choices inevitably reflecting different degrees of identification and sympathy. It is impossible to identify with all people equally, and in general it also seems troubling for a person to act more generously to perfect strangers than to his own children.[35]

Yet while many endorse the Aristotelian ideal of the good person as one who has the right desires, this view is not uncontroversial.[36] On one Kantian-inspired picture mentioned earlier in this chapter, moral virtue requires acting from duty, not desire. As Kant strikingly puts it, there are "many persons so sympathetically constituted that without any motive of vanity or selfishness they find an inner satisfaction in spreading joy and rejoice in the contentment of others." But, Kant insists, "that kind of action has no true moral worth." If, by contrast, "nature has put little sympathy into the heart of a man, and if he, though an honest man, is by temperament cold and indifferent to the sufferings of others," but nevertheless "tear[s] himself, unsolicited by inclination, out of his dead insensibility" to benefit others, only then does his action have genuine moral worth.[37]

Evaluating the relative merits of the Aristotelian and this Kantian model of the good person would require an extended discussion (in which many able philosophers have already engaged) that is beyond

---

[35] See, e.g., Galston's criticism that rescuers of victims of the Nazis sometimes put their own families at risk (1993, 131). And there's Charles Dickens's portrait in *Bleak House* of Mrs. Jellyby, who devotes her life to good works in Africa but neglects her own children (1996, ch. 4, "Telescopic Philanthropy").

[36] People will disagree, of course, about what the *right* desires are, with some assuming or arguing for a more other-directed set than others (including Aristotle). I assume that a strong dose of other-directed desires is desirable, but nothing in the argument hangs on this assumption.

[37] Kant 1997, Ak. 4, 398. Kant's reason for objecting to sympathetically motivated behavior is not, I think, that it is self-interested but rather that it is not governed by commitment to the moral law. Nevertheless, the contrast between Kant's view and the desire-based view makes it important to compare the two approaches.

the scope of this work, and I shall make only two points that bear on my purposes here. One is that the commonsense view expressing our inescapable Strawsonian reactive attitudes surely relies in large part on judgments about whether people desire and take satisfaction in the good of others. To that extent Aristotle guides common sense more than Kant. Perhaps one reason – not that this need be consciously expressed or even recognized – is that the Kantian requirement (if that is what it is) is just too demanding to serve as the basis for reasonable expectations of ordinary human beings. Another is that it seems to elevate coldness over compassion.

The other point is that this view of Kant's position may be a caricature; whatever Kant himself believed, a more nuanced picture can be constructed out of Kantian elements. Marcia Baron argues forcefully that in fact a person ought always to act from duty, but that doing so does not involve the objectionable features often attributed to Kant and does not rule out acting from the sorts of desires we have been discussing. Her argument rests on two main ideas. One is the distinction between primary and secondary motives. "A primary motive supplies the agent with the motivation to do the act in question, whereas a secondary motive provides limiting conditions on what may be done from other motives."[38] In other words, a secondary motive does not actually move a person to act but serves as a constraint: the agent would not act without its "approval." So, for example, it is permissible to help your friend out of a desire for her welfare, rather than from the belief that it is your duty to help; but if helping requires engaging in shady dealings – a violation of duty – you should not do it. This seems exactly right.

The second idea is that it is not necessary to think about the rightness of your action – whether you have a duty to do it or refrain from doing it – while acting or just before acting. What *is* necessary is that you sometimes think about rightness, and that it always governs your behavior. Just as while driving you need not explicitly think

---

[38] Baron 1984, 207. See also Baron 1995, ch. 4, for these arguments. Baron's main targets are Michael Stocker (1976), and Bernard Williams (1981).

about applying the brakes every time you do apply them, you need not explicitly think about doing your duty every time you do it.[39]

Baron agrees with Kant, then, that you should always act from duty. But, departing from the Kantian stereotype, she argues that this is compatible with desire for another's good as your primary motive and with not having duty uppermost in mind every time you act. In this way, acting from duty is compatible with our commonsense, "Aristotelian" understanding of altruistic behavior.

The probability of altruism

I have been arguing that in the only sense that matters practically, egoism is false and there is some altruism in the world. But this is compatible with a very wide range of possibilities. Altruism as I understand it is the view that some people sometimes act to benefit others without the prospect of gain for themselves. But how altruistic are people? To what extent are they willing to bear significant costs for the good of others? Stated in this way the question is absurd; there is no general answer about "people." People vary greatly in their generosity, kindness, and concern for others. And any particular person may be more or less generous at different times and will treat some people more generously than others.

We may take it as obvious – although proponents of the virtue of selfishness would disagree – that it would be better if there were more altruistically motivated people and actions in the world and that we should do what we can to increase their incidence. I shall not consider here how best to achieve this goal except to say, in keeping with the arguments made earlier, that the kind of altruism we ought to encourage, and probably the only kind with staying power, tends to be satisfying to those who practice it. More strongly, altruists tend to be invested in what they do in a way that ties their conduct to their identity and self-image. Studies of rescuers – people at the far end of the altruism spectrum, like those who at great personal risk saved

---

[39] Baron 1984, 208. The analogy Baron makes with driving comes from an unpublished paper by W.D. Falk, "Morality: Form and Content."

people from the Nazis – show that they tend not to believe their behavior is extraordinary; they feel that they have to do what they do, because it's part of who they are. Neera Badhwar argues convincingly that such people would suffer had they not performed these heroic acts; they would feel they were betraying their moral selves. In carrying out their actions, "they actualized their values, the values they endorsed and with which they were most deeply identified ... They satisfied a fundamental human interest, the interest in shaping the world in light of one's values and affirming one's identity."[40] The story of Paul Farmer, the American doctor who co-founded Partners in Health and has dedicated his life to curing infectious diseases in developing countries while seeming to live exactly the life he enjoys, comes to mind.[41] More important – given the rarity of such people and the sense that their potential as models for most of us is limited – I believe the same holds for less extraordinary agents, who nevertheless often strongly identify with, and are willing to make sacrifices for, a cause outside themselves such as the environment or the well-being of poor or otherwise disadvantaged people. Those engaged in such causes believe they ought to do what they do, but they also want to, because their acts affirm the kind of people they are and want to be and the kind of world they want to exist.

So insofar as other-directed action becomes part of a person's identity and self-image, it can be a reliable motive. Skeptics may believe that nonaltruistic motives are nevertheless more reliable as predictors of behavior, so that if we want people to benefit others – in particular, those with whom they have no special connection – we had better arrange the world so as to make it in their interest.

This skeptical challenge reminds us of the durability of a certain narrow conception of self-interest, despite the thinness of its

---

[40] Badhwar 1993, 98, 106–7. Badhwar discusses several extended studies of rescuers, including the work of Kristen Renwick Monroe, which culminated in her book *The Heart of Altruism* (1996), and of Samuel P. Oliner and Pearl M. Oliner, *The Altruistic Personality: Rescuers of Jews in Nazi Europe* (1988). Badhwar defends the strong claim that altruism "achieves its highest moral worth only by virtue of its connection with self-interest" (1993, 115–16).

[41] For Farmer's story see Kidder 2003.

supporting arguments. One view is that people are motivated by money and material benefits alone. Some economists seem committed to this picture, despite its implausibility. Surely this is not self-interest rightly understood, in Tocqueville's famous phrase.[42] When economists seem to enlarge the basket of purposes that may move people by adding "reputational effects," the question remains why people care about reputation. Is it because they have an ultimate desire to be liked or loved or respected, or only because these states tend to lead to further material benefits? Let's assume the first plays a part – that being liked, loved, and respected (which, of course, are not equivalent) are states many people want for their own sake. (It's just not plausible that all anyone wants is material goods.) Perhaps we can draw a line around these goods (material benefits, affection, respect) and a few others and take them to comprise self-interest in something like the traditional sense. Then we can think of ultimate desires to benefit others as altruistic, even though, for reasons we have seen, these desires often coincide with or lead to good feelings on the part of the agent and thus enhance her own well-being, thereby showing that the distinction between altruism and self-interest is shifting and unstable.

We should try to enhance and multiply people's altruistic motives. But we should also be aware of altruism's likely limits. Sensitivity to those limits underlies part of the motivation of this book, and explains

---

[42] "How the Americans Combat Individualism by the Principle of Self-Interest Rightly Understood": "The Americans ... are fond of explaining almost all the actions of their lives by the principle of self-interest rightly understood; they show with complacency how an enlightened regard for themselves constantly prompts them to assist one another and inclines them willingly to sacrifice a portion of their time and property to the welfare of the state. In this respect I think they frequently fail to do themselves justice, for in the United States as well as elsewhere people are sometimes seen to give way to those disinterested and spontaneous impulses that are natural to man; but the Americans seldom admit that they yield to emotions of this kind; they are more anxious to do honor to their philosophy than to themselves." Tocqueville adds that if the principle of self-interest rightly understood "were to sway the whole moral world, extraordinary virtues would doubtless be more rare; but I think that gross depravity would then also be less common" (Tocqueville 1945, vol. II, sec. II, ch. VII).

why in Chapter 6 I examined the legitimate self-regarding reasons people may have to acquire and consume things. In the next chapter I look at some ways we can capitalize on those reasons to benefit others. The ills of the world are sufficiently many and bad to justify employing whatever legitimate tools we can to eradicate them, so we should take advantage of, and perhaps not scrutinize too closely, the mix of motives that underlie human behavior when different elements of the mix can each promote the goals we have reason to advance.[43]

---

[43] Sober and Wilson defend "motivational pluralism," the view that people have both egoistic and altruistic ultimate desires, arguing that a single action may proceed from both motives (1998, 308). They attempt to show how having altruistic desires or motives could be evolutionarily advantageous, a suggestion made by Darwin. Evolutionary theory predicts that people have desires that enhance their reproductive fitness (or that at least enhanced their ancestors' reproductive fitness – like the desire for sugar and fat). The desire to take care of one's children fits this description. If human beings are egoists, then they are wired to feel good when they care for their children, and ultimately that's why they do it. If, on the other hand, parents have altruistic desires for their children's welfare, then they will be directly motivated to act, without consideration of their own well-being. Altruism is a more reliable and efficient mechanism for parental care, Sober and Wilson argue, because egoism requires a further step: the belief that helping one's children will benefit oneself. Having both altruistic and egoistic motives would further increase humans' reproductive fitness.

CHAPTER 10

Conclusion: morality for mere mortals

Most people no doubt agree that it's a very bad thing for people to live in dire poverty, and so they are disturbed, if and when they realize it, to learn that more than a billion people in the world do. What moral claims, if any, does this situation make on the world's comfortable people? It can be disagreeable to think about this question, since if you answer it by doing little you may feel guilty, and if you answer it by doing a lot you may find yourself deprived of many things you thought you wanted, needed, or were entitled to.

Despite the unease this question can produce, over the last forty years moral philosophers have thought a great deal about it. They deserve credit for daring to put an uncomfortable subject on the table. I would not have written this book had it not been for the path they have trod. Yet over the years I have become dissatisfied with the standard philosophical approaches. Their conclusions are too either/ or: either we ought to give up a great deal to alleviate global poverty, or our moral responsibilities are quite limited. I have wanted to square the circle, you might say: to admit that global poverty is a great evil that demands action on the part of the world's comfortable people, while also agreeing that morality cannot reasonably require a great deal of ordinary human beings on a regular basis. This book is my attempt to show how we might reconcile these apparently inconsistent propositions.

Summary

The claim that extreme poverty is a great evil requires little in the way of support. Perhaps a few think it improves poor people's souls, or that they deserve it; I do not take these views seriously. In Chapter 2 I described the many reasons one might have for holding that dire poverty makes moral demands on those who are in a position to remedy it: prior agreements, harm, exploitation, joint membership in a community, and pure humanitarianism. Although these reasons have varying weights and force, together they add up to a powerful case that something ought to be done. The humanitarian argument alone is very strong.

But how much, and what, ought a person to do? In Chapters 3 and 5 I may appear to be pedaling backwards by showing how philosophers who defend very strenuous moral demands on the comfortable have been led astray. There I argue that the concepts of duty and obligation – so central in contemporary moral philosophy – are not very helpful in describing or fixing our responsibilities in this realm. That's in part because of their yes/no, on/off character, suggesting a bright line where none is available. A bright line is not available, I argued, in part because the monistic theories characteristic of contemporary philosophy – utilitarianism, Kantian deontology, virtue ethics – are not convincing as complete accounts of morality. Even a pluralistic view that incorporates all these approaches falls short in establishing sharply delineated duties to benefit others except in very special circumstances. Although moral intuitions and common sense are not the last word in establishing people's moral responsibilities – and can in fact be notoriously unreliable – we cannot do without them because moral theory seems to leave the "right answers" indeterminate for many of the problems we most urgently need to resolve.

Some who are skeptical of my skepticism about moral theory might argue that we *do* have clear views about what's obligatory, offering as examples the prohibitions against murder, rape, and theft. That idea corresponds to a widespread and deeply entrenched sense that there is a distinction between "negative" duties not to harm and "positive" duties to aid. On this way of thinking, insofar as the responsibility to alleviate global poverty is a positive duty, perhaps rooted in humanitarianism, it is at best "imperfect," unlike the duties not to kill and steal, and inevitably weaker.

In Chapter 4 I challenged the viability of the distinction between negative and positive duties on a variety of grounds. One implication is that, in the contemporary world, individuals in rich countries contribute to harm in innumerable ways. Of course, it is hardly original to claim that the rich have harmed people in poor countries. (I discuss and accept this view, with some qualifications, in Chapter 2.) The relevant point here is rather that – extreme cases like killing and physical violence aside – the idea that negative duties are strict and exceptionless while positive duties are loose and imperfect does not withstand scrutiny. Disproportionate energy consumption, leading to pollution and climate change, is the most obvious example. Do we as individuals have a duty to stop – to turn down the thermostat or drive less? If so, what are the boundaries of such duties? The answers concerning these "negative" duties are no more clear than in the case of "positive" duties to aid others.

This is not to say we have no responsibilities in such cases. My point is rather that talking in terms of individual duties is not illuminating. It's both duty-talk, for reasons just mentioned, and the focus on individuals that lead us astray. We need to think in collective rather than individual terms. One reason is that to the extent that people can alleviate global poverty – whether by doing what they are presently not doing or by not doing what they are presently doing – they can act more effectively collectively than as isolated individuals. That's obvious. Another reason is less obvious: acting together with others makes many fewer demands on individuals mentally and materially. For a variety of reasons having to do with infrastructure, habituation, psychological salience, and status concerns (often perfectly justified and respectable), we do and feel what others around us do and feel, and our level of well-being and deprivation depends largely on what others around us have. This fact – a significant part of which amounts to the centrality of relative deprivation, a subject neglected by contemporary philosophers – is one of my central theses, argued at length in Chapter 6. It explains how we might radically reduce global poverty without making the kinds of onerous demands on ordinary mortals that achieving such progress might seem to call for.

Chapters 7, 8, and 9 take up objections and complications with the argument as so far set out. Chapter 7 continues the line of thinking of the previous chapter, asking why, if relative deprivation is central, we should be so concerned about global poverty rather than poverty within our own societies. The answer is that despite the importance of relative deprivation and inequality within societies, there is an absolute level of existence below which no one should be allowed to fall, so ignoring the poorest of the global poor is unacceptable. Nonetheless, recognizing the significance of relative deprivation raises difficult issues of comparison and might require painful trade-offs between the poor in developed and developing societies.

A question looming like a dark cloud over the entire project I have undertaken in this book concerns the possibility and desirability of people, governments, or institutions in rich countries alleviating poverty from without. Criticisms run the gamut: those who give aid are condescending and colonialist; those who receive it become dependent or shiftless; givers always have their own interests at heart; aid never achieves its desired goals and more often than not is counterproductive. We have seen that these criticisms are sometimes justified but sometimes not. In part, they depend on unfortunate ambiguities in terms like "aid" and "assistance," which I have analyzed in Chapters 1 and 8. In assessing the criticisms of aid, I have tried to sort the wheat from the chaff. The one-sentence answer is that some kinds of aid are good and work and others are bad and do not. More specifics can be found in Chapter 8 and below.

Finally, since this is a book in and about ethics, it seems important to dispel a common concern that might lurk in the minds of some readers: that the "moral" thing to do depends largely on a person's motive, so the idea of trying to make it easier for people to do the right thing is exactly wrong. I tackle this criticism in Chapter 9. At the same time, I certainly do not wish to repudiate – and in fact hope to encourage – behavior motivated by concern about others. I have argued that there is no reason to believe that the approach taken here will depress the standards of decent conduct or obliterate the possibility of praise-worthy behavior and virtue, and also that in the real world motives are not easily sorted into altruistic and self-interested piles.

In the remainder of this chapter I consider some practical implications of these arguments, mentioning along the way some promising approaches to ending the direst conditions of global poverty.

Encouraging collective action

Thinking about how to make it easier for people to act in ways that would reduce global poverty requires paying attention to what we know and are continually learning about the "springs of human action," to put it in the terms employed by eighteenth-century philosophers like David Hume and Jeremy Bentham (who were also the psychologists of their day). How can we increase the probability of constructive behavior? Some contemporary research by psychologists and behavioral economists concerns efforts to get people to act more prudently – to eat more healthily or save more for their old age, for example.[1] But such findings are often generalizable: they can help us to understand how people can advance not only their own interests but also the interests of others.

Probably the single most important theme of this book concerns the effects of others on a person's behavior, and especially the extent to which people do what others around them do – and have good reason to. Here I spell out several aspects of this theme and approaches suggested by it.

Support and promote good policies. An obvious corollary is to support and promote appropriate legislation and social policies, for these ensure and sometimes enforce collective action. Consider climate change. There are many reasons why people should want to abate climate change, for themselves and for the sake of their descendants, but one of the most important is that it harms the poor in poor countries more than anyone else. The effects of isolated individual efforts to reduce energy consumption are so tiny that they are likely to dampen individuals' motivation to perform them. But equally important is that the costs to individuals decline if they act together rather than alone. A general policy to produce smaller, more

---

[1] For examples see Rosenberg 2011; Thaler and Sunstein 2008; Shafir 2013.

fuel-efficient cars may lower their price. Drivers of small cars risk less injury and death if behemoth vehicles do not dominate the road. Roads themselves last longer when lighter vehicles drive on them. Social policies and publicity promoting them can reduce the status value of environmentally offending cars.

In theory, engaging in political action, lobbying leaders and the electorate, and supporting appropriate legislation could consume a lot of a person's time and energy. What Oscar Wilde is supposed to have said about socialism applies: the problem with political action is that it takes too many evenings. If so, this recommendation might seem ensnared in the "demandingness problem" I have been laboring to escape. On the other side, some might think the suggestion to support collective solutions asks too *little* of people rather than too much.

As should be clear by now, I do not think there is a straightforward answer to the question "Just how much is a person morally responsible for doing?" It's generally true that the more one can do the better. But these sorts of political efforts do not require the same kind of will-power and "virtue" that Singerian commitments to part with large chunks of one's salary and material possessions do. For most people, contributions to political causes, willingness to sign letters and petitions (almost effortless now, with the Internet), and occasional participation in political events do not demand a great deal – and of course can bring their own satisfactions. Most of us can push ourselves to work a little harder on this front without sacrificing much.

Consider the company you keep. This is not to deny that giving more of your income or wealth to organizations that responsibly promote poverty alleviation is generally a good thing. Of course, we can simply encourage or exhort each other to do that. But there are other effective approaches. Because it's easier to act when others around us do too, we should take care to consider the company we keep. What neighborhood should you move to? Which church, synagogue, or mosque should you join? Such decisions can have important consequences for your lifestyle and consumption habits. As we saw in Chapter 6, people are deeply influenced by what sociologists call their reference group. If you (and, equally, your children) hang around with others who think about nothing but clothes and gadgets and house renovations, you will find it very difficult to resist becoming preoccupied with these things too. If you live around people who are less focused on material things, that will almost inevitably affect your own inclinations.

This is not to say that you should drop your current friends. Dropping friends (unless they are genuinely not friendworthy) is itself morally problematic. Again, different observers will judge these sorts of actions (or omissions) differently – some will be more forgiving of what they will call "human nature," while others will condemn those who take the easier path. But not all options present such hard choices, and there is no question that heightened awareness of the significance of the company we choose to keep can make a difference to our consumption habits.

The respect of one's peers. In Chapter 6 I explored a variety of reasons why people do what others do. You need a car when most others around you drive cars, thereby weakening the public transportation system ("infrastructure effects"). You want shiny toys because you see them around you and they're pretty ("salience"). You feel cramped in a two-bedroom apartment because you've always lived in a big house ("habituation"). Another central reason for doing what others do concerns status. Indeed, many people wrongly think *only* of status-seeking when asked why we do as others do. Such people usually disapprove of status-seeking (even if they share the tendency). In Chapter 6 I discussed at some length why, as Adam Smith so beautifully explained, being concerned about status should not always be condemned: self-respect requires that we have certain things that others around us have. But status considerations can play an even broader role when we think about how to change behavior.

Tina Rosenberg describes how such considerations can figure at the "demand side," not just at the "supply side" – among the poor as well as those who might benefit them. The microcredit approach pioneered by Muhammad Yunus (and for which he won the Nobel Peace Prize in 2006) involves lending very small sums of money to very poor people. In the 1970s Yunus found that ordinary banks would not lend them even small amounts of money; the repayment rate was too low. The Grameen Bank, which he founded in 1983, formed its borrowers – poor women – into groups of five. The whole group had to approve every loan, "and members could only get new loans if their fellow borrowers were current on their repayments . . . Effectively, the whole group would be held hostage to one delinquent player."[2] Grameen officials eventually concluded that "it was not the threat to the group that made the women repay their loans on time – it was the simple desire to protect their reputations."[3] People have reason to do what others do, but they also have reason to care about what others think of them. We can sometimes turn this concern to social advantage – whether among the poor or those who might act to diminish poverty.[4]

Respect and self-respect. In Yunus's microcredit model, a member is motivated to repay her share of a loan because others know what she is doing or failing to do. But public knowledge is not always necessary to motivate behavior. In two large experiments, an energy company periodically sent customers reports about how their energy use compared with that of neighbors who had similarly sized houses. Households that received the reports made "significant and lasting reductions in their energy consumption."[5] In this case the information given to the subjects of the experiment was not public, so any effect it had on their behavior was not motivated by reputational concerns. The subjects internalized the message of others' lower

---

[2] Rosenberg 2011, 128.   [3] 2011, 129.

[4] Do people care about what others think of them only for instrumental reasons? This is the sort of question philosophers like to ask. It means: if a person had nothing to gain from other people's good opinion of her, would she still want to protect her reputation? But the question hardly makes sense. In the real world it's hard to imagine that one could rule out the possibility of benefiting from other people's good opinion, especially when we consider the range of possible benefits, material and immaterial.

[5] Ayres, Raseman, and Shih 2009, 3. An earlier study (Fischer 2008) failed to find such reductions, and explained this in terms of a "boomerang effect": a person who had thought her neighbors were using *less* energy than they really were would increase her own use on learning of others' behavior. The effect was neutralized by

energy consumption. They concluded that if others could do it, so could they.

Designing choice situations

The tendency for people to do what others around them do is one instance of a more general propensity. Our behavior is heavily influenced by particular features of the environment in which we act. Although radical situationism – which ascribes almost everything to the situation and almost nothing to differences between people in personality and character – is implausible, as I suggested in Chapter 6, the idea that human behavior is "heavily context dependent" is not.[6] A stronger claim than context dependence is that there is no such thing as neutral design: every environment exhibits features – a "choice architecture" – that nudge agents in some direction rather than others, making it more likely that they will do x rather than y or z.[7] Here I briefly discuss a few findings that could be useful in improving the odds that people will act more constructively to alleviate poverty.

Defaults. A striking example is the power of defaults. Employers, governments, and others who offer policies regarding retirement benefits, insurance, organ donation, and other goods can offer opt-in, opt-out, or no-default policies. The alternative chosen may have profound effects on people's decisions. In some countries, including the United States and Great Britain, you must choose (when you get or renew your driver's license) to become an organ donor; the default

communicating both "descriptive norms" (about what others actually did) and "injunctive norms" (about what it would be good to do). Injunctive norms were communicated by happy-face emoticons (!). Practically speaking, the boomerang effect could be avoided by targeting only households where it would not be expected, i.e., those predicted to use more energy than their neighbors (Ayres, Raseman, and Shih 2009, 16). For another example of the effectiveness of peer feedback (discussed in Chapter 6) see Goldstein, Cialdini, and Griskevicius 2008.

[6] The term is used by Barr, Mullainathan, and Shafir 2013, 441.

[7] Thaler and Sunstein 2008, 3. For a recent collection of interesting work demonstrating the importance of choice architecture and context dependence see Shafir 2013.

is not to donate. In many European countries, the policy is the reverse: consent to donating one's organs is presumed and one must explicitly opt out to avoid donation. In Austria, France, Hungary, Poland, and Portugal, which all have opt-out policies, effective consent rates are over 99 percent. In countries with opt-in policies, consent rates are radically lower – from 4.25 percent in Denmark to 27.5 percent in the Netherlands.[8]

In an experiment conducted by Eric Johnson and Daniel Goldstein, subjects were randomly assigned to either an opt-in, an opt-out, or a neutral system (where one had to make a choice explicitly). They were twice as likely to donate their organs when they had to opt out as when they had to opt in; in the neutral condition they were just about as likely to donate as in the opt-out condition.[9] It's easy to imagine capitalizing on the psychology of defaults in other contexts that could benefit those in need – for example, an opt-out system on income tax forms or elsewhere for donating a certain amount to reducing poverty.

Vividness and the abstract. Another finding of contemporary behavioral research that holds promise for better policies regarding poverty alleviation concerns the power of vivid as opposed to abstract information. We saw in Chapters 1 and 8 the effect of the "identifiable victim" in getting people to give more. This is not news to charitable organizations – think of the well-known sponsor-a-child programs and, more recently, the approach of microfinance organizations like Kiva that show potential donors specific individuals

---

[8] Johnson and Goldstein 2013, 418. The authors offer three (not mutually exclusive) explanations for the power of defaults: effort, implied endorsement, and loss aversion (ibid., 420–2). Sunstein and Thaler suggest another: the idea that the default is "what most people do, or what informed people do" (2003, 1180). This might appear similar to implied endorsement. But there are two differences. First, Johnson and Goldstein focus on the policymaker's endorsement, Sunstein and Thaler on the public's. Second, an agent may choose what she believes is the popular choice not because people's choosing it signifies approval of some independently valuable good but simply because she wants to do what others are doing, irrespective of whether it has merit.

[9] Johnson and Goldstein 2003.

seeking small loans. One might worry that such tactics do not benefit the vast majority of poor people who are not depicted. But highlighting real people is not incompatible with spreading the resources thereby acquired. George Loewenstein, Leslie John, and Kevin Volpp suggest that it could "turn a second-best situation (a small number of children get disproportionate support, while others languish)" into a better one that spreads the support more broadly, even while capitalizing on donors' preferences for identifiable (and cute!) individuals.[10]

The unsurprising fact that people respond more to vivid stimuli than to statistical information or other dry data has many relevant facets. Varun Gauri argues that development targets such as those embodied in the MDGs should not be expressed in terms of large numbers and percentages. He reminds us that Americans notoriously overestimate, by an order of magnitude, the amount the United States commits to development assistance: they believe it constitutes 25 percent of the US budget, and that it should be reduced to 10 percent. In fact, development assistance constitutes 1 percent of the US budget![11]

Targets for ODA, such as the "standard" target of 0.7 percent of gross national income (GNI), are doubly disadvantageous since they include both a percentage and a technical term. Gauri concludes:

> A more salient number would be dollars of development assistance per person, from each donor country, which intuitively informs people how much of their tax money is going to development assistance, and allows them to compare that contribution to how much they spend on their own purchases. Consider, for instance, how much easier it would be to imagine the impact of a decline in ODA if it were expressed, not as a reduction from 0.5% to 0.27% of GNI, but as a contribution of, say, USD\$218 per person falling to \$132 per person (roughly the decline in Austria from 2007 to 2011).[12]

---

[10] Loewenstein, John, and Volpp 2013, 373–4.

[11] World Public Opinion 2010. And much of ODA "is directed where it best suits U.S. strategic interests"; only about a quarter "goes to the world's poorest nations" (Singer 2006).

[12] Gauri 2012, 9–10.

Expressing these sums in more concrete and salient ways could potentially make a big difference in people's attitudes toward development assistance.

Another example of the importance of vivid stimuli is the image of the carbon footprint, which Elke Weber argues has "played an important role in raising awareness among members of the general public" of their effect on climate change.[13] And the possibility of getting immediate visual feedback about one's fuel consumption (as some new cars allow) can make conservation a game in which consumers compete against themselves or others.[14] Such tools, far from being manipulative, are the opposite: they are better ways to inform people.

The peanuts effect. In Chapter 3 I mentioned the "peanuts effect": "the common tendency to put little weight on very small outcomes." Fundraisers sometimes take advantage of this tendency by telling donors they can make a difference by giving just "pennies a day."[15] We can imagine more substantial efforts in this direction.

Precommitment. People engage in "hyperbolic discounting," the economist's way of saying that they overvalue present satisfactions and undervalue future ones, and increasingly as these become more distant. Richard Thaler and Shlomo Benartzi designed a program in which people could precommit to contribute to a savings-for-retirement program. In one company, those who joined the program almost quadrupled their savings rate.[16]

This approach – commit now, but give only later – can also be used to increase charitable contributions. The organization Giving What We Can asks people to publicly pledge to donate at least 10 percent of their income – until they retire – to whatever organization(s) they think will do most to reduce poverty in the developing world.[17] The approach capitalizes not only on the effectiveness of precommitment

---

[13] Weber 2013, 388–9.   [14] Weber 2013, 392.

[15] Loewenstein, John, and Volpp 2013, 364; see this article for citations to the original research on the peanuts effect.

[16] Thaler and Benartzi 2004.   [17] Giving What We Can 2013.

but also on the fact that it's public. Reneging on a public commitment could be embarrassing.

Yet despite religious injunctions to tithe, very few people give this much.[18] Moreover, the pledge requires giving 10 percent of one's income to organizations that focus on global poverty alleviation. If you want to give to public radio, the opera, your alma mater, or organizations focusing on diseases that mainly affect people in industrialized countries, such contributions would be over and above the 10 percent.[19] Still, as of February 2013, Giving What We Can has convinced 280 people to pledge more than $108,000,000.[20]

Loss aversion. A well-known finding of behavioral economics is loss aversion, first brought to light by Daniel Kahneman and Amos Tversky. People appear to be more averse to bearing losses than they are favorable to acquiring gains; they are more attached to goods they already have than they are desirous of attaining ones they lack. This phenomenon is known as the endowment effect. However, the difference between a loss and a gain is often simply a matter of how a

---

[18] Accurate figures are hard to come by. According to the Congressional Budget Office (basing its data on those from the Internal Revenue Service), in 2008, people making above $500,000 gave 3.4 percent of their income, while those making under $50,000 donated 2 percent; those in between donated 2 to 2.5 percent (Congressional Budget Office 2011, 6). But a *Chronicle of Philanthropy* article gives very different figures, asserting that "households that earn $50,000 to $75,000 give an average of 7.6 percent of their discretionary income to charity, compared with an average of 4.2 percent for people who make $100,000 or more" (Gipple and Gose 2012).

[19] At all income levels, donations to "helping meet basic needs" – and not necessarily those of the global poor – constitute only a small part of charitable contributions, even taking into account that organizations in other categories (religious, health, and "combined purpose" organizations like the United Way) may use some funds to alleviate global poverty (Congressional Budget Office 2011, 8).

[20] Giving What We Can 2013. The total amount committed is presumably based on projections of future earnings; many of those who have taken the pledge are now students. Judging from their occupations, most of these people are not rich and never will be. We should in no way denigrate the pledges of Warren Buffett, Bill Gates, and other billionaires, now numbering close to a hundred (The Giving Pledge 2013), to give away at least half of their fortunes, but such commitments demand less of those who make them in the way of personal sacrifice.

situation is described or framed.[21] So whether information or requests are presented in terms of losses incurred or gains foregone can significantly influence the choices people make. Greater attention to these tendencies in the design of policies can constructively change people's behavior. Thaler and Benartzi's savings program tied increased savings to pay raises, so savers would never see a loss in their take-home pay.[22] The same principles might work to encourage people to act in others' interests.

The bigger picture

The propensities I have been describing, and others, apply not only to self-interested but to other-directed behavior; not only to people in rich countries who might contribute more to poverty alleviation but to the poor in developing countries who could serve their own interests more effectively. So far this chapter has focused mainly on motivating comfortable people to act politically, donate more, and consume less. But work on solutions in poor communities is at least as important. Rosenberg's analysis of the women in microfinance lending groups who may be motivated to repay loans at least in part to preserve their reputations, mentioned earlier, is one example. Research carried out at the Abdul Latif Jameel Poverty Action Lab (J-PAL) at MIT, Innovations for Poverty Action, and elsewhere investigates which strategies are effective in reducing poverty – fully aware that the context dependence of human behavior means that what works in one place cannot simply be cut and pasted to another. We looked at a few of these efforts in Chapter 8 – showing, for example, the advantages of giving away bed nets to protect against malaria instead of selling them, and the effectiveness of deworming and providing school uniforms in increasing school attendance.

---

[21] Kahneman and Tversky 1984, 343–9. Plott and Zeiler (2005) argue that "subject misconceptions," rather than the endowment effect, account for the discrepancy between the amount a person would be willing to pay for a good and the amount she would be willing to accept to give up an apparently identical good. Nothing in what I say here rests on what the correct explanation is of the tendencies in question.

[22] Thaler and Benartzi 2004.

My purpose in that chapter was to counter the attention-grabbing critics who say flatly that aid doesn't work. It is, of course, easy to be discouraged when we consider the sheer numbers of very poor people. Assessing progress in reducing global poverty is indeed a glass-half-empty, glass-half-full business. The 1.3 billion people who live below the World Bank's poverty line of $1.25 a day is about equivalent to the total population of the planet in the late nineteenth century. But in 1820, 75 percent of the world's population lived below the poverty line;[23] today it's about 20 percent. Child mortality has declined by more than half since 1970, although the world's population has almost doubled. If the mortality rate had remained constant, more than 31 million children would have died in 2011 instead of 7 million.[24]

These advances no doubt result from a combination of factors: technological progress, superior organization, learning from past failures, greater resolve, and a better understanding of causal processes, including human motivation. Progress has resulted from myriad successful efforts across agriculture, health, and education, and there are strategies it is widely agreed could make a huge difference. I conclude by mentioning just a few.

Farmers in Malawi work with USAID – which in some people's minds might be associated with shipping food aid to poor countries rather than helping grow it domestically – to develop drought-resistant crops and better storage facilities that resist spoilage.[25] Geoff Lamb, president of Global Policy and Advocacy at the Gates Foundation, argues that "agricultural development is two to four times more effective at reducing hunger and poverty than any other sector." The Gates Foundation has committed more than $2 billion to such efforts; it focuses on small farmers.[26]

---

[23] Risse 2005, 10, n. 3; the figure comes from World Bank and United Nations documents.

[24] Gates 2013.   [25] Kristof 2012.

[26] World Bank 2012e; Bill and Melinda Gates Foundation 2013. See also Copenhagen Consensus 2012a: "Spending two billion dollars annually to make more productive crops would generate global returns of much more than 1600 percent. Not only would it reduce hunger, but through better nutrition, make children smarter, better educated, higher paid and hence break the cycle of poverty. At the same time, higher

Malaria kills more than a million people a year, 70 percent of them children under five. Insecticidal bed nets are the best protection from malaria; a net costs $4. The Against Malaria Foundation funds nets and works with partners that distribute them; it also monitors the use of nets to make sure they are not abandoned. At the time this book went to press, the foundation was ranked number one by GiveWell, whose work consists in conducting in-depth evaluations of charities.[27]

Diarrhea kills 2 million people a year. A highly effective preventive measure is treating drinking water with chlorine. But distributing chorine to individual households has not worked well. The problem occurs in the "last mile": getting people to change their habits and adopt technological solutions. In randomized trials in Kenya, researchers found that the example of others in the community was a crucial catalyst. With their encouragement and example, free chlorine dispensers at water collection points proved highly successful. Chlorine dispensers, supported by paid promoters, increased adoption by 53 percent, and adoption continued "30 months into the program, even after payments to promoters had ended ... The dispenser hardware provides a visual reminder to treat water when it is most salient – at the time of collection."[28] The experiment confirms two propensities we have noted: the power of the behavior of others to influence what people do, and the importance of salience – the easy availability and visibility of behavioral cues.

A remarkable fact about what works to reduce poverty and enhance economic and human development is what has become known as the "girl effect":

> A girl who doesn't attend school or marries young, for example, is at far greater risk of dying in childbirth, contracting H.I.V., being beaten by

agricultural productivity means humanity will cut down fewer forests, for the benefit of both biodiversity and earth's climate."

[27] GiveWell 2013. It was also ranked first by Giving What We Can. Giving What We Can acknowledges that it relies partly for its recommendations on GiveWell, so its high ranking was not arrived at independently.

[28] Abdul Latif Jameel Poverty Action Lab 2013. In an earlier experiment paid promoters made home visits, increasing adoption by 30 percent, but results did not endure once payments ended. The conclusions draw on research by Michael Kremer, Edward Miguel, Sendhil Mullainathan, and others (ibid.). See also Karlan and Appel 2011, 246–9, 274. Mullainathan (2010) coined the term "the last mile problem."

her husband, bearing more children than she would like, and remaining in poverty, along with her family. By contrast, an educated girl is more likely to earn higher wages, delay childbirth, and have fewer, healthier children who are themselves more likely to attend school, prosper, and participate in democratic processes.[29]

In short, "educating girls is one of the most cost-effective ways of spurring development."[30] We might generalize and speak of the "woman effect": it is widely believed that public support programs that "put money in the hands of women" rather than men are more likely to benefit children. The explanation need not lie in the greater selfishness of men over women but rather the norms and social expectations of women's role – what women are expected to do when they find themselves with extra money.[31]

There's a lot of information out there about how to eradicate global poverty. Too much, one might think. Not all of it is reliable. But in any case most people spend almost no time or effort deciding how to allocate whatever they choose to give. "Only about one third of donors surveyed recently said they did any research before donating to a charity, and those that did looked at overhead ratios above all else."[32] Investing even a few hours a year can significantly improve one's choices about what to give and do. And we don't have to start from scratch, because many intelligent and industrious people and organizations have already done a great deal of useful work.[33]

---

[29] Bornstein 2012; for evidence see Tembon and Fort 2008.

[30] Tembon and Fort 2008, xviii.   [31] Banerjee and Duflo 2011, 127–8.

[32] Association of Fundraising Professionals 2010. Charity Navigator, probably the best-known evaluator of charitable organizations, relies primarily on criteria such as administrative costs. Its methods have been criticized as simplistic and misleading (see, e.g., Bialik 2008, Karlan 2011, Pallotta 2013).

[33] The Copenhagen Consensus Center provides a great deal of good information in one place. This nonprofit organization explores and publicizes information on how governments and philanthropists can best spend aid and development money. In 2012 its expert panel, which included four Nobel Prize-winners, concluded that fighting hunger and malnutrition "should be the top priority for policymakers and philanthropists." The panel made many specific suggestions and proposals (Copenhagen Consensus 2012a, 2012b). GiveWell and Giving What We Can also provide a wealth of helpful information, both about specific organizations

Surf the web to find out more. Give what you can. Get greener. Make goodness a game. Tell others. Lobby decisionmakers. Get together. It's not that hard.

Postscript

Every proposal to improve the world that requires changing human behavior, whatever its particular content or orientation, must navigate between two hazards: the Scylla of starry-eyed idealism and the Charybdis of resigned realism. It's pointless to expect more of human beings than they are capable of delivering. But how do we tell the difference between the hegemony of entrenched norms and inescapable features of human psychology? We may suspect that those who roll their eyes, literally or metaphorically, at the appeal for reform or revolution in behavior or policy have a vested interest in the status quo or just take smug comfort in the darker picture of human nature. But surely there are also real limits to what can be reasonably expected of people.

I have tried in this book to navigate the shoals between the extremes of idealism and realism. Philosophers, of course, are thought suscep-tible to the former danger more than the latter, inhabiting an ivory tower out of touch with the so-called real world. Too much *ought*, prescription, and value; not enough *is*, description, and fact. Too much about what's desirable, not enough about what's possible. In some other lines of work, people succumb to the opposite dangers.

On the other hand, some may think I have bent too far over backwards to avoid these risks, and that my approach is too forgiving of humans as they are, stalling the alleviation of suffering and other aspects of moral progress. These critics will draw the line around what it is reasonable to expect of people in a different place. Where the line should be drawn is a debate worth having, whether for practical or purely moral reasons. (I engaged in this debate in Chapter 5.) But although it's this question that has mostly occupied the attention of philosophers, others demand our attention as well. I hope to have shed some light on a few of them.

and about the judgments and criteria that should go into choosing among them (GiveWell 2012, Giving What We Can 2013).

Works cited

Abdul Latif Jameel Poverty Action Lab. 2013. "Chlorine Dispensers for Safe Water." www.povertyactionlab.org/scale-ups/chlorine-dispensers-safe-water. Accessed February 6, 2013.

Academics Stand Against Poverty. 2013. "Illicit Financial Flows Project." www.academicsstand.org/projects/institutional-reform-goals/the-goals/illicit-financial-flows-project/. Accessed July 13, 2013.

Alkire, Sabina. 2010. "Human Development: Definitions, Critiques, and Related Concepts." Human Development Reports, Research Paper 2010/01, June 2010. New York: United Nations Development Programme.

Alperovitz, Gar and Lew Daly. 2008. *Unjust Deserts: How the Rich Are Taking Our Common Inheritance*. New York: New Press.

American Convention on Human Rights. 1969. (Adopted at the Inter-American Specialized Conference on Human Rights, San José, Costa Rica, November 22, 1969). Washington, DC: Inter-American Commission on Human Rights.

Anderson, Elizabeth and Richard H. Pildes. 2000. "Expressive Theories of Law: A General Restatement." *University of Pennsylvania Law Review* 148: 1503–75.

Anscombe, G.E.M. 1958. "Modern Moral Philosophy." *Philosophy* 33: 1–19.

Aquinas, Thomas. 1916. *Summa Theologica*. Written 1266–73. Translated by Fathers of the English Dominican Province. London: Burns Oates & Washbourne Ltd.

Aristotle. 1985. *Nicomachean Ethics*. Written 350 BCE. Translated by Terence Irwin. Indianapolis, IN: Hackett.

Arneson, Richard J. 2009. "What Do We Owe to Distant Needy Strangers?" In *Peter Singer Under Fire: The Moral Iconoclast Faces His Critics*. Edited by Jeffrey Schaler. Chicago, IL: Open Court: 267–93.

Ashford, Elizabeth. 2009. "The Alleged Dichotomy Between Positive and Negative Rights and Duties." In *Global Basic Rights*. Edited by Charles R. Beitz and Robert E. Goodin. Oxford University Press: 92–112.

Association of Fundraising Professionals. 2010. "Wise Giving: Most Donors Spend Little Time Researching Charities." www.afpnet.org/Audiences/

ReportsResearchDetail.cfm?itemnumber=4507. Accessed February 7, 2013.

Augustine. 2004. *Expositions of the Psalms 121–150*, vol. III/20. Written c. early 5th century. Edited by Boniface Ramsey. Translated by Maria Boulding. Hyde Park, NY: New City Press.

Aurelius, Marcus. 2006. *Meditations*. Written 167 CE. Translated by Martin Hammond. London: Penguin.

Ayres, Ian, Sophie Raseman, and Alice Shih. 2009. "Evidence from Two Large Field Experiments That Peer Comparison Feedback Can Reduce Residential Energy Usage." NBER Working Paper 15386. September.

Badhwar, Neera Kapur. 1993. "Altruism Versus Self-Interest: Sometimes a False Dichotomy." In *Altruism*. Edited by Ellen F. Paul, Fred D. Miller, Jr., and Jeffrey Paul. Cambridge University Press: 90–117.

Banerjee, Abhijit V. and Esther Duflo. 2007. "The Economic Lives of the Poor." *Economic Perspectives* 21:141–67. doi: 10.1257/jep.21.1.141.

    2011. *Poor Economics: A Radical Rethinking of the Way to Fight Global Poverty*. New York: Public Affairs.

Barnard, Anne. 2007. "Soft Spot for the South Bronx." *New York Times*. October 21.

Baron, Marcia. 1984. "The Alleged Moral Repugnance of Acting from Duty." *Journal of Philosophy* 81: 197–220.

    1995. *Kantian Ethics Almost Without Apology*. Ithaca, NY: Cornell University Press.

Barr, Michael S., Sendhil Mullainathan, and Eldar Shafir. 2013. "Behaviorally Informed Regulation." In *The Behavioral Foundations of Public Policy*. Edited by Eldar Shafir. Princeton University Press: 440–61.

Barry, Brian. 1979. "And Who Is My Neighbor?" *Yale Law Journal* 88: 629–58.

Batson, C. Daniel. 1991. *The Altruism Question: Toward a Social-Psychological Answer*. Hillsdale, NJ: Lawrence Erlbaum Associates.

Bauer, Peter. 1981. *Equality, the Third World and Economic Delusion*. London: Weidenfeld and Nicolson.

Beauchamp, Tom. 2008. "The Principle of Beneficence in Applied Ethics." *Stanford Encyclopedia of Philosophy*. http://plato.stanford.edu/archives/fall2008/entries/principle-beneficence/. Accessed November 18, 2012.

Beitz, Charles. 2009. *The Idea of Human Rights*. Oxford University Press.

Benvenisti, Eyal and George W. Downs. 2007. "The Empire's New Clothes: Political Economy and the Fragmentation of International Law." *Stanford Law Review* 60: 595–631.

Bialik, Carl. 2008. "Charity Rankings Giveth Less Than Meets the Eye." *Wall Street Journal*. December 19.

Bill and Melinda Gates Foundation. 2013. "Agricultural Development: Strategy Overview." August. www.gatesfoundation.org/What-We-Do/Global-Development/Agricultural-Development. Accessed June 7, 2013.

Bittman, Mark. 2009. "Loving Fish, This Time With the Fish in Mind." *New York Times*. June 9.

Bornstein, David. 2012. "Africa's Girl Power." *New York Times*. March 7. http://opinionator.blogs.nytimes.com/2012/03/07/africas-girl-power/. Accessed February 5, 2013.

Brinton, Crane. 1965. *The Anatomy of Revolution*. New York: Vintage.

Brock, Gillian. 2009. *Global Justice: A Cosmopolitan Account*. Oxford University Press.

Brown, Alyssa. 2012. "With Poverty Comes Depression, More Than Other Illnesses." *Gallup*. www.gallup.com/poll/158417/poverty-comes-depression-illness.aspx. Accessed May 30, 2013.

Buckley, Cara. 2007. "Man Is Rescued by Stranger on Subway Tracks." *New York Times*, January 3. www.nytimes.com/2007/01/03/nyregion/03life.html?_r=1&ex=1325480400&en=bfb239e4fab06ab5&ei=5090&partner=rssuserland. Accessed May 10, 2013.

Butler, Joseph. 1969. *Fifteen Sermons*. Originally published 1726. London: G. Bell & Sons.

Celizic, Mike. 2007. "'Baby Jessica' 20 Years Later." *NBCNews Today*, June 11. http://today.msnbc.msn.com/id/19165433/ns/today-today_news/t/baby-jessica-years-later/#.UGMgToLrMk8. Accessed December 21, 2012.

Cialdini, Robert. 2001. *Influence: Science and Practice*. 4th edn. Boston, MA: Allyn & Bacon.

Colbert, Elizabeth. 2008. "Turf Wars." *The New Yorker*. July 21.

Colbert, Stephen. 2011. "'Poor' in America." *The Colbert Report*. July 19. www.colbertnation.com/the-colbert-report-videos/393168/july-26-2011/-poor-in-america. Accessed May 10, 2013.

Collier, Paul. 2007. *The Bottom Billion: Why the Poorest Countries Are Failing and What Can Be Done About It*. Oxford University Press.

Collins, Chuck, Mike Lapham, and Scott Klinger. 2004. *I Didn't Do It Alone: Society's Contribution to Individual Wealth and Success*. Boston, MA: United For a Fair Economy. www.faireconomy.org/files/pdf/notalonereportfinal.pdf. Accessed December 21, 2012.

Congressional Budget Office. 2011. *"Options for Changing the Tax Treatment of Charitable Giving."* Statement of Frank Sammartino before the U.S. Senate Committee on Finance. October 18. Washington, DC.

Convention on the Rights of the Child. 1989. (Registration: September 2, 1990, No. 27531.) New York: United Nations.

Copenhagen Consensus 2012a. *Nobel Laureates: More Should Be Spent on Hunger, Health.* Lowell, MA: Copenhagen Consensus Center USA, Inc. www.copenhagenconsensus.com/sites/default/files/CC12%2BResults%2BPress%2BRelease%2BFinal_0.pdf. Accessed May 10, 2013.

2012b. *The Expert Panel Findings.* Lowell, MA: Copenhagen Consensus Center USA, Inc. www.copenhagenconsensus.com/sites/default/files/Outcome_Document_Updated_1105.pdf. Accessed February 6, 2013.

Cullity, Garrett. 2004. *The Moral Demands of Affluence.* Oxford University Press.

Daly, Martin, Margo Wilson, and Shawn Vasdev. 2001. "Income Inequality and Homicide Rates in Canada and the United States." *Canadian Journal of Criminology* 43(2): 219–36.

Dancy, Jonathan. 2009. "Moral Particularism." *Stanford Encyclopedia of Philosophy.* http://plato.stanford.edu/entries/moral-particularism/. Accessed April 25, 2012.

Darley, John and Bibb Latané. 1968. "Bystander Intervention in Emergencies: Diffusion of Responsibility." *Journal of Personality and Social Psychology* 8: 377–83.

and Daniel Batson. 1973. "From Jerusalem to Jericho: A Study of Situational and Dispositional Variables in Helping Behavior." *Journal of Personality and Social Psychology* 27: 100–8.

Daskal, Steven. 2012. "Confining Pogge's Analysis of Global Poverty to Genuinely Negative Duties." *Ethical Theory and Moral Practice* 11: 15–36.

Dawkins, Richard. 1976. *The Selfish Gene.* New York: Oxford University Press.

Dawson, E. Murrell and Elfreda Chatman. 2001. "Reference Group Theory With Implications for Information Studies: A Theoretical Essay." *Information Research* 6. http://informationr.net/ir/6-3/paper105.html. Accessed April 26, 2012.

de Waal, Alex. 2009. *Famine Crimes: Politics and the Disaster Relief Industry in Africa.* London: Africa Rights and the International African Institute.

de Waal, Frans. 2010. "Morals Without God?" *New York Times* online, October 17. http://opinionator.blogs.nytimes.com/2010/10/17/morals-without-god/. Accessed May 10, 2013.

Deaton, Angus. 2003a. "Health, Income, and Inequality." *NBER Reporter Research Summary.* www.nber.org/reporter/spring03/health.html. Accessed April 28, 2012.

2003b. "Health, Inequality, and Economic Development." *Journal of Economic Literature* 41: 113–58.

2010. "Instruments, Randomization, and Learning About Development." *Journal of Economic Literature* 48: 424–55.

Deshaney v. Winnebago County Social Services Department. 1989. 489 U.S. 189.

Dickens, Charles. 1996. *Bleak House.* Originally published 1853. London: Penguin.

Doris, John. 2002. *Lack of Character: Personality and Moral Behavior.* Cambridge University Press.

Downey, Kirsten. 2007. "Virginia Tech Shootings: Liviu Librescu." *Washington Post.* April 17.

Duesenberry, James. 1949. *Income, Saving and the Theory of Consumer Behavior.* Cambridge, MA: Harvard University Press.

Dugger, Celia W. 2006. "U.S. Plan to Lure Nurses May Hurt Poor Nations." *New York Times,* May 24.

Easterlin, Richard. 1974. "Does Economic Growth Improve the Human Lot?: Some Empirical Evidence." In *Nations and Households in Economic Growth: Essays in Honor of Moses Abramovitz.* Edited by Paul A. David and Melvin W. Reder. New York: Academic Press: 89–125.

   1995. "Will Raising the Incomes of All Increase the Happiness of All?" *Journal of Economic Behavior and Organization* 27: 35–47.

Easterly, William. 2006. *The White Man's Burden: Why the West's Efforts to Aid the Rest Have Done So Much Ill and So Little Good.* New York: Penguin.

Ebrahim-zadeh, Christine. 2003. "Dutch Disease: Too Much Wealth Managed Unwisely." *Finance and Development* 40(1). www.imf.org/external/pubs/ft/fandd/2003/03/ebra.htm. Accessed December 21, 2012.

Economic Policy Institute. 2012. *The State of Working America: Inequality.* Washington, DC: Economic Policy Institute. http://stateofworkingamerica.org/fact-sheets/inequality-facts/. Accessed December 19, 2012.

Economist. 2009. "Fertility and Living Standards: Go Forth and Multiply a Lot Less." October 29.

Elster, Jon. 2004. *Closing the Books: Transitional Justice in Historical Perspective.* Cambridge University Press.

Emerson, Ralph Waldo. 1876. "Gifts." In *Essays,* Second Series. Boston, MA: James Munroe and Company: 173–80.

European Convention on Human Rights. 1950. (Entered into force: September 3, 1953.) Rome: Council of Europe.

Evans, Peter. 2005. "The Challenges of the 'Institutional Turn': New Interdisciplinary Opportunities in Development Theory." In *The Economic Sociology of Capitalism.* Edited by Victor Nee and Richard Swedberg. Princeton University Press: 90–117.

Feinberg, Joel. 1970. "Justice and Personal Desert." In *Doing and Deserving: Essays in the Theory of Responsibility.* Princeton University Press: 55–87.

Ferguson, Ronald F. 1998. "Teachers' Perceptions and Expectations and the Black-White Test Score Gap." In *The Black-White Test Score Gap.* Edited by Christopher Jencks and Meredith Phillips. Washington, DC: Brookings Institution: 273–317.

Fischer, Corinna. 2008. "Feedback on Household Electricity Consumption: A Tool for Saving Energy?" *Energy Efficiency* 1: 79–104.

Foot, Philippa. 1993. "Justice and Charity." *The Gilbert Murray Memorial Lecture 1992*. Oxford: Oxfam.

Frank, Robert. 1985. *Choosing the Right Pond: Human Behavior and the Quest for Status*. New York: Oxford University Press.

1997. "The Frame of Reference as a Public Good." *The Economics Journal* 107: 1832–47.

1999. *Luxury Fever: Weighing the Cost of Excess*. Princeton University Press.

and Thomas Gilovich, and Dennis Regan. 1993. "Does Studying Economics Inhibit Cooperation?" *Journal of Economic Perspectives* 7: 159–71.

Frederick, Shaun and George Loewenstein. 1999. "Hedonic Adaptation." In *Well-Being: The Foundations of Hedonic Psychology*. Edited by Daniel Kahneman, Ed Diener, and Norbert Schwartz. New York: Russell Sage Foundation: 302–29.

Friedman, Milton. 1962. *Capitalism and Freedom*. University of Chicago Press.

Fullinwider, Robert K. and Judith Lichtenberg. 2004. *Leveling the Playing Field: Justice, Politics, and College Admissions*. Lanham, MD: Rowman and Littlefield.

Galston, William. 1993. "Cosmopolitan Altruism." In *Altruism*. Edited by Ellen F. Paul, Fred D. Miller, Jr., and Jeffrey Paul. Cambridge University Press: 118–34.

Gapminder. 2005. "Human Development Trends, 2005." www.gapminder.org/downloads/human-development-trends-2005/. Accessed December 18, 2012.

Gates, Melinda. 2013. "Next, Focus on the Newborn." *Economist: The World in 2013*: 88.

Gauri, Varun. 2012. "MDGs that Nudge: The Millennium Development Goals, Popular Mobilization, and the Post-2015 Development Framework." World Bank Policy Research Working Paper 6282. November.

George, Patricia and Rosa Aronson. 2003. "How Do Educators' Cultural Belief Systems Affect Underserved Students' Pursuit of Postsecondary Education?" Paper prepared for the Pathways to College Network. www.pathwaystocollege.net/pdf/EducatorsCulturalBeliefs.pdf. Accessed May 10, 2013.

Gimein, Mark. 2011. "Wealth Debate: How Two Economists Stacked the Deck." *Fiscal Times*, March 25.

Gipple, Emily and Ben Gose. 2012. "America's Generosity Divide." *Chronicle of Philanthropy*, August 19.

GiveWell. 2012. *Standard of Living in the Developing World*. www.givewell. org/international/technical/additional/Standard-of-Living. Accessed December 24, 2012.

2013. http://www.givewell.org. Accessed February 7, 2013.

The Giving Pledge. 2013. http://givingpledge.org/#enter. Accessed February 3, 2013.

Giving What We Can. 2013. www.givingwhatwecan.org. Accessed February 3, 2013.

Goldstein, Noah J., Robert B. Cialdini, and Vladas Griskevicius. 2008. "A Room With a Viewpoint: Using Normative Appeals to Motivate Energy Conservation in a Hotel Setting." *Journal of Consumer Research* 35(3): 472–82.

Goodin, Robert. 2009. "Demandingness as a Virtue." *Journal of Ethics* 13: 1–13.

Gouldner, Alvin. 1960. "The Norm of Reciprocity." *American Sociological Review* 25: 161–78.

Greene, Joshua D., R. Brian Sommerville, Leigh E. Nystrom, John Darley, and Jonathan D. Cohen. 2001. "An fMRI Investigation of Emotional Engagement in Moral Judgment." *Science* 293: 2105–8.

Guevara, Che. 1964. Speech delivered at the 19th General Assembly of the United Nations, New York, December 19. www.marxists.org/archive/guevara/1964/12/11.htm. Accessed May 10, 2013.

Hadwiger, Kenneth E. and Darin Garard. 1993. "Review of *America Calling: A Social History of the Telephone to 1940*, by Claude S. Fischer." *Illinois Historical Journal* 86: 198–200.

Hamilton, William D. 1964. "The Genetical Evolution of Social Behaviour I and II." *Journal of Theoretical Biology* 7: 1–52.

Hampton, Jean. 1993. "Selflessness and the Loss of Self." In *Altruism*. Edited by Ellen F. Paul, Fred D. Miller, Jr., and Jeffrey Paul. Cambridge University Press: 135–65.

Hancock, Graham. 1994. *Lords of Poverty: The Power, Prestige, and Corruption of the International Aid Business*. New York: Atlantic Monthly Press.

Hart, H.L.A. 1955. "Are There Any Natural Rights?" *Philosophical Review* 64: 175–91.

and A.M. Honoré. 1985. *Causation in the Law*. 2nd edn. Oxford: Clarendon Press.

Hassoun, Nicole. 2012. *Globalization and Global Justice: Shrinking Distance, Expanding Obligations*. Cambridge University Press.

Hayek. F.A. 1963. "Introduction." In *The Collected Works of John Stuart Mill*, vol. XII. Edited by Francis E. Mineka. University of Toronto Press.

Health Impact Fund. 2012. http://healthimpactfund.org. Accessed December 21, 2012.

Hirsch, Fred. 1976. *Social Limits to Growth*. Cambridge, MA: Harvard University Press.

Hochschild, Adam. 2005. *Bury the Chains: Prophets and Rebels in the Fight to Free an Empire's Slaves*. Boston, MA: Houghton Mifflin.

Hoff, Karla and Joseph E. Stiglitz. 2001. "Modern Economic Theory and Development." In *Frontiers of Development Economics: The Future in Perspective*. Edited by Gerald M. Meier and Joseph E. Stiglitz. New York: Oxford University Press, for the World Bank: 389–459.

Hoffman, Elizabeth, Kevin McCabe, and Vernon L. Smith. 1996. "Social Distance and Other-Regarding Behavior in Dictator Games." *American Economic Review* 86: 653–60.

Howse, Robert and Ruti Teitel. 2010. "Global Justice, Poverty, and the International Economic Order." In *The Philosophy of International Law*. Edited by Samantha Besson and John Tasioulas. Oxford University Press: 437–52.

Hume, David. 1978. *A Treatise of Human Nature*. 2nd edn. Originally published 1739. Edited by L.A. Selby-Bigge. Oxford: Clarendon Press.

  1998. *An Enquiry Concerning the Principles of Morals*. Originally published 1751. Edited by Tom L. Beauchamp. Oxford University Press.

Inequality.org. 2012a. Inequality Data and Statistics. http://inequality.org/inequality-data-statistics/. Accessed December 19, 2012.

  2012b. Inequality and Health. http://inequality.org/inequality-health/. Accessed December 19, 2012.

International Covenant on Civil and Political Rights. 1966. (Registration: March 23, 1976, No. 14668.) New York: United Nations.

International Covenant on Economic, Social and Cultural Rights. 1966. (Registration: January 3, 1976, No. 14531.) New York: United Nations.

Isen, A.M. and P.F. Levin. 1972. "Effect of Feeling Good on Helping: Cookies and Kindness." *Journal of Personality and Social Psychology* 21: 384–8.

Jacobellis v. Ohio. 1964. 378 U.S. 184.

Jenni, Karen and George Loewenstein. 1997. "Explaining the 'Identifiable Victim Effect.'" *Journal of Risk and Uncertainty* 14: 235–57.

Johnson, Eric J. and Daniel G. Goldstein. 2003. "Do Defaults Save Lives?" *Science* 302(5649): 1338–9.

  2013. "Decisions by Default." In *The Behavioral Foundations of Public Policy*. Edited by Eldar Shafir. Princeton University Press: 417–27.

Jones, Charlotte A., Arjuna Perera, Michelle Chow, Ivan Ho, John Nguyen, and Shahnaz Davachi. 2009. "Cardiovascular Disease Risk Among the Poor and Homeless: What We Know So Far." *Current Cardiology Reviews* 5: 69–77.

Kahneman, Daniel and Amos Tversky. 1984. "Choices, Values, and Frames." *American Psychologist* 39: 341–50.

Kant, Immanuel. 1996. *Critique of Practical Reason*. Originally published 1788. Edited by Paul Guyer and Allen W. Wood. Translated by Mary J. Gregor. Cambridge University Press.

1997. *Foundations of the Metaphysics of Morals*. Originally published 1785. Translated by Lewis White Beck. Indianapolis, IN: Bobbs-Merrill.

Karlan, Dean. 2011. "Why Ranking Charities by Administrative Expenses Is a Bad Idea." *Freakonomics*. June 9. www.freakonomics.com/2011/06/09/why-ranking-charities-by-administrative-expenses-is-a-bad-idea/. Accessed February 7, 2013.

and Jacob Appel. 2011. *More than Good Intentions: How a New Economics Is Helping to Solve Global Poverty*. New York: Dutton.

Kelly, Morgan. 2000. "Inequality and Crime." *Review of Economics and Statistics* 82: 530–9.

Kennedy, David. 2005. *The Dark Sides of Virtue: Reassessing International Humanitarianism*. Princeton University Press.

Kennedy, J. Michael. 1987. "Jessica Makes It to Safety – After 58½ Hours." *Los Angeles Times*. October 17.

Kidder, Tracy. 2003. *Mountains Beyond Mountains: The Quest of Dr. Paul Farmer, A Man Who Would Cure the World*. New York: Random House.

Kittay, Eva Feder. 1999. *Love's Labor: Essays on Women, Equality, and Dependency*. New York: Routledge.

Kopczuk, Wojciech, Emmanuel Saez, and Jae Song. 2010. "Earnings Inequality and Mobility in the United States: Evidence from Social Security Data Since 1937." *Quarterly Journal of Economics* 127: 91–128.

Kristof, Nicholas. 2012. "Obama's Fantastic Boring Idea." *New York Times*. July 11.

Krugman, Paul. 2010. "Income and Life Expectancy." *New York Times*. November 10.

Kuper, Andrew. 2002. "More Than Charity: Cosmopolitan Alternatives to the 'Singer Solution.'" *Ethics & International Affairs* 16: 107–20.

Kuran, Timur and Cass R. Sunstein. 1998. "Availability Cascades and Risk Regulation." *Stanford Law Review* 51: 683–768.

Kwok, Roberta. 2008. "Is Local Food Really Miles Better?" *Salon.com*. June 24. www.salon.com/2008/06/24/food_miles/. Accessed May 10, 2013.

Lacohée, Hazel, Nina Wakeford, and Ian Pearson. 2003. "A Social History of the Mobile Telephone With a View to Its Future." *BT Technology Journal* 21: 203–11.

Lancaster, Carol. 1999. *Aid to Africa: So Much to Do, So Little Done*. Chicago, IL: University of Chicago Press.

Latané, Bibb and John Darley. 1968. "Group Inhibition of Bystander Intervention in Emergencies." *Journal of Personality and Social Psychology* 10: 215–21.

1970. *The Unresponsive Bystander: Why Doesn't He Help?* New York: Appleton-Century-Crofts.

Latané, Bibb and Judith Rodin. 1969. "A Lady in Distress: Inhibiting Effects of Friends and Strangers on Bystander Intervention." *Journal of Experimental Social Psychology* 5: 189–201.

Layard, Richard. 2003. "Happiness: Has Social Science a Clue?" Lionel Robbins Memorial Lecture, Part 1, London School of Economics, London, March.

Levine, James A. 2011. "Poverty and Obesity in the U.S." *Diabetes* 60(11): 2667–8.

Lichtenberg, Judith. 1983. "The Right, the All Right, and the Good." *Yale Law Journal* 92: 544–63.

1996. "Consuming Because Others Consume." *Social Theory and Practice* 22: 273–97. Reprinted in *Ethics of Consumption: The Good Life, Justice, and Global Stewardship.* Edited by David Crocker and Toby Linden. Lanham, MD: Rowman and Littlefield: 155–75.

2004. "Absence and the Unfond Heart: Why People Are Less Giving Than They Might Be." In *The Ethics of Assistance: Morality and the Distant Needy.* Edited by Deen Chatterjee. Cambridge University Press: 75–97.

2009a. "Famine, Affluence, and Psychology." In *Peter Singer Under Fire: The Moral Iconoclast Faces His Critics.* Edited by Jeffrey Schaler. Chicago, IL: Open Court: 229–58.

2009b. "How to Judge Soldiers Whose Cause Is Unjust." In *Just and Unjust Warriors.* Edited by David Rodin and Henry Shue. Oxford University Press: 112–30.

and David Luban. 1997. "The Merits of Merit." *Report from the Institute of Philosophy and Public Policy* 17.

Loewenstein, George, Leslie John, and Kevin G. Volpp. 2013. "Using Decision Errors to Help People Help Themselves." In *The Behavioral Foundations of Public Policy.* Edited by Eldar Shafir. Princeton University Press: 361–79.

Lowrey, Annie. 2013. "Is It Crazy to Think We Can Eradicate Poverty?" *New York Times.* April 30.

Luban, Daniel. 2012. "Adam Smith on Vanity, Domination, and History." *Modern Intellectual History* 9: 275–302.

Luban, David. 2003. "Integrity: Its Causes and Cures." *Fordham Law Review* 72: 279–310.

Luttmer, Erzo F. P. 2005. "Neighbors as Negatives: Relative Earnings and Well-Being." *Quarterly Journal of Economics* 120: 963–1002.

Macaulay, Thomas Babington. 2013. "Against a Legal Duty to Rescue." Originally published 1837. In *Philosophical Problems in the Law,* 5th edn. Edited by David M. Adams. Belmont, CA: Wadsworth Cengage: 704–6.

Maimonides, Moses. 2003. *Gifts for the Poor (Treatise on Tzedakah)*. Written c. 1177. Edited by Marc Lee Raphael. Translated by Joseph B. Meszler. Williamsburg, VA: Department of Religion, The College of William and Mary. http://rabbimeszler.com/yahoo_site_admin/assets/docs/Gifts_for_the_Poor.27083736.pdf. Accessed February 8, 2013.

Maren, Michael. 1997. *The Road to Hell: The Ravaging Effects of Foreign Aid and International Charity*. New York: Free Press.

Margalit, Avishai. 1996. *The Decent Society*. Cambridge, MA: Harvard University Press.

Marmot, Michael. 2004. *The Status Syndrome: How Social Standing Affects Our Health and Longevity*. New York: Times Books.

Marx, Karl. 1847. *Wage Labour and Capital*. Translated by Friedrich Engels. www.marxists.org/archive/marx/works/1847/wage-labour/ch06.htm. Accessed April 26, 2012.

Mauss, Marcel. 1990. *The Gift: The Form and Reason for Exchange in Archaic Societies*. Originally published 1925. Translated by W.D. Halls. New York: Norton.

May, Joshua. 2011. "Psychological Egoism." *Internet Encyclopedia of Philosophy*. www.iep.utm.edu/psychego/#SH3a. Accessed May 10, 2013.

May, Larry and Stacey Hoffman, eds. 1991. *Collective Responsibility: Five Decades of Debate in Theoretical and Applied Ethics*. Lanham, MD: Rowman and Littlefield.

McDonough, Peggy, Greg J. Duncan, David Williams, and James House. 1997. "Income Dynamics and Adult Mortality in the United States, 1972 through 1989." *American Journal of Public Health* 87(9): 1476–83.

McNeil, Donald G., Jr. 2011. "Malaria: World Health Organization Says Deaths Have Dropped 25 Percent in Last Decade." *New York Times*, December 26.

Merton, Robert K. and Alice Rossi. 1968. "Contributions to the Theory of Reference Group Behavior." *Social Theory and Social Structure*, enlarged edn. by Robert K. Merton. New York: Free Press.

Milanovic, Branco. 2011. *The Haves and the Have-Nots: A Brief and Idiosyncratic History of Global Inequality*. New York: Basic Books.

Mill, John Stuart. 1941. *On Social Freedom*. [Authorship uncertain.] Reprinted from *Oxford and Cambridge Review*, June 1907, with an introduction by Dorothy Fosdick. New York: Columbia University Press.

1978. *On Liberty*. Originally published 1859. Indianapolis, IN: Hackett.

1979. *Utilitarianism*. Originally published 1861. Indianapolis, IN: Hackett.

Miller, Richard. 2010. *Globalizing Justice: The Ethics of Poverty and Power.* Oxford University Press.

Monroe, Kristen Renwick. 1996. *The Heart of Altruism.* Princeton University Press.

Moyo, Dambisa. 2010. *Dead Aid: Why Aid Is Not Working and How There Is a Better Way for Africa.* New York: Farrar Straus & Giroux.

Mulgan, Tim. 2001. *The Demands of Consequentialism.* Oxford University Press.

Mullainathan, Sendhil. 2010. "Solving Social Problems With a Nudge." TED talk. www.ted.com/talks/sendhil_mullainathan.html. Accessed June 6, 2013.

and Eldar Shafir. 2013. "Decision Making and Policy in Contexts of Poverty." In *The Behavioral Foundations of Public Policy.* Edited by Eldar Shafir. Princeton University Press: 281–97.

Murphy, Liam. 1993. "The Demands of Beneficence." *Philosophy & Public Affairs* 22: 267–92.

Murray, Christopher J.L., Catherine Michaud, Matthew T. McKenna, and J.S. Marks. 1998. *U.S. Patterns of Mortality by County and Race: 1965–94.* Cambridge, MA: Harvard Center of Population and Development Studies.

Nagel, Thomas. 1970. *The Possibility of Altruism.* Oxford: Clarendon Press.

1975. "Libertarianism Without Foundations." *Yale Law Journal* 86: 136–49.

2005. "The Problem of Global Justice." *Philosophy & Public Affairs* 33: 113–47.

Nickel, James. 2007. *Making Sense of Human Rights.* 2nd edn. Oxford: Blackwell.

2010. "Human Rights." *Stanford Encyclopedia of Philosophy.* http://plato.stanford.edu/entries/rights-human/. Accessed April 15, 2012.

Norton, Michael I. and Dan Ariely. 2011. "Building a Better America – One Wealth Quintile at a Time." *Perspectives on Psychological Science* 6: 9–12.

Nozick, Robert. 1974. *Anarchy, State, and Utopia.* New York: Basic Books.

Offenheiser, Raymond. 2011. "Dear Friends." *Oxfam Exchange.* Fall.

Okasha, Samir. 2009. "Biological Altruism." *Stanford Encyclopedia of Philosophy.* http://plato.stanford.edu/entries/altruism-biological/. Accessed May 10, 2013.

Oliner, Samuel P. and Pearl M. Oliner. 1988. *The Altruistic Personality: Rescuers of Jews in Nazi Europe.* New York: Free Press.

Olson, Nate. 2012. "Ties That Bind: Respect and Relationship-Based Responsibilities." Dissertation, Georgetown University.

O'Neill, Onora. 2005. "The Dark Side of Human Rights." *International Affairs* 81: 427–39.

OPHI. 2013. *Oxford Poverty & Human Development Initiative*. www.ophi.org. uk. Accessed February 8, 2013.

Pallotta, Dan. 2013. "The Way We Think About Charity Is Dead Wrong." TED talk. www.ted.com/talks/dan_pallotta_the_way_we_think_about_charity_is_dead_wrong.html. Accessed March 18, 2013.

Parfit, Derek. 1984. *Reasons and Persons*. Oxford University Press.

Petersen, John. 2008. "A Green Curriculum Involves Everyone on the Campus." *Chronicle of Higher Education*, June 20.

Plott, Charles R. and Kathryn Zeiler, 2005. "The Willingness to Pay-Willingness to Accept Gap, the 'Endowment Effect,' Subject Misconceptions, and Experimental Procedures for Eliciting Valuations." *American Economic Review* 95: 530–45.

Pogge, Thomas. 2001. "How Should Human Rights Be Conceived?" In *The Philosophy of Human Rights*. Edited by Patrick Hayden. St. Paul, MN: Paragon House: 187–211. Reprinted from *Jahrbuch fur Recht und Ethik* 3: 103–20 (1995).

2002. *World Poverty and Human Rights*. Cambridge: Polity Press.

2005. "Recognized and Violated by International Law: The Human Rights of the Global Poor." *Leiden Journal of International Law* 18: 717–45.

2009. "World Poverty and Human Rights." In *Ethics & International Affairs: A Reader*. 3rd edn. Edited by Joel H. Rosenthal and Christian Barry. Washington, DC: Georgetown University Press: 307–16.

2010. *Politics As Usual: What Lies Behind the Pro-Poor Rhetoric*. Cambridge: Polity Press.

Population Reference Bureau. 2007. *2007 World Population Data Sheet*. Washington, DC: Population Reference Bureau. www.prb.org/pdf07/07WPDS_Eng.pdf. Accessed December 21, 2012.

Rand, Ayn. 1964. *The Virtue of Selfishness*. New York: Signet.

Rawls, John. 1971. *A Theory of Justice*. Cambridge, MA: Harvard University Press.

Rector, Robert and Rachel Sheffield. 2011. *Air Conditioning, Cable TV, and an Xbox: What Is Poverty in the United States Today?* Washington, DC: Heritage Foundation. www.heritage.org/Research/Reports/2011/07/What-is-Poverty. Accessed May 10, 2013.

Rieff, David. 2002. *A Bed for the Night: Humanitarianism in Crisis*. New York: Simon & Schuster.

Risse, Mathias. 2005. "Do We Owe the Global Poor Assistance or Rectification?" *Ethics & International Affairs* 19: 9–18.

Rodgers, Richard and Oscar Hammerstein II. 1943. *Oklahoma*. New York: R & H Theatricals.

Rorty, Richard. 1993. "Human Rights, Rationality, and Sentimentality." In *On Human Rights: The Oxford Amnesty Lectures 1993*. Edited by Stephen Shute and Susan Hurley. New York: Basic Books: 111–34.

Rosenberg, Tina. 2011. *Join the Club: How Peer Pressure Can Transform the World*. New York: Norton.

Ross, Lee and Richard Nisbett. 2011. *The Person and the Situation: Perspectives of Social Psychology*, 2nd edn. London: Pinter and Martin.

Rousseau, Jean-Jacques. 1997. *Discourse on the Origin and Foundations of Inequality Among Men*. Originally published 1755. In *"The Discourses" and Other Early Political Writings*. Edited by Victor Gourevitch. Cambridge University Press: 111–232.

Rowntree, B. Seebohm. 1902. *Poverty: A Study of Town Life*. 2nd edn. London: Macmillan.

Runciman, W.G. 1966. *Relative Deprivation and Social Justice: A Study of Attitudes to Social Inequality in Twentieth-Century England*. Berkeley, CA: University of California Press.

Sachs, David. 1981. "How to Distinguish Self-Respect from Self-Esteem." *Philosophy & Public Affairs* 10: 346–60.

Sachs, Jeffrey. 2005. *The End of Poverty: Economic Possibilities for Our Time*. New York: Penguin.

Salmon, Felix. 2011. "Swedish Inequality Datapoint of the Day." *Reuters*, March 25. http://blogs.reuters.com/felix-salmon/2011/03/25/swedish-inequality-datapoint-of-the-day/. Accessed May 10, 2013.

Sauvigny, Guillaume de Bertier de. 1999. *La Restauration*. Paris: Flammarion.

Scheffler, Samuel. 1986. "Morality's Demands and Their Limits." *Journal of Philosophy* 83: 531–7.

  1994. *The Rejection of Consequentialism: A Philosophical Investigation of the Considerations Underlying Rival Moral Conceptions*. 2nd rev. edn. Oxford: Clarendon Press.

  1995. "Individual Responsibility in a Global Age." *Social Philosophy and Policy* 12: 219–36.

Schwartz, Barry. 1967. "The Social Psychology of the Gift." *American Journal of Sociology* 73: 1–11.

Sen, Amartya. 1981. *Poverty and Famines: An Essay on Entitlement and Deprivation*. Oxford: Clarendon Press.

  1983. "Poor, Relatively Speaking." *Oxford Economic Papers* 35: 153–69.

  1999. *Development as Freedom*. New York: Random House.

Seneca, L. Annaeus. 1935. *On Benefits*. Written first century CE. Translated by John W. Basore. Cambridge, MA: Harvard University Press.

Shafir, Eldar, ed. 2013. *The Behavioral Foundations of Public Policy*. Princeton University Press.

Shue, Henry. 1988. "Mediating Duties." *Ethics* 98: 687–704.

1996 (1980). *Basic Rights: Subsistence, Affluence, and U.S. Foreign Policy.* 2nd edn., with a new foreword. Princeton University Press.

Sidgwick, Henry. 1907. *Method of Ethics.* 7th edn. London: Macmillan.

Simon, Herbert. 2012. "Public Administration in Today's World of Organizations and Markets." https://research.mbs.ac.uk/hsi/Aboutus/ HerbertSimonsLastPublicLecture.aspx. Accessed December 21, 2012. Also in *PS: Political Science and Politics* 33(2000), 756.

Singer, Peter. 1972. "Famine, Affluence, and Morality." *Philosophy & Public Affairs* 1: 229–43. Reprinted in *International Ethics.* Edited by Charles Beitz, Marshall Cohen, Thomas Scanlon, and A. John Simmons. Princeton University Press, 1985.

1981. *The Expanding Circle: Ethics and Sociobiology.* New York: Farrar, Straus and Giroux.

2006. "What Should a Billionaire Give – And What Should You?" *New York Times.* December 17. Reprinted in *Giving Well: The Ethics of Philanthropy.* Edited by Patricia Illingworth, Thomas Pogge, and Leif Wenar. Oxford University Press, 2011: 13–25.

2009. "Reply to Judith Lichtenberg." In *Peter Singer Under Fire: The Moral Iconoclast Faces His Critics.* Edited by Jeffrey Schaler. Chicago, IL: Open Court: 259–66.

2010. *The Life You Can Save: Acting Now to End World Poverty.* New York: Random House.

and William Easterly. 2009. Dialogue on bloggingheads.tv, December 24. http://bloggingheads.tv/videos/2384. Accessed March 8, 2013.

Slovic, Paul. 2007. "If I Look at the Mass I Will Never Act: Psychic Numbing and Genocide." *Judgment and Decisionmaking* 2: 79–95.

Small, Deborah A., George Loewenstein, and Paul Slovic. 2007. "Sympathy and Callousness: The Impact of Deliberative Thought on Donations to Identifiable and Statistical Victims." *Organizational Behavior and Human Decision Processes* 102: 143–53.

Smith, Adam. 1994. *An Inquiry into the Nature and Causes of the Wealth of Nations.* Originally published 1726. Edited by Edwin Cannan. New York: Modern Library.

2002. *The Theory of the Moral Sentiments.* Originally published 1759. Edited by Knut Haakonssen. Cambridge University Press.

Sober, Elliot and David Sloan Wilson. 1998. *Unto Others: The Evolution and Psychology of Unselfish Behavior.* Cambridge, MA: Harvard University Press.

Sogge, David. 2002. *Give and Take: What's the Matter With Foreign Aid?* London: Zed Books.

Solnick, Sarah J. and David Hemenway. 1998. "Is More Always Better?: A Survey on Positional Concerns." *Journal of Economic Behavior & Organization* 37: 373–83.

Specter, Michael. 1999. "The Dangerous Philosopher." *The New Yorker*, September 6.

Stern, N.H., Jean-Jacques Dethier, and F. Halsey Rogers. 2005. *Growth and Empowerment: Making Development Happen*. Cambridge, MA: MIT Press.

Stern, Robert. 2004. "Does 'Ought' Imply 'Can'? And Did Kant Think It Does?" *Utilitas* 16: 42–61.

Stocker, Michael. 1976. "The Schizophrenia of Modern Ethical Theories." *Journal of Philosophy* 63: 453–66.

Stohr, Karen. 2011. "Kantian Beneficence and the Problem of Obligatory Aid." *Journal of Moral Philosophy* 8: 45–67.

Stouffer, Samuel A., Edward A. Suchman, Leland C. DeVinney, Shirley A. Star, and Robin M. Williams, Jr. 1949. *The American Soldier: Adjustment During Army Life. Studies in Social Psychology in World War II, vol. 1*. Princeton University Press.

Strawson, Peter F. 1962. "Freedom and Resentment." *Proceedings of the British Academy* 48. Reprinted in Peter Strawson, *Freedom and Resentment and Other Essays*. London: Routledge, 2008: 1–28.

Strudler, Alan and Eleonora Curlo. 1997. "Consumption as Culture." In *Ethics of Consumption: The Good Life, Justice, and Global Stewardship*. Edited by David Crocker and Toby Linden. Lanham, MD: Rowman and Littlefield: 269–86.

Sunstein, Cass R. and Richard H. Thaler. 2003. "Libertarian Paternalism Is Not an Oxymoron." *University of Chicago Law Review* 70: 1159–1202.

Tawney, R.H. 1980. *Religion and the Rise of Capitalism*. Originally published 1926. New York: Penguin.

Telegraph. 2012. "Professor James Urmson." April 4. www.telegraph.co.uk/news/obituaries/9186962/Professor-James-Urmson.html. Accessed May 10, 2013.

Tembon, Mercy and Lucia Fort. 2008. *Girls' Education in the 21st Century: Gender Equality, Empowerment, and Economic Growth*. Washington, DC: World Bank.

Thaler, Richard and Cass Sunstein. 2008. *Nudge: Improving Decisions about Health, Wealth and Happiness*. New Haven, CT: Yale University Press.

and Shlomo Benartzi. 2004. "Save More Tomorrow: Using Behavioral Economics to Increase Employee Saving." *Journal of Political Economy* 112: S164–87.

Tierney, John. 2011. "Do You Suffer From Decision Fatigue?" *New York Times*. August 17.

Tocqueville, Alexis de. 1945. *Democracy in America, vol. II.* Originally published 1840. Translated by Henry Reeve. New York: Alfred A. Knopf.

    2011. *The Ancien Régime and the French Revolution.* Originally published 1856. Translated by Arthur Goldhammer. Cambridge University Press.

Trivers, Robert L. 1971. "The Evolution of Reciprocal Altruism." *Quarterly Review of Biology* 46: 35–57.

Twain, Mark. 1894. *The Tragedy of Pudd'nhead Wilson and the Comedy of those Extraordinary Twins.* Hartford, CT: American Publishing Company.

UN Millennium Campaign. 2013. "End Poverty 2015." www.endpoverty2015. org/. Accessed June 2, 2013.

Unger, Peter. 1996. *Living High and Letting Die: Our Illusion of Innocence.* New York: Oxford University Press.

UNICEF. 2012. *Levels and Trends in Child Mortality. Estimates Developed by the UN Inter-agency Group for Child Mortality Estimation.* New York: United Nations Children's Fund. http://apromiserenewed.org/files/UNICEF_2012_child_mortality_for_web_0904.pdf. Accessed February 8, 2012.

United Nations. 2001. *Report of the Third United Nations Conference on the Least Developed Countries.* Brussels: United Nations.

United Nations Development Programme. 2010. *Human Development Report 2010, 20th Anniversary Edition. The Real Wealth of Nations: Pathways to Human Development.* Basingstoke: Palgrave Macmillan.

United States Census Bureau. 2012a. *"Poverty."* www.census.gov/hhes/www/poverty/about/overview/index.html. Accessed December 18, 2012.

    2012b. *"Historical Estimates of World Population."* www.census.gov/population/international/data/worldpop/table_history.php. Accessed October 19, 2012.

Universal Declaration of Human Rights. 1948. (Adopted and proclaimed by UN General Assembly resolution 217 A (III) of December 10, 1948.) New York: United Nations General Assembly.

Urmson, James O. 1958. "Saints and Heroes." In *Essays in Moral Philosophy.* Edited by A.I. Melden. Seattle, WA: University of Washington Press: 198–216.

U.S. v. Carroll Towing Co. 1947. 159 F.2d 169 (2d Cir.).

Veblen, Thorstein. 2007. *The Theory of the Leisure Class.* Originally published 1899. Oxford University Press.

Waldron, Hilary. 2007. "Trends in Mortality Differentials and Life Expectancy for Male Social Security-Covered Workers, by Average Relative Earnings." *U.S. Social Security Administration, Social Security Bulletin* 67 (3): 1–28.

Weber, Elke. 2013. "Doing the Right Thing Willingly: Using the Insights of Behavioral Decision Research for Better Environmental Decisions." In *The Behavioral Foundations of Public Policy*. Edited by Eldar Shafir. Princeton University Press: 380–97.

Weber, Max. 1958. *The Protestant Ethic and the Spirit of Capitalism*. Originally published 1905. New York: Scribner's.

Wenar, Leif. 2008. "Property Rights and the Resource Curse." *Philosophy & Public Affairs* 36: 2–32.

2011. "Poverty Is No Pond: Challenges for the Affluent." In *Giving Well: The Ethics of Philanthropy*. Edited by Patricia Illingworth, Thomas Pogge, and Leif Wenar. Oxford University Press: 104–32.

Wertheimer, Alan. 1996. *Exploitation*. Princeton University Press.

Westermarck, Edward. 1908. *The Origin and Development of the Moral Ideas*. London: Macmillan.

Wilkinson, Richard. 1996. *Unhealthy Societies: The Afflictions of Inequality*. London: Routledge.

Wilkinson, Will. 2007. "In Pursuit of Happiness Research: Is It Reliable? What Does It Imply for Policy?" *Policy Analysis* 590.

Williams, Bernard. 1973. "A Critique of Utilitarianism." In *Utilitarianism: For and Against*. Edited by J.J.C. Smart and Bernard Williams. Cambridge University Press: 77–150.

1981. *Moral Luck*. Cambridge University Press.

Wolf, Susan. 1982. "Moral Saints." *Journal of Philosophy* 79: 419–39.

World Bank. 2008. *Poverty Data: A Supplement to World Development Indicators 2008*. Washington, DC: The World Bank. http://siteresources.world bank.org/DATASTATISTICS/Resources/WDI08supplement1216.pdf. Accessed May 13, 2013.

2011. *Africa Development Indicators Factoids 2011*. Washington, DC: The World Bank. http://siteresources.worldbank.org/INTAFRICA/Resources/ Africa-factoids_hi-res_FINAL_Sept_9-2011_11.pdf. Accessed October 19, 2012.

2012a. "Poverty and Equity Data." http://povertydata.worldbank.org/ poverty/home/. Accessed December 21, 2012.

2012b. "PovcalNet." http://iresearch.worldbank.org/PovcalNet/index. htm?1. Accessed October 16, 2012.

2012c. "New Estimates Reveal Drop in Extreme Poverty 2005–2010." http://go.worldbank.org/4K0EJIDFA0. Accessed December 21, 2012.

2012d. *Inequality in Focus* 1(1). April. Washington, DC: The World Bank. http://siteresources.worldbank.org/EXTPOVERTY/Resources/ Inequality_in_Focus_April2012.pdf. Accessed February 8, 2013.

2012e. "Japan and Republic of Korea Pledge Additional $60 Million to Boost Food Security in World's Poorest Countries." www.worldbank.org/en/news/press-release/2012/10/12/japan-republic-of-korea-pledge-additional-60-million-boost-food-security-worlds-poorest-countries. Accessed June 8, 2013.

World Health Organization. 2012. "Underweight in Children." www.who.int/gho/mdg/poverty_hunger/underweight/en/index.html. Accessed December 18, 2012.

World Public Opinion. 2010. "American Public Vastly Overestimates U.S. Foreign Aid." November 29. www.worldpublicopinion.org/pipa/articles/brunitedstatescanadara/670.php?nid=&id=&pnt=670&lb=. Accessed February 2, 2013.

Index

Italicized numbers refer to footnotes on that page.